Leo Laporte's

2005 Gadget Guide

Leo Laporte & Michael Miller

que®

800 East 96th Street
Indianapolis, IN 46240

Leo Laporte's 2005 Gadget Guide

Copyright © 2005 by Que Publishing

International Standard Book Number: 0-7897-3208-4

Library of Congress Catalog Card Number: 2004107073

Printed in the United States of America

First Printing: September 2004

07   06 05 04   4 3 2 1

Trademarks

All terms mentioned in this book that are known to be trademarks or service marks have been appropriately capitalized. Que Publishing cannot attest to the accuracy of this information. Use of a term in this book should not be regarded as affecting the validity of any trademark or service mark.

Warning and Disclaimer

Every effort has been made to make this book as complete and as accurate as possible, but no warranty or fitness is implied. The information provided is on an "as is" basis. The authors and the publisher shall have neither liability nor responsibility to any person or entity with respect to any loss or damages arising from the information contained in this book.

Bulk Sales

Que Publishing offers excellent discounts on this book when ordered in quantity for bulk purchases or special sales. For more information, please contact

U.S. Corporate and Government Sales

1-800-382-3419

corpsales@pearsontechgroup.com

For sales outside of the U.S., please contact

International Sales

international@pearsoned.com

Publisher
Paul Boger

Associate Publisher
Greg Wiegand

Executive Editor
Rick Kughen

Development Editor
Todd Brakke

Managing Editor
Charlotte Clapp

Project Editor
Andy Beaster

Production Editor
Megan Wade

Indexer
Erika Millen

Proofreader
Tracy Donhardt

Team Coordinator
Sharry Lee Gregory

Photo Acquisitions
Sharry Lee Gregory

Interior Designer
Anne Jones

Cover Designer
Commercial Artisan Design

Page Layout
Bronkella Publishing

Graphics
Tammy Graham

Contents at a Glance

Introduction xi

1 Computer Gadgets 1

2 Portable Gadgets. 55

3 Digital Photography Gadgets 125

4 Home Movie Gadgets 149

5 Home Audio/Video Gadgets 171

6 Telephone Gadgets 197

7 Game Gadgets 225

8 Automotive Gadgets 239

Index 261

Table of Contents

1 **Computer Gadgets** 1

Mice and Keyboards 2

Backup Devices 7

TV Tuners and DVRs 11

Speakers 15

Scanners 19

Webcams 23

USB Gizmos 27

Keychain Storage Devices 34

Digital Media Readers 39

Portable Computer Accessories 42

Other Cool Computer Gadgets 48

2 **Portable Gadgets** 55

Palm OS PDAs 56

Pocket PC PDAs 60

PDA Accessories 63

Portable Music Players 67

iPod Accessories 72

Headphones 80

Earbuds 84

Noise-Canceling Headphones 88

Portable Video Players 91

Portable DVD Players 94

Digital Voice Recorders 98

Handheld GPS Devices 101

High-tech Watches 105

Battery-Related Gadgets 110

Cases and Bags 114

Other Cool Portable Gadgets 118

3 **Digital Photography Gadgets** **125**

Point-and-Shoot Digital Cameras 126

High-end Digital Cameras 130

Digital SLRs 134

Specialty Digital Cameras 137

Digital Camera Accessories 141

Other Cool Digital Photography Gadgets 146

4 Home Movie Gadgets **149**

    Basic Camcorders 150

    High-end Camcorders 154

    Camcorder Accessories 158

    Video Capture Devices 162

    Tape-to-DVD Burners 166

    Other Cool Moviemaking Gadgets 168

5 Home Audio/Video Gadgets **171**

    Digital Media Hubs 172

    DVD Recorders 178

    Home Theater in a Box Systems 182

    Universal Remote Controls 186

    Satellite Radio 190

    Other Cool Audio/Video Gadgets 193

6 **Telephone Gadgets**. **197**

    Mobile Phones 198

    Camera Phones 202

    Smart Phones 206

    Headsets 210

    Cases and Holders 214

    Chargers/Batteries 217

    Other Cool Phone Gadgets 220

7 **Game Gadgets** **225**

    Game Controllers 226

    Adapters and Switchers 232

    Other Cool Game Gadgets 235

8 **Automotive Gadgets**. **239**

    GPS Navigation Systems 240

    Hands-free Car Phone Kits 243

    Satellite Radio Receivers 246

    DVD Video Systems 250

    Other Cool Automotive Gadgets 254

Index **261**

About the Authors

Leo Laporte is the former host of two shows on TechTV: *The Screen Savers* and *Call for Help*. Leo is a weekend radio host on Los Angeles radio KFI AM 640. He also appears regularly on many other television and radio programs, including ABC's *World News Now* and *Live with Regis and Kelly* as "The Gadget Guy." He is the author of *Leo Laporte's 2003 Computer Almanac* and *Leo Laporte's 2004 Screensavers Technology Almanac*, both of which have been bestsellers. Leo also is the author of three newly published books on consumer technology in his Leoville Press series: *Leo Laporte's Guide to TiVo*, *Leo Laporte's Mac Gadget Guide*, and *Leo Laporte's 2005 Gadget Guide*, all published by Que.

Michael Miller has written more than 50 nonfiction books over the past 15 years. His books for Que include *Bargain Hunter's Guide to Online Shopping*, *Absolute Beginner's Guide to Computer Basics*, and *Absolute Beginner's Guide to eBay*. He was also a contributor to *Leo Laporte's 2003 Technology Almanac*.

Acknowledgments

Thanks to the usual suspects at Que, including but not limited to Greg Wiegand, Rick Kughen, Todd Brakke, Andy Beaster, and Megan Wade. Special thanks to Sharry Gregory, who wrangled all the pictures you see in these pages. And additional thanks to the companies who provided pictures, information, and—most important—the cool gadgets you're going to read about.

Photo Credits

All product photos used in this book are owned by the respective manufacturers, including, but not limited to 3M, Abacus, Addlogix, Addonics, ADS Technologies, Alpine, Altec Lansing, Anycom, AOS Technologies, Ansmann Energy, Apex, Apple Computer, Archos, ATI Technologies, Audiovox. Auravision, AVerMedia, Bellagio Designs, Belkin, Beltronics, Bianchi, Blaupunkt, Boeckeler, Bose, Canon, Canopus, Cardo, Casio, CCM, CH Products, CEIVA, Cobra, Compact Power Systems, Inc., Corex, CMS Products, Creative, Creditel, Crumpler, D-Link, Davis Instruments, Delphi Electroncics, Dexia Design, Digital Dream, Eagletron, Egato, Egg Solution, Elton Corp., Epson, Escient, Essex Electronics, Etymotic Research, Eyetop, Excalibur Electronics, Ezonics, FastDraw Products, Felicidade, FlowCam, Focus Enhancements, FoneFree, Fujifilm, Freecom, FrontX, Future Sonics, GameShark, Garmin, Grado Labs, Gravis, Griffin Technology, Gyration, Harman/Kardon, Hauppauge, Hewlett Packard, Hoodman, iBIZ Technology, Infinium Labs, Innovative Solutions & Technologies, Iomega, IOGEAR, I.R.I.S., iRiver, iRobot, iSkin, Inc., isun, JAKKS Pacific, Inc., JBL, JVC, Kensington, Kenwood, Klipsch, Knock-in-Key, Koss, Kyrocera Imaging, Lacie, Laughing Rabbit, Inc., LG Electronics, Line 6, Linksys, LOAS, Logitech, Lowrance, Magna Donnelly, Magellan, Marware, Inc., Matias Corp., Maxtor, Measurement Specialties, Meritline, Metz, MHL Communications, MIB, Microsoft, Microtek, Minolta, Mirra, Monster Cable, Motorola, Natural Point, Navman, NETGEAR, Nikon, Nirotek America, Norazza Nyko, Olympia, Olympus, One for All/Universal Electronics, PalmOne, Panasonic, Personal Electronics Concealment, Pelican, Philips, PhoneLabs, Photo3-D, Pioneer, Pinnacle Systems, Planon, Plantronics, Plextor, Proctor & Gamble, Pyramat, Rayovac, RCA, Research in Motion, Roku, Royal, Safety Technology, Samsung, SanDisk, Sanyo, Sealife, Sennheiser, Sidewinder, Siemens, Shure, Slim Devices, Smith-Victor Corp., Solid Alliance, SoniqCast, Sony, Sony Erissson, Speedtech Instruments, Star Case, Streamzap, Tapwave, Targus, TEN Technology, Terk Technologies, ThinkGeek, Thrustmaster, Tiffen, Timex, Tivoli Audio, ToCAD, TomTom, Toshiba, TrackIT Corp., Tune Belt, Turtle Beach, Unrealtoys, Vantec, Veo, Victorinox, VidPro, Western Digital, Wireless Garden, Wurlitzer, Yamaha, Xact, Xantrex, Zio Corp., ZIP-LINQ.

We Want to Hear from You!

As the reader of this book, *you* are our most important critic and commentator. We value your opinion and want to know what we're doing right, what we could do better, what areas you'd like to see us publish in, and any other words of wisdom you're willing to pass our way.

As an associate publisher for Que, I welcome your comments. You can email or write me directly to let me know what you did or didn't like about this book—as well as what we can do to make our books better.

Please note that I cannot help you with technical problems related to the topic of this book. We do have a User Services group, however, where I will forward specific technical questions related to the book.

When you write, please be sure to include this book's title and authors, as well as your name, email address, and phone number. I will carefully review your comments and share them with the authors and editors who worked on the book.

Email:	feedback@quepublishing.com
Mail:	Greg Wiegand
	Que Publishing
	800 East 96th Street
	Indianapolis, IN 46240 USA

For more information about this book or another Que title, visit our website at www.quepublishing.com. Type the ISBN (excluding hyphens) or the title of a book in the Search field to find the page you're looking for.

Introduction

Gadgets are fun.

It doesn't matter whether you're talking about one of those cheap little keychain memory gizmos or an expensive robot vacuum cleaner, gadgets tickle my fancy. They don't even have to be practical—in fact, it's sometimes better if they're not. To capture my attention, a gadget only has to be interesting and innovative and imaginative—in a single word, *cool*.

So, this book is all about cool gadgets, of all shapes and sizes. Gadgets you attach to your computer. Gadgets you carry around on a belt clip. Gadgets that ride along with you in your car. Gadgets you talk into, or type on, or shoot pictures with. Gadgets that have absolutely no useful purpose at all, and gadgets that actually help you do something more efficiently.

In short, *Leo Laporte's 2005 Gadget Guide* is a "wish book" of more than 300 of my very favorite gadgets. I find all the gadgets here terribly interesting, and some of them either quite useful or hilariously funny—or both. (You can't beat the USB Duck for both novelty and practicality.) These are gizmos you can marvel at, laugh at, and drool over. With only a few exceptions, they're actual honest-to-goodness consumer products, which means you can purchase them for your own personal use. Or not.

How This Book Is Organized

I've organized the gadgets in this book into eight major categories:

- **Part I, "Computer Gadgets"**—Includes mice and keyboards, backup devices, TV tuners and DVRs, speakers, scanners, Webcams, USB gizmos (one of my favorite types of gadget), keychain storage devices, digital media readers, portable computer accessories, and other cool computer gadgets

- **Part II, "Portable Gadgets"**—Includes Palm OS PDAs, Pocket PC PDAs, PDA accessories, portable music players, iPod accessories, headphones, earbuds, noice-canceling headphones, portable video players, portable DVD players, digital voice recorders, handheld GPS devices, high-tech watches, battery-related gadgets, cases and bags, and other cool portable gadgets

- **Part III, "Digital Photography Gadgets"**—Includes point-and-shoot digital cameras, high-end digital cameras, digital SLRs, specialty digital cameras, digital camera accessories, and other cool digital photography gadgets

- **Part IV, "Home Movie Gadgets"**—Includes basic camcorders, high-end camcorders, camcorder accessories, video capture devices, tape-to-DVD burners, and other cool movie-making gadgets

- **Part V, "Home Audio/Video Gadgets"**—Includes digital media hubs, DVD recorders, home-theater-in-a-box systems, universal remote controls, satellite radio, and other cool audio/video gadgets

- **Part VI, "Telephone Gadgets"**—Includes mobile phones, camera phones, smart phones, headsets, cases and holders, chargers/batteries, and other cool phone gadgets

- **Part VII, "Game Gadgets"**—Includes game controllers, cables, adapters, switchers, and other cool game gadgets

- **Part VIII, "Automotive Gadgets"**—Includes GPS navigation systems, hands-free car kits, satellite radio receivers, DVD video systems, and other cool automotive gadgets

Each category includes several types of gadgets, as I just listed. Each type of gadget is introduced with some general information; then I list my favorite gadgets of that type. The absolute coolest gadgets are highlighted as "Leo's Picks"; you want to give these gizmos special consideration, just because.

At the end of each gadget listing is a box with detailed information about that gadget, including the model number, manufacturer, website, and price. Given how things go, all this information is subject to change. The price I list is generally the manufacturer's suggested retail price; if you shop around, you can probably find most of these gadgets for a bit less than that.

In case you're wondering, I've accepted no payment or consideration of any sort to list these particular gadgets in this book. The fact that I've included—or not included—a specific gadget reflects no objective review of the gadget's merit, only that it caught my fancy. In other words, these are my favorite gadgets at this point in time. That's all.

Where Does He Get Such Wonderful Toys?

If you see a gadget here that you think is particularly neat, you probably have one more question—where can I buy it? Well, many of these gadgets are available from major computer and consumer electronics retailers, such as CompUSA and Best Buy. Other gadgets—especially some of the more off-the-wall ones—can be purchased online at sites like Gadget Universe (www.gadgetuniverse.com) and ThinkGeek (www.thinkgeek.com). Finally, some gadgets can be purchased directly from the manufacturer; visit the company's website for more information.

And if you're a real gadget hound, take a gander at the Gizmodo (www.gizmodo.com) and GadgetMadess (www.gadgetmadness.com) blogs. These sites feature up-to-the-minute information about all sorts of new gadget releases, as well as links to the gadgets' manufacturers. They're the first places to read about the coolest new gadgets.

Computer Gadgets

1

Mice and Keyboards

If you're still using the standard-issue mouse and keyboard that came with your PC, you're missing out on some really cool input devices. Despite what you might think, not all mice and keyboards are alike; some perform better than others, some offer unique features, and some are hip and trendy looking. You just have to know what's available and what you really want and need.

The biggest trend in input devices today is cordless connectivity. If you like to lean back and put your feet up while computing, you know how constricting it is to be tethered to your computer by the standard too-short connecting cable. When you go cordless, you can put your keyboard on your lap and your mouse on a coffee table, if that's you want. Cordless equals more flexibility.

The hottest cordless devices use the new Bluetooth standard. Bluetooth is a specific type of 2.4GHz connectivity, but don't bother about the technology. What's important is that Bluetooth is more reliable than other cordless technologies, and—as the buzzword du jour—will cost you a little more than traditional cordless products, which themselves are more expensive than corded gadgets.

Beyond cordless, look for mice and keyboards with enhanced ergonomics, as well as those with wholly nonfunctional (but cool-looking) lights and colors. And don't limit yourself to mice and keyboards; some of the neatest input devices break the paradigm completely, letting you communicate with your computer via trackball or pen.

As you'll see, some of the most innovative input devices come from a single company—Logitech. I don't want to sound like a shill for the company, which I'm not, but it's hard not to be impressed by Logitech's offerings. Even the company's run-of-the-mill mice and keyboards have a better feel than most competing products, and their cutting-edge models show you what all the other manufacturers will be producing next year.

Outside of Logitech and Microsoft (the other major mouse/keyboard supplier), several smaller companies are doing cool things. Look for mice that work without a desktop and keyboards that glow like neon fixtures in a Las Vegas casino. And, while you're shopping, keep an eye out for devices that connect via USB; they're a lot easier to connect than devices that use the standard PS/2 mouse and keyboard connectors.

Logitech diNovo Media Desktop

When every mouse and keyboard starts to resemble every other mouse and keyboard, Logitech's diNovo Media Desktop stands out from the crowd. This mouse and keyboard combo features hip styling and the latest Bluetooth wireless technology; it's cutting-edge in more ways than one.

We'll start with the mouse, which is of the rechargeable variety. This means you don't have to worry about replacing batteries every few weeks; the Bluetooth receiver doubles as the mouse's recharging station. Like all Logitech mice, this one has a nice feel and includes the ubiquitous scroll wheel and programmable back and forward buttons.

The keyboard (which uses regular batteries) is eye-catching in its design, with very clean lines and a flat look that's unique among today's computer keyboards. Naturally, the keys are full-sized and have a nice full-travel feel; there are a variety of programmable keys you can use to provide direct access to your favorite programs or documents.

The really unique part of the Media Desktop, however, is a separate piece that docks to the keyboard, called the MediaPad. It's more than just a numeric keypad, although it's that, too; you can use the MediaPad to control all your digital media—to play music files, display digital photos, and so on. It also displays email and instant message notifications and includes a time and date display.

If you think that one keyboard or mouse is the same as the next, think again. Give the diNovo Media Desktop a spin, and you'll never go back to generic input devices.

Model: diNovo Media Desktop
Manufacturer: Logitech (www.logitech.com)
Price: $249.95

Nyko Air Flo Mouse

Suffer from sweaty palms? Then check out Nyko's Air Flo Mouse, which has a built-in fan that pushes air through holes in the shell. This cools your hand during heavy computing sessions. (Don't knock it till you've tried it—accurate computing requires a cool hand!)

Aside from the air vents, this is a nice wired optical mouse, incorporating a two-button design and a scroll wheel. The rubber grips and added weight give the mouse a very solid feel. Versions are available for both PC and Mac platforms.

Model: Air Flo Mouse
Manufacturer: Nyko (www.nyko.com)
Price: $14.99

Gyration Ultra GT Cordless Optical Mouse

Cordless mice are nice, but they still require you to roll the controller around a desktop or other flat surface. If you want to totally break away from the desktop, you need a mouse that doesn't need a desk—like the Gyration Ultra GT.

The Ultra GT mouse works by waving it around, more or less. It incorporates motion-sensing technology—actually, a miniature gyroscope—that lets you use natural hand movements to control your cursor. All it takes is a flick of the wrist to launch a program or scroll down a web page. No more wires, no more desktops; you can truly do your computing from a comfortable chair clear across the room from your PC.

Model: Ultra GT Cordless Optical Mouse
Manufacturer: Gyration (www.gyration.com)
Price: $79.99

IOGEAR Phaser Handheld Wireless Mouse

The Logitech Cordless Presenter introduced the concept of the cordless controller; the IOGEAR Phaser ups the coolness factor considerably. This dingus looks like a *Star Trek* phaser and includes two buttons and a thumb-operated trackball. It also has a built-in laser pointer, and there's nothing cooler than aiming your phaser and firing off that red laser light.

Naturally, it operates via RF transmissions, and you can connect multiple devices to the same base. It feels good in your hand, too—it's definitely not wimpy.

Model: Phaser Mouse
Manufacturer: IOGEAR (www.iogear.com)
Price: $59.95

Logitech Cordless Presenter

If you give a lot of PowerPoint presentations, you'll love the Logitech Cordless Presenter. As the name implies, it's a cordless controller with two buttons (back and forward) you can use to switch from slide to slide. It also doubles as a simple two-button optical mouse—and it features a built-in laser pointer.

The Cordless Presenter communicates with your PC via Bluetooth technology, so the connection is extremely reliable. It comes with its own carrying case, so you won't damage it when you're on the road.

Model: Cordless Presenter
Manufacturer: Logitech
(www.logitech.com)
Price: $199.95

Auravision EluminX Illuminated Keyboard

The EluminX keyboard doesn't do anything different or better than hundreds of other computer keyboards—but it looks cooler. The EluminX is lit from within by a glowing blue light. The manufacturer claims that this "internal luminescence" makes the keyboard easier to use and reduces eyestrain, which is pretty much a load of hooey. What the lighting does is make your keyboard look like something out of a science-fiction movie—or a hip martini bar. That's reason enough to buy it, especially if you tend to compute in a darkened room. The effect is visually stunning.

Model: EluminX Illuminated Keyboard
Manufacturer: Auravision
(www.auravisionllc.com)
Price: $69.99

Logitech io Personal Digital Pen

This section reads like a love letter to Logitech, but give the guys there credit; they come up with some truly innovative input devices. Case in point: the io Personal Digital Pen. This gadget combines a normal ballpoint pen with an optical sensor and a small amount of computer memory. Anything you write is automatically stored digitally inside the pen; when you place the pen back in its cradle, it all is transferred to your PC. Included software helps you organize your notes and integrate with Microsoft Outlook and Lotus Notes. It's a neat convergence of pen-and-paper technology with the digital world.

Model: io
Manufacturer: Logitech
(www.logitech.com)
Price: $199.95

Backup Devices

In the caveman days of personal computing, you could back up all your important files on a single floppy disk. But that was before you started adding graphics to all your memos, and before the days of multi-megabyte digital music files and megapixel digital picture files.

In today's world of 200+GB hard drives, it's increasingly difficult to back up your crucial computer files. It would take thousands of floppies to back up today's typical hard drive; there's so much data involved, it's not even practical to burn to backup DVDs. (A 100GB hard drive would require almost two dozen recordable DVDs!)

No, if you're serious about backing up your big hard drive, you need a different solution. In fact, what you need to back up a hard drive is another hard drive. Fortunately, as hard drive prices have dropped, this alternative has become increasingly feasible.

All the major hard drive manufacturers now market hard drive–based backup devices. Most of these solutions include an external hard drive, a USB 2.0 or FireWire connection, and some sort of backup software. The best units totally automate the backup process, making backups either automatically via software or via a big front-panel backup button. I happen to like the

push-button approach; it makes what used to be a complex process quite easy.

What really makes all this easy is the fact that, thanks to big hard disks, all you have to do is copy all your files from one hard drive to another. It's not like the old days, when you had to winnow down the files to copy and then bother with inserting and removing multiple media. Nope, just press a button and turn the backup drive into a mirror of your main drive. What could be easier than that?

A few of the devices here take slightly different approaches to backing up your data. Iomega remains a rebel in its support of removable media, and its REV drive is the true oddball product in this group, designed for those who want to take their files with them. Also unique, but in a totally different fashion, is Mirra, which offers backup via a full-featured personal computer server. This approach might be overkill for most users, but it does provide some additional functionality, if you're interested.

Otherwise, stick to one of the external hard drive backup solutions. Just plug it in to your PC's USB or FireWire jack (FireWire is faster), configure the backup software, and let it do its thing. It's that easy.

Western Digital Media Center

Whether you want to back up the contents of your hard drive or just need more storage for all your digital media files, you can't go wrong with Western Digital's Media Center external hard drives. The Media Center connects to your PC via either USB 2.0 or FireWire and includes a front-mounted power switch. It's available in 160GB, 200GB, and 250GB versions.

Western Digital calls the Media Center a "dual-option" device, which means you can choose to back up files manually or perform automated backups. Backing up is fast (7200rpm) and quiet. It's a slim unit that you can stand horizontally or vertically, and it's small enough to carry from computer to computer.

What makes the Media Center unique is that it's more than just a backup device. It also functions as an 8-in-1 digital media reader and a two-port USB hub. Use it to download your latest digital photos via memory card or to connect other USB peripherals. Better to have this one gadget on your desktop than three separate devices taking up valuable space!

Model: Media Center
Manufacturer: Western Digital (www.wdc.com)
Capacity: 160GB, 200GB, and 250GB versions
Price: $299.99 (160GB), $349.99 (200GB), $399.99 (250GB)

CMS Velocity

If you want a really fast hard disk backup, check out the CMS Velocity. This external hard disk uses a high-speed Serial ATA (SATA) interface for backups that are more than three times faster than with USB or FireWire connections. CMS offers 80GB, 120GB, and 200GB versions.

And here's something else cool—the Velocity functions as an externally bootable backup device for Windows. If your hard disk fails, you can boot from the Velocity backup disk (using the included BounceBack Professional software) and restore your data from there.

Model: Velocity
Manufacturer: CMS Products
(www.cmsproducts.com)
Capacity: 80GB, 120GB, and 200GB versions
Price: $269 (80GB), $299 (120GB), $409 (200GB)

Maxtor OneTouch

The cool thing about the Maxtor OneTouch is that it's truly a one-button backup device. Just press the big button on the front of the unit, and the backup commences via the included Dantz Retrospect Express backup software. It's perhaps the easiest-to-use external hard drive available today.

Maxtor offers 80GB and 120GB USB versions, as well as larger-capacity models that connect via either USB or FireWire. You can even buy an optional carrying case, quite useful if you use the OneTouch with multiple computers—or like to keep your backup disk in a different physical location from your PC.

Model: OneTouch
Manufacturer: Maxtor (www.maxtor.com)
Capacity: 80GB, 120GB, 160GB, 200GB, 250GB, and 300GB versions
Price: $149.95 (80GB), $179.95 (120GB), $199.95 (160GB), $279.95 (200GB), $299.95 (250GB), $349.95 (300GB)

Iomega REV Drive

Not all backup solutions use external hard drives. The Iomega REV utilizes a removable disk cartridge that can store either 35GB (uncompressed) or 90GB (compressed) of data. The REV advantage is price; a REV cartridge costs just a fraction of a comparable external hard drive. Plus, transporting data from one drive to another is as simple as popping a REV disk into your pocket.

Iomega currently makes USB 2.0 and ATAPI versions of the REV Drive; FireWire, SCSI, and SATA versions are planned. It includes software such as Iomega Automatic Backup Pro and Norton Ghost (for creating full-system backups).

Model: REV Drive
Manufacturer: Iomega (www.iomega.com)
Capacity: 35GB (uncompressed)/90GB (compressed) per disk
Price: $399.99; REV disks cost $59.99 each

Mirra Personal Server

Now here's a different approach to data backup: Instead of using a simple external hard drive or backup cartridge, Mirra uses a Linux-based server for continuous hands-free backup of all your computer's data. You connect the Personal Server to your network hub or router or hook it up to the Internet to share files with other users.

Mirra makes the whole process easy enough that the typical home user can do it; included firewall software provides the necessary level of security. The Mirra Personal Server also makes it easy to move files from one computer to another or simply to store all your digital files in a single location. And you get to tell all your techie friends that you're running your own computer server!

Model: Mirra Personal Server
Manufacturer: Mirra (www.mirra.com)
Capacity: 80GB, 120GB, and 250GB versions
Price: $399 (80GB), $499 (120GB), $749 (250GB)

TV Tuners and DVRs

The hottest consumer electronics gadget is the digital video recorder (DVR). DVRs, such as the popular TiVo units, record television programming digitally on hard disks. This lets you not only record a television program for later viewing, but also manipulate a program while you're watching it—you can pause and rewind live TV or even fast forward through commercials.

Of course, you're not really pausing live TV. When you press the Pause button, you freeze the picture onscreen while the DVR keeps recording the live program. Press Play again, and you return to what the DVR just recorded. So you're no longer watching "live" TV, although it's close.

All this is cool enough, but what does it have to do with computers? Simple—because DVRs are hard disk recorders, why not use the hard disk in your computer for the same function? If you can turn your computer into a DVR, you don't need to buy a separate TiVo unit—or pay the monthly (or lifetime) TiVo subscription fees.

To turn your PC into a DVR, you first have to turn it into a TV. That means adding a television tuner to your computer, either with an external device (typically connected via USB) or with an internal video/TV card. Then you need special software to save that television signal to hard disk and to display the necessary television program guide (to make recording specific shows easy).

The other thing you need to turn your PC into a DVR is a big hard disk. Using the standard MPEG2 compression, a 1-hour program takes up 2GB of disk space. So, for example, if you have 20GB free, you can record only 10 hours of programming; the more hard disk space you have, the more programs you can record and store.

When you're buying a TV/DVR device or card, look at the types of inputs it accepts. Yes, you want the standard coaxial input to connect to an antenna or a cable system, but you might also want to connect a VCR or DVD player. So, look for composite video and S-Video inputs for the most flexibility. And, after you get everything hooked up, consider copying your old videotapes to hard disk and then burning them to DVD for posterity. Most of these products come with all the software you'll need to perform this task; just plug everything in, press a few buttons, and start recording!

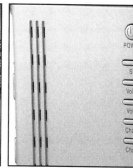

Pinnacle PCTV Deluxe

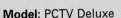

Pinnacle's PCTV Deluxe turns your computer into a full-fledged television and DVR, without the need to open your PC and install a new video card. All you have to do is connect your antenna, cable, or satellite signal to the PCTV breakout box and then connect the breakout box to your PC (via USB), and you're ready to go. The breakout box has both composite video and S-Video inputs, as well as left and right audio inputs. It functions as a state-of-the-art television tuner, controlled by software you install on your PC.

PCTV Deluxe also incorporates high-quality DVR tech-nology to record TV programming to your computer's hard disk in either MPEG2 or lower-quality MPEG1 for-mat. (You can store twice as much programming with the lower-quality format.) You can use the PCTV Deluxe to record your favorite shows, pause live TV programming, skip commercials, or create your own instant replays. It has TiVo-like performance, but with-out the monthly subscription fees.

You can also use the PCTV Deluxe to copy your old videotapes to hard disk or burn them to DVD. You can even connect your camcorder to copy your home movies to your computer's hard drive. It's easy to use and provides quality results at a surprisingly affordable price.

Model: PCTV Deluxe
Manufacturer: Pinnacle Systems
(www.pinnaclesys.com)
Price: $199.99

WinTV-PVR-350 Video Card

Hauppauge's WinTV-PVR-350 is essentially the internal version of the company's outboard WinTV-PVR-USB2 unit; all the connections are on the card itself, accessible from the back of your PC. Like the outboard unit, the WinTV-PVR-350 lets you watch television programs, record programs to your hard disk, pause live shows, and create your own instant replays. You just have to install the card inside your computer.

Bundled software includes WinTV-Editor for video editing, WinTV-Scheduler for recording, and Ulead DVD MovieFactory for authoring and burning DVDs.

Model: WinTV-PVR-350
Manufacturer: Hauppauge
(www.hauppauge.com)
Price: $199

WinTV-PVR-USB2

Hauppauge's WinTV-PVR-USB2 is a lot like Pinnacle's PCTV Deluxe and offers the same TV/DVR functionality. The main unit includes both composite and S-Video inputs and connects to your PC via USB. It includes a 125-channel cable-ready TV tuner, as well as an FM radio tuner.

The included WinTV-Scheduler software lets you schedule your recordings in advance; there's also support for the TitanTV online electronic program guide. For recording your old videotapes to hard disk (and subsequent burning to DVD), Hauppauge includes Ulead DVD MovieFactory software.

Model: WinTV-PVR-USB2
Manufacturer: Hauppauge
(www.hauppauge.com)
Price: $199

All-In-Wonder 9800 PRO Video Card

ATI's TV tuner/DVR top-of-the-line offering is the All-In-Wonder 9800 PRO video card. It's a full-featured HDTV unit that's great for watching and recording TV or playing the latest 3D game graphics.

The included TV-on-Demand software lets you record TV programs on your PC's hard drive and pause live programming; dual 125-channel tuners provide PIP capability. You can look up TV schedules with the Gemstar GUIDE Plus+ software and use the Pinnacle Studio software to create your own movies, music videos, and slideshows. Best of all, ATI's Thruview technology displays TV and DVD programming in translucent desktop windows for easy viewing and even easier access.

Model: All-In-Wonder 9800 PRO
Manufacturer: ATI Technologies, Inc.
(www.ati.com)
Price: $399

AVerMedia TVBox 9 TV Tuner

AVerMedia's TVBox 9 is different from the other gadgets here, in that it doesn't need a computer to work. Instead, the TVBox 9 is a TV tuner that turns any computer monitor into a full-featured television set. Connect your antenna, cable, or satellite signal—as well as signals from a video game or DVD player—and put that old monitor to use. You can even use it as an input device for your new projection or plasma monitor!

Features include picture in picture (PIP), multiple-channel preview (up to 13 channels onscreen simultaneously), progressive scan output, and 3:2 pull-down (converts 24 frames-per-second movie signals to 30 frames-per-second video signals). The TVBox 9 supports displays up to 1280 × 1024 resolution and comes with its own infrared remote control.

Model: TVBox 9
Manufacturer: AVerMedia (www.aver.com)
Price: $179.99

Speakers

Back when I was a youngster, our PCs had just one small, tinny-sounding speaker, and we were glad to have it! (I also walked five miles to school every day, uphill, in the snow—so there.) Of course, all the speaker did was bleep and bloop a little, so the fact that it sucked wasn't that big a deal.

Today, we expect our PC speakers to do a lot more than bleep and bloop. We use our PCs to listen to CDs and digital music we download; we use our PCs to watch surround sound movies on DVD; and we use our PCs to play ultra-realistic games with heart-pounding sounds. And you can't do any of that—or at least, not well—with a tinny-sounding built-in speaker.

For that reason, multiple-speaker systems are some of the most popular add-ons for personal computers today. Ideally, you want a speaker system that sounds good when you're playing music, when you're watching movies, and when you're playing games.

Music reproduction is probably the simplest task for a speaker system. You need two speakers, right and left, and maybe a third speaker—called a *subwoofer*—for the low bass. This type of system is called a *2.1 system*; the right and left speakers are the 2, the subwoofer is the 1, and the dot is a separator.

When you start talking about movies and games, you get into *surround sound*, which requires two or more speakers to be placed behind you. A *4.1 system* has right and left front speakers, right and left rear speakers, and a subwoofer. A *5.1 system* adds a fifth speaker center front; this is the most common system for movie watching. A *6.1 system* adds a center rear speaker to the mix, and a *7.1 system* has the three front speakers plus two surrounds on the left and right sides and two in the rear.

All PC speaker systems are built around powered speakers. Unlike home audio systems that use a *power amplifier* (sometimes built in to a multi-function *receiver*) to power the speakers, your PC doesn't have a power amplifier built in. Instead, the amps are in the speakers themselves or, in some cases, in a control unit to which the speakers are connected. It's not always a truism, but in most cases more power means better sound.

If you decide on a surround sound system, make sure you have the wherewithal to run the proper cables from the front to the rear. Also make sure your PC's sound card supports multichannel sound; you'll need a card with digital outputs to feed most high-end surround sound speaker systems.

    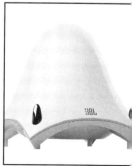

Logitech Z-680

Now, this is one heck of a sound system—whether you're listening to CDs or playing your favorite shoot'em-up games.

First, the Z-680 is a THX-certified 5.1 system with fairly powerful amplification. The center speaker checks in at 69 watts, the four satellites are 62 watts/channel, and the subwoofer delivers a floor-shaking 188 watts. The system includes both Dolby Digital and DTS surround sound decoding, as well as Dolby Pro Logic II technology to simulate surround sound from a stereo input.

The Z-680 lets you connect up to four audio sources simultaneously; the unit includes digital optical, digital coaxial, six-channel direct, and stereo mini connectors. That means you can use it not only with your PC, but also with any video game system, DVD player, CD player, and satellite receiver.

The coolest thing about the Z-680 system is the Digital SurroundTouch Control Center, an outboard controller with its own LCD display. You can use the controller to select which input to listen to, the desired sound effect (Dolby Digital, DTS, stereo, and so on), volume level, and other settings (surround delay, center channel width, and so on). It also features an auxiliary jack you can use to connect a portable music player. And you get a wireless remote control, too.

Great sound, great connections, great control—any wonder why this is Leo's Pick system?

Model: Z-680
Manufacturer: Logitech (www.logitech.com)
Speakers: 5.1
Price: $399.95

Klipsch ProMedia Ultra 5.1

This system demonstrates just what a traditional audio manufacturer can do in the PC speaker arena. Klipsch is well-known for its high-end home speakers, and the ProMedia Ultra 5.1 system delivers that same award-winning sound to any PC-based sound source.

The ProMedia Ultra 5.1 is, as you might suspect, a 5.1 system. The center and satellite speakers feature a horn tweeter and a 3" midrange; the subwoofer has dual 8" side-firing drivers. All this is driven by a 500-watt BASH amplifier, making the ProMedia Ultra 5.1 one of the most powerful personal audio systems available today. It'll blow you away.

Model: ProMedia Ultra 5.1
Manufacturer: Klipsch (www.klipsch.com)
Speakers: 5.1
Price: $399.99

Creative GigaWorks S750

Five speakers (and a subwoofer) not enough for you? Then check out the GigaWorks S750, one of the first 7.1 systems on the market. That's right, you get a center speaker, six satellites (two front, two side, two rear), and a subwoofer for the most surrounding surround sound you can imagine—terrific for hardcore gamers.

Don't have a 7.1 sound card? Don't fret; Creative uses proprietary CMSS upmix technology to simulate 7.1 surround sound from ordinary 5.1 and 6.1 sound cards. And it's all THX-certified, so even George Lucas will be satisfied with the results.

Model: GigaWorks S750
Manufacturer: Creative (www.creative.com)
Speakers: 7.1
Price: $499.99

Harman/Kardon SoundsticksII

It might seem paradoxical to praise speakers for their looks, but SoundsticksII might be the coolest-looking PC speakers made today. Look closely at that picture; that's right, these are *transparent* speakers. They're unlike anything you've ever seen.

And guess what? These speakers sound as good as they look. The left and right speakers (this is a stereo system, so there's no surround sound) each features four 1" drivers. The bass is delivered by the separate 6" subwoofer, although you probably want to rethink the typical under-the-desk placement; the darned thing is too cool-looking to hide away in a corner!

Model: SoundsticksII
Manufacturer: Harman/Kardon
(www.harmankardon.com)
Speakers: 2.1
Price: $199.95

JBL Creature II

Also quite cool is JBL's Creature II, another two-channel system with subwoofer. These speakers look like...well, they look like some sort of alien creature, that's for sure.

The Creature's sound quality is on par with the Soundsticks', which is fine for listening to music or playing games. You also get a touch volume control to turn things up—or quiet them down. And here's a bonus feature: Because the Creature II is self-powered (like all the systems here), you can connect your portable music player and use it to play all your digital music; the looks of this system make it an ideal companion to Apple's cool-white iPod.

Model: Creature II
Manufacturer: JBL (www.jbl.com)
Speakers: 2.1
Price: $99.95

Scanners

In the scheme of things, scanners are probably the least sexy part of a computer system. (Okay, parallel ports are maybe even less hip. It's a toss-up.) In most cases, a scanner does exactly what it's supposed to do. It scans a sheet of paper into a digital reproduction. If there's text on the paper, a good scanner (and good optical character recognition software) translates the text into characters for a word processing document. If there's a picture on the page, the scanner creates a digital graphics file containing the picture. A good scanner does the job quickly, relatively accurately, and with a minimum of fuss and muss. It also does it for less than $200—far less, in many cases.

So, what could possibly be cool about scanning? Well, you'd be surprised. First, there are actually a few scanners that do what they do in style, utilizing interesting industrial design. Second, some scanners are cool because they specialize in a particular type of task—scanning photos or business cards or some such. And third, some scanners are cool because they're small and compact and fit in your pocket, and anything that fits in your pocket is intrinsically cool. (Leo's Rule of Coolness #17: Small Is Cool.)

In the pages that follow, I present five scanners that definitely aren't boring. Not that they necessarily outperform the other, less-cool scanners on the market; spend a hundred bucks or so and you'll get a decent scanner, cool or not. But these are scanners you won't feel embarrassed to own. In fact, you might deem them displayworthy, just cool enough to show off to your techie friends.

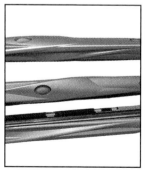
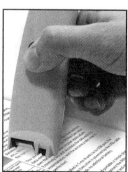

HP Scanjet 4670

Leo's Pick

I never thought I'd call a scanner cool, but then HP introduced the Scanjet 4670. This puppy makes you want to ditch your old-fashioned desktop scanner, even if it's in perfect working condition, just so you can show off the 4670's cool see-through design.

First, the 4670 doesn't lay flat on your desktop—it stands up vertically on its stand, like a picture frame. And the scanner itself is see-through, which turns it into an attractive piece of equipment. To make a scan, you fold open the unit and slip the paper inside. You can also take the scanner off the stand and slip it over the original for "free" scanning. Oh, and there's an adapter you can use to scan 35mm slides and negatives.

Performance-wise, this unit delivers acceptable 2400 × 2400 dpi resolution and 48-bit color. It connects to your PC via USB 2.0 and comes with a variety of imaging and OCR software.

But all that doesn't really matter. Admit it, you want this scanner because it looks cool—which is good enough for me.

Model: Scanjet 4670
Manufacturer: Hewlett-Packard (www.hp.com)
Price: $199.99

Epson Perfection 4870 Photo

Most desktop scanners only do a so-so job scanning photo prints, and some don't scan negatives or slides at all. For serious photo scanning, you need a dedicated photo scanner—like the Epson Perfection 4870 Photo. This unit is made especially for scanning 35mm slides, negatives, and photo prints; it delivers a stunning 4800 × 9600 dpi resolution, with 48-bit color.

The Perfection 4870 Photo features a built-in transparency unit that accommodates film up to 4" × 5" or up to twenty-four 35mm negatives at a time. Even cooler, Epson's DIGITAL ICE technology removes dust, scratches, and tears from photo prints. If you have a lot of slides or prints to scan, this is the gadget for you.

Model: Perfection 4870 Photo
Manufacturer: Epson (www.epson.com)
Price: $449

Corex CardScan Executive

Here's another specialty scanner, perfect for the busy businessperson. Corex's CardScan Executive is the world's best-selling business-card scanner; just pop a card into the slot, and the CardScan Executive scans all the important information. Even better, the information then is translated and automatically inserted into the correct fields of the included address book software—no manual editing necessary.

You can connect the CardScan Executive to your PC via USB or sync the address book software with your PDA or smartphone. CardScan is compatible with Microsoft Outlook, Lotus Notes, ACT!, and other similar programs.

Model: CardScan Executive
Manufacturer: Corex (www.corex.com)
Price: $199.99

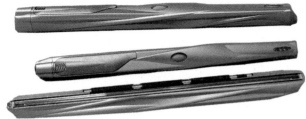

Planon DocuPen

Scanners don't have to take up an entire desktop. Here's one that looks just like a ballpoint pen; the Planon DocuPen is just 8" long and 1/2" in diameter. It's small enough to fit in your shirt pocket.

The DocuPen is battery-operated and contains 2MB of flash memory. Drag it across the document you want to scan; it scans a full page in just 4–8 seconds. Connect the DocuPen to your PC via USB to download the scanned images.

Model: DocuPen
Manufacturer: Planon (www.planon.com)
Price: $199.99

IRISPen Executive

Use a lot of forms? Then check out the IRISPen Executive. This is a handheld scanner that's perfect for capturing text, figures, bar codes, and even handwritten numbers. Just slide the scanner over the text you want to enter, and the text is automatically scanned and entered into the current application. It reads any font in any type style, from 6-point to 22-point, at up to 1,000 characters per second.

You connect the IRISPen to your PC via USB. The pen unit features two programmable buttons you can use to assign common keyboard commands. Just scan and click!

Model: IRISPen Executive
Manufacturer: I.R.I.S (www.irisusa.com)
Price: $219.99

Webcams

Webcams—sometimes called *Internet cameras*—have become increasingly popular. Part of that popularity is due to price; these aren't terribly expensive peripherals, all things considered. Part is due to more and more users wanting to put their own video on the Web. And part is due to the fact that these are neat-looking gadgets, and it's kind of cool to have one of these puppies sitting on your computer monitor, even if you never launch your own Webcam website or partake in live videoconferencing.

Let's start by talking about how you might use a Webcam. One of the most common uses is for video instant messaging. Most of the major instant messaging systems—Windows Messenger, Yahoo! Messenger, and the like—let you connect a Webcam and add live video to your instant messages. Most people find it easier to speak than type; plus it's always cool to transmit pictures of yourself across the Web, especially when they're in real time. Using a Webcam with Yahoo! Messenger and the like is typically as easy as turning on your camera, clicking the appropriate button or link, and smiling for your friends.

Then there's the concept of sending video-enabled email messages—called *video email*. Obviously, you can't send *live* video via email,

but you can record short videos of yourself and attach the video files to your email messages. Most Webcams come with software that makes this task relatively simple.

Finally, we have the concept of Webcam-enabled websites—themselves called *Webcams*. One of the first, and for a long while the most popular, of these sites was the Jennicam, which 24/7 chronicled the life of a young woman named Jenni via a half-dozen or so live cameras scattered throughout her apartment. Today, you can find Webcams broadcasting continuously outside public buildings, over busy intersections, aimed at fish tanks and coffee machines (don't ask), and—more notoriously—documenting (for a fee) various X-rated shenanigans. It's all based on the same technology, using the same hundred-dollar Webcams you can buy at your local CompUSA.

There's one more use for Webcams, which I'll touch on with a product or two—surveillance. Position a Webcam, hook it up to a private website (only you have the URL), and watch what goes on while you're out of the house. It's actually kind of a blurry line; any consumer Webcam can be used for surveillance, and some so-called surveillance cams actually make fine consumer Webcams. It's pretty much the same technology, at any rate.

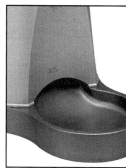

Logitech QuickCam Orbit

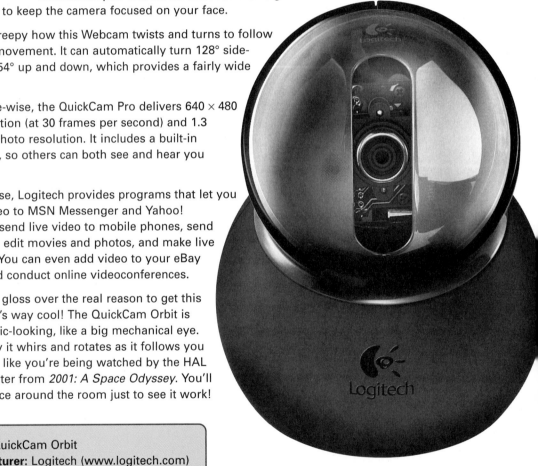

Leo's Pick

Don't feel like positioning your camera manually? Then check out the QuickCam Orbit, the Webcam that follows you as you move around the room. That's right, this camera features automatic face tracking software and a mechanical pan-and-tilt mechanism with digital zoom to keep the camera focused on your face.

It's almost creepy how this Webcam twists and turns to follow your every movement. It can automatically turn 128° side-to-side and 54° up and down, which provides a fairly wide stage.

Performance-wise, the QuickCam Pro delivers 640 × 480 video resolution (at 30 frames per second) and 1.3 megapixel photo resolution. It includes a built-in microphone, so others can both see and hear you online.

Software-wise, Logitech provides programs that let you add live video to MSN Messenger and Yahoo! Messenger, send live video to mobile phones, send video email, edit movies and photos, and make live video calls. You can even add video to your eBay auctions and conduct online videoconferences.

But let's not gloss over the real reason to get this Webcam—it's way cool! The QuickCam Orbit is very futuristic-looking, like a big mechanical eye. And the way it whirs and rotates as it follows you around...it's like you're being watched by the HAL 9000 computer from *2001: A Space Odyssey*. You'll want to dance around the room just to see it work!

Model: QuickCam Orbit
Manufacturer: Logitech (www.logitech.com)
Price: $129.99

Logitech QuickCam Pro 4000

If you don't mind positioning your Webcam manually, check out Logitech's QuickCam Pro. It's the best-selling Webcam today, and for good reason—the QuickCam Pro is a solid performer in a compact package that's easy to use, is easy to connect, and delivers a host of useful features.

The QuickCam Pro includes a built-in digital zoom, as well as mechanical panning and tilting, all controlled from your PC via the included software. It comes with all the software bundled with the pricier QuickCam Orbit, so you can use it to do just about anything you can think of. The PC connection is via USB.

Model: QuickCam Pro 4000
Manufacturer: Logitech
(www.logitech.com)
Price: $99.95

D-Link SecuriCam DCS-5300W Wireless Internet Camera

Here's a wireless camera designed for surveillance use that also makes a darned good PC-based Webcam. Thanks to the Wi-Fi operation, you can put the camera anywhere in your house and not bother with running a cable to your PC.

What's really cool about the SecuriCam is its built-in motion detection and motorized operation. You can pan and tilt the unit from any PC connected to the Internet or with the unit's remote control. Autopan mode enables the camera to move 270° horizontally, and the special Patrol mode cycles the unit through 24 preset positions. You can even program the camera to email you when it's activated!

Model: SecuriCam DCS-5300W
Manufacturer: D-Link (www.dlink.com)
Price: $399.95

Eagletron TrackerPod

You don't have to buy a high-priced Webcam to get fancy panning and tilting. Instead, you can mount your Webcam on the TrackerPod, a robotic tripod that provides pan, tilt, and zoom operations.

All functions can be controlled over the Internet via the included TrackerCam software, or you can use its motion tracking technology to track the nearest person to the camera. You can even program the TrackerPod for surveillance operation, in which it scans a room in any pattern you specify. It works with any USB Webcam.

Model: TrackerPod
Manufacturer: Eagletron
(www.trackercam.com)
Price: $174.99

iSeePet

This gadget might seem comically odd at first, but I guarantee it'll win you over—especially if you're a pet lover. The manufacturer calls iSeePet a "remotely controlled pet communication system," and that's as good a description as any. You connect the unit to the Internet, via your PC, and fill it with food and water. Then you can use any Internet-connected computer to call your pet, release some food, and watch Fido or Fluffy via the built-in Webcam.

It sounds goofy, but it's a cool way to pet sit while you're away from home. Just open your Web browser, click a few buttons, and see what your dog or cat is up to. It's a fairly brilliant idea, IMHO.

Model: iSeePet
Manufacturer: AOS Technologies
(www.iseepet.com)
Price: $500

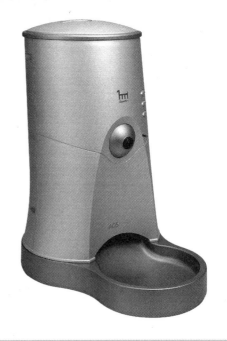

USB Gizmos

This is my favorite category in this entire book. Why? Because it contains some of the goofiest gadgets you'll ever imagine—and they're all powered by USB.

The driving force behind all these devices is USB power. USB is a unique connector in that it not only transfers computer signals and data, but also passes through a small amount of electricity. That electricity is used to provide power to the USB devices you connect to your computer. So, if you connect a Webcam via USB, for example, you don't have to plug the Webcam in to a power outlet; the USB connection provides all the operating power it needs.

That simple fact has inspired designers the world over—but particularly in Japan, for some reason—to come up with all manner of devices that can feed off the USB power source. The devices don't have to be particularly useful; the only common denominator is that they don't have separate power connections, just a simple USB connector.

What kind of gizmos are we talking about? It's a wide, wild variety. As you'll see, a USB device can be anything from a useful USB Wi-Fi adapter to a completely useless USB heating pad. There are USB lights and fans, USB beverage warmers and air purifiers, and even USB aquariums. And they're all powered by that little cable connected to your PC's USB port.

The one thing I noticed about these USB gadgets is that the less useful they are, the more likely they are to come from small and quirky Japanese manufacturers. I'm not sure why this is the case, but the Japanese seem to have an infatuation with USB devices, and the more bizarre, the better. All power to the Japanese, I say; I love strange USB devices.

Unfortunately, the more unusual the USB device, the harder it is to find and purchase. In fact, some of gizmos I discuss can only be purchased from the Japanese manufacturer. Maybe there's a USB-powered yen-to-dollar conversion device you can use, if you're interested.

That said, I find ThinkGeek (www.thinkgeek.com) to be a good source for the quirkier of these USB devices. And for the latest new product announcements, you can't beat Gizmodo (www.gizmodo.com), which I thank for bringing to my attention some of the odder gizmos listed here. So read on—and prepare to be entertained.

Griffin PowerMate

My favorite USB gadget is simple to describe: It's a big freakin' knob. So, why do you need a big freakin' knob? Well, you can program the PowerMate to control just about anything you want on you computer. The most obvious use is as a volume knob, but you can also use it as a video editing jog/shuttle wheel, to scroll through Word or Excel documents, to scrub through songs in music sequencing applications, to browse through email messages, and more. It works by sending keyboard shortcut commands to your PC, so all you have to do is program in the appropriate shortcuts to make it work.

What I really like about the PowerMate is how it feels in your hand. It's made out of heavy machined aluminum, which gives it an extremely solid feel. You can order it in either brushed aluminum or flat black.

The PowerMate also provides visual confirmation of what you're doing via a cool blue light that glows underneath the knob. Turn up the volume and the glow gets brighter; dial it down and the glow dims. Press the Mute button and the light turns off. And, while your computer sleeps, the glow pulses hypnotically.

It looks cool, it feels cool, and it actually does something useful—which is more than you can say for most USB gadgets.

Model: PowerMate
Manufacturer: Griffin Technology
(www.griffintechnology.com)
Price: $45

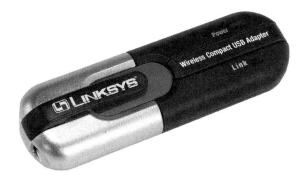

Linksys Wireless Compact USB Adapter

The Linksys Wireless Compact USB Adapter is a long name for a simple, quite useful, little device. The USB Adapter is an 802.11b Wi-Fi adapter in the form of a USB keychain device. Just plug the USB Adapter in to the USB port of your notebook or desktop PC and get instant access to all nearby Wi-Fi networks. The adapter is hot-swappable, so you can easily move it between different computers.

Linksys includes a neck strap to make it easy to carry around, as well as a USB extension cable in case you need to plug it in to the back of a desktop PC. This is truly plug-and-play Wi-Fi access!

Model: WUSB12
Manufacturer: Linksys (www.linksys.com)
Price: $69 (Photo courtesy of Linksys)

USB Vacuum Cleaner

You can use USB power for just about anything, so why not use it to keep your desktop clean? The USB Vacuum Cleaner is a small handheld vac sized just right for cleaning your computer keyboard and the front of your system unit. It comes with a fairly long coiled cord, so you have a little bit of flexibility. The USB connection provides adequate power for sucking dust off the keys.

Don't laugh at this one—just take a look at your keyboard and see how much dust you have building up at the corners. Why not use USB power to clean things up a bit?

Model: USB Vacuum Cleaner
Manufacturer: LOAS (www.loas.co.jp)
Price: N/A

FlyFan USB Fan

Kensington's other USB gizmo is the FlyFan, a small, personal, USB-powered fan. It provides just enough breeze to cool you off in stuffy meetings or on crowded airplanes, and you can precisely position the fan thanks to its flexible gooseneck. It's quiet, it's safe (the blades are made of a soft nylon), and it doesn't use a lot of power.

The FlyFan is a great way to cool your own personal space—wherever you might be computing.

Model: FlyFan
Manufacturer: Kensington
(www.kensington.com)
Price: $9.99

FlyLight USB Notebook Light

Here's the first of two practical USB gizmos from Kensington that are designed especially for notebook users. The FlyLight is a small LED flashlight on a flexible gooseneck, powered by your computer's USB port. All you have to do is plug it in and you have personal lighting no matter where you might happen to be—on an airplane, in a dark conference room, or in your home office with the lights turned off.

The FlyLight is small, is easy-to-use, doesn't consume a lot of power (less than 90 seconds of notebook battery charge for each hour of use), and is priced right.

Model: FlyLight
Manufacturer: Kensington
(www.kensington.com)
Price: $19.99

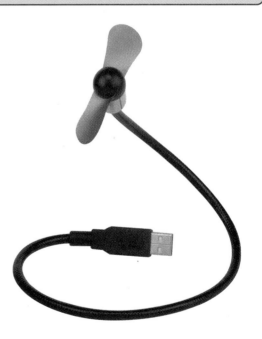

USB Ashtray

Here's another oddball USB accessory from the folks at ThinkGeek, perfect for all you smokers out there. The USB Ashtray is a so-called smoke-less ashtray, with USB-powered absorbing fan and filter. The ashtray section can be easily removed for quick cleaning, and you turn it on and off by opening and closing the cover. There's even a cute little Japanese creature inside, whose significance totally eludes me.

In any case, the USB Ashtray is sure to cut down on smoke and odors at least a little, in a geeky sort of way.

Model: USB Ashtray
Manufacturer: ThinkGeek
(www.thinkgeek.com)
Price: $34.99

USB Air Purifier

If you like the idea of a personal fan, go one step further with this USB-powered air purifier. It plugs in to your computer's USB slot and pro-vides constant air freshening by removing smoke, dust, germs, and other airborne contami-nants. It's small enough to not get in the way (just 3" × 2.5"); just plug it in and let it silently do its job.

Cleaner air is definitely a good thing—especially when it's enabled by clean USB power!

Model: USB Air Purifier
Manufacturer: ThinkGeek
(www.thinkgeek.com)
Price: $29.99

USB Beverage Warmer

If you thought a USB ashtray was odd, how about a USB-powered beverage warmer? This gizmo is a low-voltage heat pad with Velcro fastener that you can wrap around cups, mugs, and even baby bottles. Plug it in to your computer's USB port, and you can keep beverages hot about 30 minutes longer than otherwise.

The only problem with the USB Beverage Warmer is that it only comes with a 5" cable, which doesn't give you a lot of sipping room. If you're serious about using this gadget, you'll probably need to attach it to a USB extension cable—or use a really long straw.

Model: USB Beverage Warmer
Manufacturer: Addlogix
(www.addlogix.com)
Price: $12.95

USB Heating Blanket

And now for something almost completely useless—a USB-powered heating blanket, courtesy of a Japanese company that specializes in oddball computer gadgets. What they call the *electricknee* is actually a small mat that heats up when you connect it to your PC's USB port. I assume you place it on your lap to keep your private parts warm.

As MIB puts it on their Web site (translated from the Japanese, thanks to Babelfish), "Feeling good temperature is maintained due to the heat source element!" They go on to claim that "blood circulation of the body is promoted," and "warming the body to the core, you improve many cold characteristic constitution in the woman." I'm all for improving cold womanly constitutions, but I fail to see a real need for this one. If you disagree, MIB offers this gadget in two patterns, as well as a *Sesame Street* Elmo version (undoubtedly unlicensed), all in 100% polyester.

Model: UHK-01A/B
Manufacturer: MIB
(www.mib.co.jp/onlineshop/)
Price: 4,980 yen (approx. $45)

USB Glowing Aquarium

This gadget is so strange that it's strangely appealing. What you have here is a miniature fake aquarium, completely powered from your computer's USB port. The USB powers the aquarium's high-intensity blue LED light, as well as the small motor used to generate the small water current.

The Glowing Aquarium comes with the plexi-glass tank, two "fish," and a USB cable. Just add water to the tank, attach it to your computer via USB, and watch the fake fish swim around. It's just kitschy enough to be cool.

> **Model:** USB Glowing Aquarium
> **Manufacturer:** Addlogix
> (www.addlogix.com)
> **Price:** $22

Illuminated USB Cables

Finally, if you're going to be hooking up a lot of USB gadgets, you might as well do it in style. ThinkGeek offers these illuminated USB cables, with your choice of blue, red, or white lights at the ends. The cables are 6' long and available as both A-B type cables or as extension cables with two A-type connectors.

Imagine computing in the dark with your glowing blue USB cables, your glowing blue PowerMate knob, your glowing blue USB Aquarium, and your glowing blue EluminX keyboard. Just you in the dark with a lot of blue stuff glowing all around you. How cool would that be?

> **Model:** Illuminated USB Cables
> **Manufacturer:** ThinkGeek
> (www.thinkgeek.com)
> **Price:** $5.99

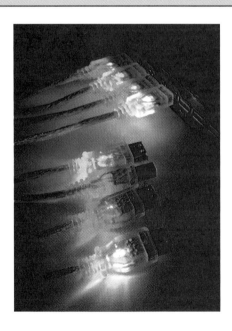

Keychain Storage Devices

Leaving behind the more useless USB gadgets, let's turn to a much more useful, much more popular category—USB memory devices. These gadgets contain various amounts of flash memory and connect to your computer via the USB port. When connected, your computer views the device just like another disk drive. You can then transfer files from your computer to the flash memory and back again.

What's especially cool about these USB memory devices is that they pack so much storage in such a small form factor. Most of these gizmos are truly keychain-sized; you can slip them in your pocket and carry them from PC to PC. That makes for truly portable mass storage. And, because they're pretty much plug-and-play, transferring your files from one computer to another is easy, which is great if you use multiple PCs or travel to various locations.

Some of the early USB memory devices didn't have much memory onboard—8MB and 16MB devices were common. But as the price of flash memory has come down, manufacturers have packed more and more memory into these little doodads. Some models today have upwards of 512MB and 1GB of storage, which is big enough to store all but the biggest files.

Of course, the more storage offered, the higher the price. Today's lowest-priced USB memory devices give you 32MB of storage for $30 or so. Get into the 256MB range and you'll spend closer to $100, and the big 1GB gizmos will set you back several hundred bucks.

Of course, when a device becomes a commodity, fashion comes into play. You can go with a plain-Jane USB memory device or one in fluorescent colors with a stylish neck chain. You can even find USB memory devices attached to Swiss army knives and built in to expensive ballpoint pens. My favorite USB memory device is the i-Duck, which is shaped like a little rubber ducky. The shape isn't particularly useful, but I really like the idea of plugging a duck into my computer!

Fujifilm USB Drive

There are tons of USB flash drives on the market, but the Fujifilm USB Drive gets my thumbs up because it comes in such a wide variety of capacities. You can get USB Drives in capacities ranging from 32MB to a whopping 1GB, and they're all small and cute and easy to schlep around.

Using a USB Drive is as easy as removing the cap and plugging it into one of your computer's USB ports. You don't need to connect any power cables or install any software. Just plug it in and your computer reads it like any other drive. It's a convenient way to transfer files of all sorts from one computer to another.

Fujifilm's 32MB and 64MB USB Drives are USB 1.1 compatible, whereas the larger-capacity models are compatible with both USB 1.1 and 2.0. You can use any model with PCs, Macs, and Linux machines, and they come in cool blue plastic casings.

Model: USB Drive
Manufacturer: Fujifilm
(www.fujifilmusbdrive.com)
Capacity: 32MB, 64MB, 128MB, 256MB, 512MB, 1GB
Price: $30 (32MB), $40 (64MB) $70 (128MB), $110 (256MB), $170 (512MB), $340 (1GB)

Sandisk Cruzer Mini USB Flash Drive

What I like about the Sandisk Cruzer Mini is that it's smaller than most other high-capacity USB drives. The Cruzer's thin design doesn't obstruct the stacked USB ports found on many computers, as other keychain devices tend to do. If space is tight, this drive will fit.

Each unit comes with two extra color caps and a neck strap, if that sort of thing appeals to you. It's compatible with both USB 1.1 and 2.0.

Model: Cruzer Mini
Manufacturer: Sandisk (www.sandisk.com)
Capacity: 128MB, 256MB
Price: $49.99 (128MB), $79.99 (256MB)

Iomega Micro Mini

Here's another small form-factor keychain drive, the Iomega Micro Mini. This is an ultra-small drive that is small enough to fit comfortably in any pocket.

The Micro Mini (is that name redundant?) is also ultra-fashionable. It comes with three changeable color covers, neck chain, key clip, and illuminating USB extension cable. It's a USB 2.0 device, so file transfers are fairly fast. Like other similar devices, no installation software is required.

Model: Micro Mini
Manufacturer: Iomega (www.iomega.com)
Capacity: 64MB, 128MB
Price: $49.95 (64MB), $69.95 (128MB)

Freecom USB Card

Freecom's USB Card is different from other keychain devices, in that it's not designed to fit on a keychain. Instead, the USB Card is designed to fit in your wallet; it's shaped like a thin credit card. When it comes time to connect it to your PC, the USB adapter folds out of the body of the card.

What I like about the USB Card, in addition to its shape, is its speed. This flash memory device provides ultra-fast 5MB/second transfer rates—significantly faster than keychain memory devices. It also comes with a preloaded software suite and built-in security password protection.

Model: USB Card
Manufacturer: Freecom
(www.freecom.com)
Capacity: 128MB, 256MB, 512MB
Price: $99.99 (128MB), $139.99 (256MB),
$229.99 (512MB)

SWISSMEMORY USB
Swiss Army Knife

Leave it to the Swiss to utilize flash memory in a highly functional fashion. The SWISSMEMORY is a USB memory device built in to a multifunction Swiss army knife—complete with red LED, a blade, a nail file with screwdriver, scissors, and a ballpoint pen. I guess this means that computer memory is as indispensable as a screwdriver, at least to the Swiss.

In case the name doesn't mean anything to you, Victorinox is the company that makes "official" Swiss army knives. So, you're getting the real deal here, along with your flash memory. And in case you're wondering, the USB drive can be detached from the rest of the knife—so you don't have to have that big toolkit hanging off your PC.

Model: SWISSMEMORY 0.6076.T
Manufacturer: Victorinox
(www.victorinox.com)
Capacity: 64MB
Price: $69

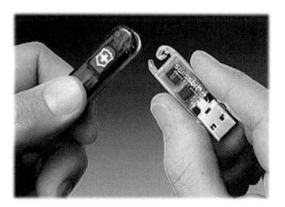

© 2004 CNET Networks, Inc.

Meritline Mobile Pen Drive

Meritline offers some interesting applications of flash memory technology, chief of which is the Mobile Pen Drive. This gadget is a functioning ballpoint pen with flash memory added. The memory and USB adapter are built in to the cap of the rather elegant pen; the body of the pen is the pen.

The Mobile Pen Drive truly puts computer storage in your pocket. Think about it; what could be more natural than sliding a pen into your pocket—with or without a geeky pocket protector? It's a fairly clever idea to let USB memory piggyback along for the ride.

Model: Mobile Pen Drive
Manufacturer: Meritline
(www.meritline.com)
Capacity: 128MB
Price: $65

i-Duck

If coolness is more important than compactness, the i-Duck is the USB drive for you. The i-Duck is a uniquely Japanese flash memory device that looks like a little ducky. Plug it in to your PC's USB port and the ducky lights up. Six colors are available: pink, yellow, blue, tangerine, Army (camouflage), and Heart (with little red hearts on it).

The i-Duck comes in three capacities, from 16MB to 512MB. All the ducks are USB 1.1-compatible, and the 512MB version is also compatible with USB 2.0. But what's really important is that you can plug a lighted ducky in to your PC. A ducky!

Model: i-Duck
Manufacturer: Solid Alliance
(www.dynamism.com/iduck/)
Capacity: 16MB, 256MB, 512MB
Price: $49 (16MB), $149 (256MB), $329 (512MB)

Digital Media Readers

Digital media cards are all the rage. If you have a digital camera, it stores its pictures on some sort of media card. If you have some types of digital music players, they store their files on media cards. If you have a PDA, chances are it stores its files on some sort of media card.

The problem, of course, is how to transfer files from that little media card to your PC. The solution is to use a digital media reader; insert the card into the reader, connect the reader to the PC, and your PC views the media card as just another drive. You can then transfer files back and forth, quick as anything.

A complicating factor is that there isn't just one type of digital media card. These gizmos come in all shapes and sizes, not to mention various capacities, so a single slot won't handle all the different variations.

Although you can purchase very inexpensive single-format readers, you probably should spend a few more bucks and get one that reads all the types of media cards in use today. That includes Compact Flash I and II (they're subtly different), Smart Media, Secure Digital, MultiMediaCard, Memory Stick, Memory Stick Pro, IBM Microdrive, and xD-Picture Card. The more formats read, the better. In any case, before you make a purchase, make sure the digital media reader handles the type of cards you use in all your devices.

Most digital media readers connect to your PC via USB. They all tend to perform similar functions, chief of which is transferring data from the media card to your PC, and vice versa. Some media readers let you transfer data from one type of card to another, without passing through the PC. One reader, the Addonics 18-in-1, even includes a DVD/CD-R/RW drive and lets you transfer data from memory card direct to recordable CDs.

In any case, you don't have to spend a lot of money on a digital media reader. Just be sure you pick one that handles the card formats you use and that fits the way you use it.

 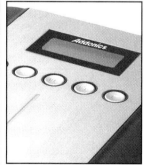   

Addonics MFR 18-in-1 Multi Function Recorder

Leo's Pick

This one device does just about everything.

The Addonics MFR 18-in-1 Multi Function Reader is a DVD player, a CD-R/CD-RW player/burner, a standalone MP3 player, and an 8-in-1 digital media reader, all in a single compact and portable device. By putting all your media together in a single drive, you have the option of backing up your memory cards directly to CDs. You can also bypass your PC completely and play back any digital images you have in flash memory (or on CD) through a TV or projector.

The MFR is a USB 2.0 unit, and it comes with its own remote control unit. It also features a 2.5-hour rechargeable battery pack, so you can use it anywhere.

And just what are those 18 functions? Well, I think Addonics uses creative counting, but here's what they say. First, it reads eight types of flash memory media: Compact Flash I, Compact Flash II, Smart Media, Secure Digital, MultiMediaCard, Memory Stick, Memory Stick Pro, IBM Microdrive, and xD-Picture Card. (That's actually nine types of media, by my count.) It performs eight player functions: DVD to TV, DVD to PC, CD, VCD, still photo on TV, still photo via projector, S-Video, and MP3. (I think they double-count some of these.) Finally, it works with two types of optical recording media: CD-R and CD-RW. (Definitely double-dipping here.)

However you count it, though, the MFR Multi Function Reader is one versatile device. It's great when space or connections are at a premium—or when you just want one gadget instead of several.

> **Model:** MFR Multi Function Recorder
> **Manufacturer:** Addonics (www.addonics.com)
> **Price:** $235

Dazzle Hi-Speed 10-in-1 Universal Reader/Writer

The Dazzle 10-in-1 is a versatile, extremely fast digital media reader. The speed comes from the USB 2.0 connection, and the versatility comes from the formats it supports: CompactFlash I, CompactFlash II, IBM Microdrive, SmartMedia, Memory Stick, Magic Gate Memory Stick, Memory Stick PRO, MultiMediaCard, Secure Digital, and xD-Picture Card.

You can use the Dazzle 10-in-1 with both PCs and Macs. It comes with OnDVD software, which you can use to create photo slideshows.

Model: DM-24001
Manufacturer: Zio Corporation
(www.ziocorp.com)
Price: $69.95

Sandisk ImageMate 8-in-1 Reader/Writer

The Sandisk ImageMate is a cool-looking digital media reader; you can lay it horizontally on your desktop or stand it vertically in the included stand. The main unit is fairly portable so you can carry it with you from one PC to another.

It's a USB 1.1/2.0 device, so it works with any PC. And it reads and writes the following digital formats: CompactFlash I, CompactFlash II, Memory Stick, Memory Stick PRO, SmartMedia, xD-Picture Card, MultiMediaCard, and SD Card.

Model: ImageMate 8-in-1 Reader/Writer
Manufacturer: Sandisk (www.sandisk.com)
Price: $39.99

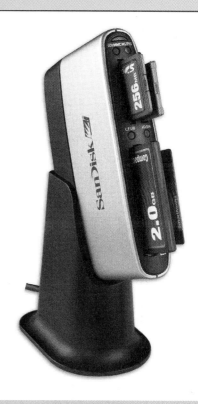

Portable Computer Accessories

One of the reasons I like notebook PCs is that there are all sorts of gadgets you can buy for them—and, in case you can't tell, I like buying gadgets! Notebook gadgets are mostly small, often (but not always) low-priced, and sometimes quite cool. My only problem is that if I buy every notebook gadget that catches my eye, I'll need more space to haul the gadgets than I do to haul my notebook PC!

What types of notebook gadgets are we talking about? There are three main categories: security, power, and storage/display—along with the normal miscellaneous gadgets, of course.

Security-related gadgets are designed to protect your notebook from theft. The simplest devices work to strap your PC to a presumably immovable object; the fancier ones incorporate some sort of antitheft alarm. All do a pretty good job of deterring would-be thieves.

You use power-related gadgets to provide power to your notebook. These gadgets supplement your PC's built-in batteries or power supply when you're on the road. Some devices replace the clunky factory-supplied AC power adapter; others let you connect to various DC power sources. All are essential if you're a frequent traveler.

Storage and display gadgets function as racks or docking stations when you use your notebook in the office. Some of these items are quite fashionable; others, such as the LapCool (with built-in cooling fan), provide unique functionality.

The two largest manufacturers of portable computer accessories are Kensington and Targus. You've already seen some of Kensington's products, such as the USB FlyLight and FlyFan. Targus is big in the security and power categories and also supplies a full line of notebook cases. I recommend perusing each of their websites to see what catches your eye.

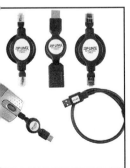

Vantec LapCool Notebook Cooler

Here's a really cool notebook computer gadget—obvious pun intended. The LapCool notebook cooler helps cool down hot-running notebooks, thanks to two ultra-quiet fans in the base. Set your notebook PC on the LapCool, flip on the fans, and bring down the heat level almost immediately. The two fans are separately adjustable, so you can dial in just the right amount of cooling that you want.

The LapCool has a flat 300mm × 263mm surface, so just about any notebook fits on top; four rubber feet ensure that the LapCool stays firmly in place. And the slight angle of the unit positions your notebook keyboard at a comfortable angle.

If that isn't neat enough, the LapCool also functions as a four-port USB 2.0 hub, so you can get double duty from the desktop footprint. The USB ports let you use the LapCool as a kind of notebook docking station—and the built-in cooling is just a plus.

Cool!

Model: LapCool
Manufacturer: Vantec
(www.vantecusa.com)
Price: $42.95

Targus DEFCON Security Devices

Leo's Pick

One of the big problems with portable computers is that they're portable enough for sneaky thieves to make off with if you're not paying close attention. It's a particular problem in airports, coffeehouses, and other public venues; it's getting so you don't ever want to turn your back on your expensive PC investment.

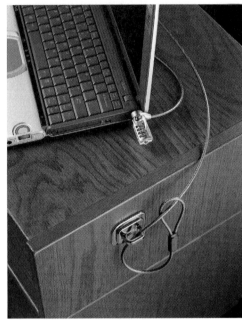

This situation has inspired a raft of notebook security products, some of the best of which are manufactured by Targus. In fact, two Targus products get my Leo's Pick in this category.

The simplest way to secure your notebook PC is to chain it down. To that end, Targus's DEFCON CL Notebook Computer Cable Lock functions pretty much like an old-fashioned bicycle chain; attach it to your notebook's lock slot and then loop and lock it around any secure object. The Cable Lock is 6.5' of cut-resistant galvanized steel, with a combination lock attached. A thief would have to have a chainsaw to cut through this puppy.

If you want even more security, check out Targus's DEF-CON 1 Ultra Notebook Computer Security System. This system combines a 3' steel cable with a four-digit combination lock and high-decibel alarm unit, complete with motion sensor. If the cable is severed or the alarm unit otherwise disturbed, it sets off an ear-shattering alarm (95dB worth) that will scare off all but the most determined thieves. The unit itself is quite compact, and the steel cable retracts into the alarm unit at the press of a button.

> **Model:** DEFCON CL Notebook Computer Cable Lock (PA410U; $34.99), DEFCON 1 Ultra Notebook Computer Security System (PA400U; $49.99)
> **Manufacturer:** Targus (www.targus.com)

TrackIT Portable Anti-Theft System

Don't want to bother with chains and locks? Then attach your notebook PC to the TrackIT Portable Anti-Theft System. The TrackIT unit is synched to a keychain receiver that you carry with you at all times. If you're separated from your PC—that is, if the TrackIT gets too far from the receiver—a 110dB alarm sounds. It's that simple.

The TrackIT can be used to monitor notebook PCs, briefcases, purses, luggage, or any similar item. The hand unit includes a panic button you can press to activate the alarm remotely. Just remember to turn off the TrackIT when you leave your office for the evening!

Model: TrackIT
Manufacturer: TrackIT Corp.
(www.trackitcorp.com)
Price: $59.95

3M Privacy Computer Filters

From the folks who brought you Scotch tape and Post-It notes comes this neat little gizmo that keeps prying eyes from your computer screen. The privacy filter fits over your notebook's screen and blacks out the display to anyone viewing from an angle. You see the full display; passersby see a dark black screen.

The privacy filter snaps over any notebook screen (different sizes are available) and stays in place even when the notebook is closed. 3M also makes sizes to fit desktop LCD monitors.

Model: Notebook/LCD Privacy Computer Filters
Manufacturer: 3M (www.3m.com)
Price: $75

Targus Power Accessories

In addition to its security products, Targus manufactures a full range of useful notebook accessories. I'm particularly fond of its AC and DC power adapters.

The Mobile 70 Universal AC Power Adapter serves as a backup or on-the-road battery for just about any notebook PC. It comes with a variety of power tips to fit different brands and models; additional tips are available.

The Universal Auto/Air Notebook Power Adapter lets you plug your notebook computer or other portable device in to just about any DC power outlet—car batteries, airline power jacks, and so on. Like the AC Power Adapter, the Notebook Power Adapter comes with a variety of power tips to fit different PCs and portable devices.

Model: Mobile 70 Universal AC Power Adapter (APA10US; $79.99), Universal Auto/Air Notebook Power Adapter (PAPWR200U; $99.99)
Manufacturer: Targus (www.targus.com)

ZIP-LINQ Road Warrior Kit

ZIP-LINQ's Road Warrior Kit is the bundle of notebook accessories that every road warrior needs. You get a USB optical mouse with retractable cable, USB light on flexible gooseneck, retractable modem cable, retractable Ethernet cable, and retractable USB extension cable, all for a single low price.

You might not need all these accessories all the time, but I bet you'll need some of them sometime. I can't tell you how many times I have checked into a hotel room and found no waiting Ethernet cable for high-speed Internet service or been without a modem cable for dial-up connections. And using a real mouse—even a small one, like this one—beats extended use of my notebook's touchpad any day.

Model: Road Warrior Kit
Manufacturer: ZIP-LINQ (www.ziplinq.com)
Price: $59.99

Kensington Wi-Fi Finder

In a strange city and looking for the nearest Wi-Fi hotspot? Then you need Kensington's Wi-Fi Finder, a handheld device that detects all available Wi-Fi networks at the touch of a button. Three lights indicate signal strength; it detects Wi-Fi hotspots up to 200 feet away. And the Wi-Fi Finder is smart enough to filter out other 2.4GHz wireless signals, including cordless phones, Bluetooth networks, and microwave ovens. Just pop the Wi-Fi Finder in your pocket and start wandering around town; press the button to see whether there's a hotspot nearby.

Model: 33063
Manufacturer: Kensington
(www.kensington.com)
Price: $39.95

Dexia Laptop Rack

The Dexia Rack is one of the coolest-looking and most practical accessories for the desk-bound notebook PC user. The rack puts your notebook screen 7.6" off the top of the desktop, which leaves more than enough space to slide an auxiliary keyboard underneath.

It's a beautiful stand, with a clear-coat aluminum top with your choice of black or aluminum legs. You can even fold it up and take it with you; the Dexia Rack is only 3/4" thick at its most compact.

Fashionable and functional—the ideal accessory for every notebook user!

Model: Dexia Rack
Manufacturer: Dexia Design
(www.dexiadesign.com)
Price: $45.95

Other Cool Computer Gadgets

We'll end our list of computer gadgets with the catch-all category of "other cool computer gadgets." These are widgets and doodads that don't fit in any of the previous categories but are interesting enough to warrant your attention. In fact, some of these gizmos are downright fascinating, even if they appeal only to a small segment of the market.

The one thing many of these gadgets have in common is that they connect to your PC via USB. They're not necessarily USB-powered devices, as we discussed previously, but they utilize USB for an easy plug-and-play connection. What did we ever do before USB? These days you need a half-dozen or more USB connectors on your PC to connect all these

devices—which means you might need to purchase an add-on USB hub. Fortunately, USB hubs are a dime a dozen, not even worth mentioning in this book, but necessary nonetheless.

I won't go into any more detail about these other computer gadgets; you can read the individual listings yourself. But know that you won't always find these gadgets at your local Best Buy or CompUSA. No, these tend to be specialty items, which means you'll probably need to access the manufacturers' websites for ordering information. As much as I might like to wish, a USB guitar port just isn't a mass market item, so direct ordering is the way to go. As always, go to the websites listed for more information.

Streamzap PC Remote

If you listen to a lot of music on your PC—via CDs, Internet radio stations, or downloaded digital media files—you know how lame it is to control your listening with a normal computer keyboard or mouse. What you need is the same type of wireless remote control you use to control your home audio system. Right?

Well, that type of remote control is exactly what you get with the Streamzap PC Remote. This is a full-featured wireless remote, complete with numeric keypad, up and down buttons, forward and reverse buttons, and mute buttons—35 buttons in all, including 4 programmable macro buttons.

You can use the Streamzap remote to start and stop audio playback, move back and forth through tracks and playlists, and turn the volume up and down. It's also great for watching DVD movies on your PC.

The Streamzap remote works with all major digital media players, including Windows Media Player, iTunes, RealPlayer, Winamp, and MusicMatch Jukebox. You can even use it to control PowerPoint presentations—from up to 40 feet away from your PC!

Model: Streamzap PC Remote USBIR2
Manufacturer: Streamzp, Inc.
(www.streamzap.com)
Price: $39.95

Sony Puppy Fingerprint Identity Token

Keep unauthorized users from accessing your PC, programs, or documents with the Sony Puppy Fingerprint Identity Token. The Sony Puppy looks like a keychain USB device and attaches to any PC's USB port. You program the Puppy with your fingerprint and the appropriate PC and program passwords. Then, instead of entering a password, all you have to do is press your finger to the Puppy's touchpad. If your fingerprint matches, you get access; if not, you're locked out.

Using a fingerprint identity system is a lot easier—and more foolproof—than entering passwords. And this Puppy is portable, so you can use it on multiple machines; it's a great way to carry your Internet authentication with you from PC to PC.

> **Model:** FIU-180 Puppy Fingerprint Identity Token
> **Manufacturer:** Sony
> (www.sony.com/puppy/)
> **Price:** $169.99

Griffin ControlKey

Worried about your kids accessing inappropriate material on the Internet? Think they're spending too much time on the PC? Then check out Griffin's ControlKey, a keychain-sized security device that plugs in to the USB port of any PC.

You start by configuring the ControlKey software to allow specific types of access. When the ControlKey is inserted, you can use your computer normally. But when your child accesses the PC without the ControlKey, access is limited to those programs you specify—and Internet access is blocked completely. And without the ControlKey, your kids can't change your computer's settings!

> **Model:** ControlKey
> **Manufacturer:** Griffin Technologies
> (www.controlkey.com)
> **Price:** $59.99

Olympia Soundbug

Don't have space for a big speaker system? Want big sound from a notebook PC? Then check out Olympia's Soundbug. This neat little gadget turns any smooth, hard surface into a loudspeaker. Just plug the Soundbug in to your PC's audio jack (or the headphone jack of any portable music player) and lay it on a flat surface. The Soundbug translates the audio signal into vibrations that create a sounding-board out of whatever it's up against.

You can even use the Soundbug with vertical surfaces, such as walls, windows, or glass picture frames. It comes with a sucker push ring to keep it attached when you turn up the volume. Use two of them for stereo sound!

Model: Soundbug
Manufacturer: Olympia
(www.soundbug-us.com)
Price: $39.95

GuitarPort

The GuitarPort lets you connect your electric guitar to your computer; just plug your guitar in to the GuitarPort and connect the GuitarPort to your PC's USB port and to an amplifier or a powered speaker system. You can then feed your guitar into any PC-based music mixing or sequencing program.

The GuitarPort software lets you model 15 different amp/cabinet combinations and 18 pedal and studio effects, and it even includes a built-in chromatic tuner. It's a great way to integrate your guitar with your computer—and mix your guitar tracks digitally!

Model: GuitarPort
Manufacturer: Line 6 (www.guitarport.com)
Price: $169

PhoneBridge Cordless Internet Phone

Eliminate long-distance charges with the PhoneBridge cordless Internet phone. Just connect any cordless phone to the PhoneBridge device, and then connect the PhoneBridge to your PC's sound card. You can then use your PC to place VOIP phone calls, using your regular phone to talk.

Optionally, the PhoneBridge can use your PC's speakers and microphone to create a giant speakerphone. It's a full-duplex device for optimal call quality.

Model: PhoneBridge
Manufacturer: MHL Communications, Inc. (www.phonebridge.com)
Price: $129.95

Super Cantenna Wireless Network Antenna

This gadget is cooler than it looks—which is good because it looks like a long metal can. The Super Cantenna is a powerful antenna for wireless networks, a lot more powerful than the antennas you get with most wireless routers and access points.

You can use the Super Cantenna to boost the range of your wireless network, or as a user to connect to other wireless networks in your neighborhood. It's a directional antenna, compatible with both 802.11b and 802.11g networks.

Model: Super Cantenna
Manufacturer: Wireless Garden (www.cantenna.com)
Price: $19.95

IOGEAR MiniView III KVMP Switch

When you need to share USB devices between two PCs, you need the IOGEAR MiniView III. The MiniView is a KVMP switch—that is, it lets you switch keyboards, video monitors, mice, and other USB peripherals. It's a great way to control two PCs from the same keyboard or mouse or use two PCs with the same monitor. Just push a button to switch a device from one PC to another.

Model: MiniView III KVMP Switch (GCS1712)
Manufacturer: IOGEAR (www.iogear.com)
Price: $159.95

FrontX Front Panel Computer Port

Tired of digging around behind your PC to connect all your peripherals? Then check out FrontX, a panel that moves selected ports to the front of your PC. It installs into any 5.25" drive bay.

The really neat thing about FrontX is that you can have the company custom-make any combination of ports. Want all USB ports? Or a mix of USB and audio jacks? Or how about two USBs, one FireWire, and a headphone jack? FrontX can do it, up to eight ports total. Check out its website for ordering details.

Model: FrontX
Manufacturer: FrontX (www.frontx.com)
Price: Configurations start at $13.60

Royal CD/Media Destroyer and Paper Shredder

You're probably used to shredding your paper documents, but what about all the sensitive data you've recorded on CD-R/RW discs? Throw a used disc in the trash, and any schmoe with a CD-ROM drive can read everything you've written.

Royal comes to the rescue with the MD 100 CD/media destroyer. Feed in your CD or DVD discs, and the MD 100 makes mincemeat of them. You can also use it as a simple paper shredder or to shred your old plastic credit cards.

Model: MD 100
Manufacturer: Royal (www.royal.com)
Price: $99.99

C.H.I.M.P. Monitor Mirror

Our last computer gadget isn't computerized at all. The C.H.I.M.P. monitor mirror is a small rear-view mirror for your computer, so you can see your boss coming before he taps on your shoulder. Just attach it to the top of your monitor and keep an eye on what's happening behind you.

By the way, C.H.I.M.P. stands for "chimp has invisible monkey powers," whatever that means. All I know is that it'll keep you from getting busted for playing Doom in the office!

Model: C.H.I.M.P. Monitor Mirror
Manufacturer: ThinkGeek
(www.thinkgeek.com)
Price: $9.99

Portable Gadgets

2

Palm OS PDAs

When it comes to personal digital assistants (PDAs), you have your choice of units that use the Palm operating system (Palm OS) or Microsoft's Pocket PC operating system. Palm OS devices tend to be lower-priced than Pocket PCs, although some of the high-end models are every bit as expensive. Features tend to be comparable between the two types of devices, although you should go the Pocket PC route if you need to work with Word or Excel files; Pocket PCs incorporate "pocket" versions of both programs.

The big player in the Palm OS market is palmOne, as Palm now calls itself. palmOne manufactures the Tungsten line for business users and the Zire line for general consumer use. Sony used to be a player but recently discontinued their line of Clié PDAs.

Today's Palm OS devices come with a slew of features you need to sift your way through. In addition to considering size and weight, determine whether you're okay with the normal stylus-based entry or if you want to enter data with your thumbs via a mini-keyboard. Also look for either Bluetooth or Wi-Fi wireless connectivity; the former for connecting to your PC, and the latter for connecting to the Internet at Wi-Fi hotspots.

Most users use their PDAs pretty much for managing contacts, scheduling appointments, and making to-do lists. (Oh, and playing games—there's nothing like a quick game of solitaire during a long, boring meeting.) Palm OS PDAs synch with the Palm Desktop software for all these functions; most Palm PDAs also come with utility programs that let you synch with Microsoft Outlook, if that's what you prefer.

Most Palm PDAs also function as digital music players, with built-in player software. Because the built-in speaker typically leaves a lot to be desired, you'll probably want to do your listening via headphones. And for the ultimate coolness, check out the models with built-in digital cameras.

In addition to the Palm OS models I list here, check out the Garmin iQue 3600 GPS/PDA on p. 104, as well as the combination cell phone/PDAs on p. 206. And don't forget to stock up on PDA accessories; I list a bunch, starting on p. 63.

palmOne Tungsten T3

This is one neat PDA. It's fast, it's good-looking, and it features a truly unique display.

The T3's Stretch Display offers 50% more viewing area than other palmOne handhelds. The total display area is 320 × 480 pixels; slide the bottom of the unit down to access the extra display space. Even better, the Stretch Display also rotates from portrait to landscape mode at a tap of a button. This makes the T3 ideal for viewing spreadsheets and other wide documents.

Technology-wise, a 400MHz Intel XScale processor drives the T3, which is the top-of-the-line for PDAs these days. It also features built-in Bluetooth wireless technology and comes with the RealOne Desktop Player for audio and video playback. And if you're an MS Office user, know that the T3 is compatible with your Word, Excel, and PowerPoint files.

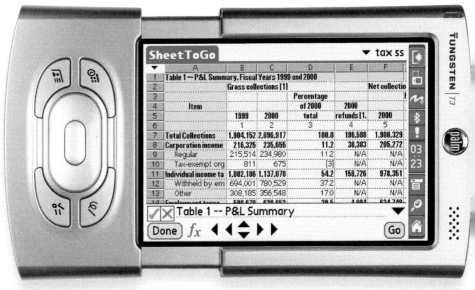

Despite all that's inside, the T3 is surprisingly compact and light. The unit comes with a gray leather flip cover that attaches on the back and flips over the top.

Model: Tungsten T3
Manufacturer: palmOne (www.palmone.com)
Price: $399

palmOne Tungsten C

The Tungsten C runs the same 400MHz processor as the Tungsten T3 but adds a unique QWERTY mini-keyboard that makes typing and entering data easier. (The keys are pretty small, though, so you'll probably end up typing with your thumbs.) It also features built-in Wi-Fi wireless technology for fast connection to Wi-Fi hotspots.

The color display is a conventional 320 × 320 size, unlike the T3's Stretch Display. All in all, this is an attractive business-like PDA, with all the features you need to take your business on the road.

Model: Tungsten C
Manufacturer: palmOne
(www.palmone.com)
Price: $399

palmOne Zire 72

Tungsten is palmOne's business line; Zire models are aimed at the general consumer market, which means they're a little hipper and more stylish. Case in point: the Zire 72, a feature-packed PDA in a cool blue, rubberized case.

The Zire 72's entertainment focus is evident from the built-in 1.2-megapixel digital camera that lets you shoot photos and video clips. You can also record voice memos and play digital audio files; Bluetooth wireless connectivity is built-in.

Although the Zire 72 isn't quite as powerful as the Tungsten handhelds, its multimedia capabilities make it appealing to young professionals who want to mix some fun with their business activities.

Model: Zire 72
Manufacturer: palmOne
(www.palmone.com)
Price: $299

palmOne Zire 31

If you want a decent Palm OS PDA at a bargain price—and don't care too much about all the bells and whistles—the Zire 31 is the model for you. The Zire 31 is small and light but still has an easy-to-read color screen. The case is an attractive metallic blue.

Inside, you get software to do all the normal stuff—store contacts, create schedules and to-do lists, and so on. It even does double duty as a portable MP3 player, if that's your thing. Unlike the Zire 72, there's no built-in camera, but then again it only costs half as much as the other model, so there.

Model: Zire 31
Manufacturer: palmOne
(www.palmone.com)
Price: $149

Tapwave Zodiac

The Tapwave Zodiac is a Palm OS PDA specifically designed for game playing. The high-resolution widescreen 480 × 320 3.8" color display is easy on the eyes, whether you're playing games, viewing digital photos, or watching full-motion video. Inside, the Motorola ARM9 processor is plenty fast for advanced game play, the ATI Imageon graphics accelerator is optimized for game graphics, and the FatHammer X-Forge 3D graphics engine delivers console-quality performance.

Tapwave bills the Zodiac as "a game console that fits in your pocket." I think that's an apt description. This is evident even in the wireless department, where the built-in Bluetooth technology lets you connect with up to seven other units for wireless multiplayer gaming. Two models are available, with either 32MB or 128MB of memory.

Model: Zodiac
Manufacturer: Tapwave
(www.tapwave.com)
Price: $299.99 (32MB), $399.99 (128MB)

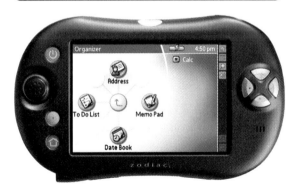

Pocket PC PDAs

The Pocket PC is Microsoft's answer to the Palm PDA. Pocket PCs tend to be a little more business-oriented and a little more powerful than Palm PDAs—and little more expensive, as well.

Features-wise, all Pocket PCs come with a stereo headphone jack and Windows Media Player software, so you can use the device as a portable music player. You also get Pocket Word, Pocket Excel, and Pocket Money, so you can use your Pocket PC to edit the same files you use on your desktop PC. You can also synch your Pocket PC contact and appointment lists with Microsoft Outlook; the synchronization happens automatically when you insert the PDA into its cradle.

Performance-wise, most Pocket PCs come with either 32MB or 64MB of RAM (for files) and anywhere from 16MB to 48MB of ROM (for the operating system and programs). Most of today's Pocket PCs use an Intel microprocessor running at 300MHz or 400MHz. And you get the latest version of the operating system, which Microsoft

now calls Microsoft Windows Mobile 2003 Premium for Pocket PC. (Microsoft has never been known for snappy names.)

As with Palm OS PDAs, look for a bevy of optional features to play havoc with the purchase price. In particular, look for mini-keyboards and Bluetooth and Wi-Fi wireless connectivity. Also consider the screen; some models have a slightly larger display, which is always nice.

Pocket PCs are manufactured by HP, Dell, Toshiba, and ViewSonic—although HP makes the most innovative models and has the bulk of the market. That explains why my list of cool Pocket PCs is all-HP; I tried to find cooler models from the other companies but couldn't. That doesn't mean you should look for only HP models, of course. In particular, Dell makes some Pocket PCs that deliver a lot of features for the price. But HP's models, while a tad more expensive, are also a tad cooler—and coolness is what this book is all about, right?

HP iPAQ h5550/h5555

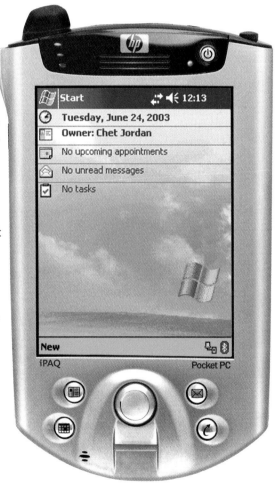

Leo's Pick

The iPAQ h5550/h5555 is *the* PDA for power users. You get a fast processor, high-resolution color display, a built-in microphone, more memory than any other Pocket PC, and both Wi-Fi and Bluetooth wireless connectivity built in. The color LCD display is a big 3.8" diagonal and looks great.

Even neater, this unit uses biometric fingerprint recognition technology to protect your data. Just press your fingertip to the screen to access protected files.

This is also a very expandable Pocket PC, thanks to HP expansion packs. It can accept both PCMCIA cards and CF cards via PC Card expansion sleeves.

HP equips this model with a user-replaceable battery, something you don't always find. You also get a nice leather belt-mountable case, which makes the PDA easy to carry around.

On the downside, this is one expensive puppy. But if you want top-of-the-line performance and flexibility, nothing else will do.

(By the way, the dual model numbers for this and other HP Pocket PCs reflects HP's dual-channel sales strategy. They assign one model number for the consumer channel and another for the business channel—even though it's the same PDA inside the box.)

Model: iPAQ h5550/h5555
Manufacturer: HP (www.hp.com)
Price: $649.99

HP iPAQ h1940/h1945

If you want a more affordable Pocket PC, check out the iPAQ h1940/h1945. This is a slim (4.5" × 2.8" × 0.5") and lightweight (4.3 oz.) model, ideal for schlepping around in your shirt pocket. It features built-in Bluetooth, enough internal memory to get the job done, and a nice display. And if you need Wi-Fi, just use an add-on card.

Yes, you sacrifice some speed and features, but you spend half the cash as you do with other Pocket PC models. And sometimes saving money is cooler than getting a state-of-the-art gadget.

Model: iPAQ h1940/h1945
Manufacturer: HP (www.hp.com)
Price: $299.99

HP iPAQ h4350/h4355

The iPAQ h4350/4355 is a good choice for business users. It includes both Wi-Fi and Bluetooth wireless connectivity, a decent 3.5" color display, and excellent battery life. (Battery life declines rapidly, however, when you're using either of the wireless modes.)

The defining feature is the miniature QWERTY keyboard at the bottom of the unit, which makes entering data a snap. The keys have blue back-lighting for typing in the dark. Of course, the addition of the keyboard makes the unit a little bulkier than competing models, but that's a small price to pay to bypass stylus entry.

Model: iPAQ h4350/h4355
Manufacturer: HP (www.hp.com)
Price: $499.99

PDA Accessories

When you plunk down your $300 (or $400 or $500) for a brand-spanking new PDA, you might as well keep your wallet out. That's because there are a ton of cool stuff you can buy to accessorize your PDA—and cool accessories cost money.

The first accessory you need is a good protective case. I list a bunch of cool cases starting on p. 114, but a good place to start is the Targus website (www.targus.com). Targus makes great cases for just about every portable device, and it has PDA cases starting at just $10.

Next, you should consider an add-on keyboard. Stylus-based entry just doesn't cut it if you have a lot of data to enter or if you need to type a long report. Nothing beats typing on a keyboard, and you have your choice of models to choose from—including a wireless model from Targus that works with any PDA.

Of course, cables are essential—especially when you're on the road. ZIP-LINQ's Sync-N-Charge cables let you connect your PDA to your notebook PC's USB port and then synch your contact/appointment data and recharge your PDA at the same time. It saves you from carrying your PDA cradle or AC adapter with you when you travel.

Which other accessories you buy depends on how you want to use your PDA. For example, if you want to turn your PDA into a digital camera, consider Veo's Photo Traveler add-on camera. And if you want to use your PDA for navigating, consider TomTom's Navigator GPS add-on.

Other PDA accessories can be found at your manufacturer's website (palmOne is especially good at hawking add-ons) and from companies like Belkin (www.belkin.com) and Targus. Also good are sites that sell all kinds of accessories and software, such as PDAZoo (www.pdazoo.com), PalmGear.com (www.palmgear.com), and Pocket PC Central (www.pocketpccentral.net).

TomTom Navigator Bluetooth GPS

Turn your PDA into a full-fledged GPS navigation system with the TomTom Navigator. This cool gizmo connects to your PDA via Bluetooth wireless technology; you can carry the remote GPS unit in your hand or mount it on your dashboard and then read the results on your PDA's screen.

The Navigator not only shows you where you are, but also offers door-to-door 2D or 3D navigation and voice-guided turn-by-turn instructions. And if you take a wrong turn, it takes that into account and recalculates your route automatically.

I particularly like the "avoid roadblock" feature that provides instant rerouting around major construction and traffic congestion. The Navigator even displays the total distance for your trip and your estimated time of arrival. Neat!

TomTom's navigation software includes tons of U.S. maps, liberally sprinkled with gas stations, restaurants, and other points of interest. You can use the software to plan trips to and from any location.

You can use the Navigator as either a handheld or automotive GPS device. TomTom offers models for both Palm and Pocket PC units.

Model: Navigator
Manufacturer: TomTom (www.tomtom.com)
Price: $349

Targus Universal Wireless Keyboard

You can add a keyboard to any Palm or Pocket PC model without worrying about connectors, thanks to Targus's Universal Wireless Keyboard. This is a fold-out, full-size QWERTY keyboard that connects with your PDA via a wireless infrared connection.

All you have to do is sit your PDA into a small cradle above the keyboard. The IR connection is automatic, and the keyboard folds up for easy transport. It's universal, so you can use it with any PDA you have handy—or even most smart phones.

> **Model:** Universal Wireless Keyboard PA870U
> **Manufacturer:** Targus (www.targus.com)
> **Price:** $79.99

iBIZ XELA Case/Keyboard

After trying to enter data via tapping on a touch screen, it sure is nice to type on a keyboard. To that end, check out the XELA, a combination case/keyboard for your Palm PDA. It features a flip-stand for your PDA, attached above a folding keyboard. When you slide your PDA into the stand, it automatically connects it to the keyboard, and you're ready to type. Fold it up, and it functions as a hard case for your PDA.

I especially like the way the keyboard hinges in three parts to angle into tight spaces. XELA keyboards are available for all major Palm OS models.

> **Model:** XELA Case/Keyboard
> **Manufacturer:** iBIZ Technology Corporation (www.ibizpda.com)
> **Price:** $69.99

ZIP-LINQ Sync-N-Charge Cables

Here's a neat idea—recharge your PDA from your laptop PC, so you don't have to carry that bulky PDA recharger with you when you travel. Instead, use ZIP-LINQ's Sync-N-Charge cable to connect your PDA to your PC, via USB. Once connected, the cable automatically syncs your data and recharges your PDA. The cable itself includes a retractable doohickey, so when you're not using it it's nice and compact.

Sync-N-Charge cables are available for most major Palm and Pocket PC models, as well as selected smart phones. Check ZIP-LINQ's website for more information.

Model: Sync-N-Charge
Manufacturer: ZIP-LINQ (www.ziplinq.com)
Price: $20

Veo Photo Traveler Camera

Add a digital camera to your PDA with Veo's Photo Traveler. The Photo Traveler is a 1.3-megapixel camera with 4X digital zoom; it can also be used to shoot moving videos. It features a swivel lens that pivots from front to back, so you can take pictures of yourself. You can fine-tune your image with the unit's focus dial.

The Photo Traveler connects to the expansion slot on the top of your PDA. Versions are available for most major Palm and Pocket PC models.

Model: Photo Traveler for Pocket PC/Palm OS
Manufacturer: Veo (www.veo.com)
Price: $79.99

Portable Music Players

If you want your music to go, you need a portable music player that stores and plays back digital audio files. Download music from the Web or rip songs from CDs; then transfer the files to your portable music player. Even the smallest portable players hold hundreds of songs, and the largest devices can archive your entire music collection. And, best of all, these gadgets fit in the palm of your hand; no more carrying around bulky portable CD players.

Another advantage to these digital music players is that you can program them to play back your own personalized music mix, in the form of customized playlists. Put together one mix for your drive to work, another mix for your drive home, and a third to listen to on weekends. It's normally as simple as dragging and dropping specific songs in a PC-based music player program and then transferring the songs—and the playlist—to your portable device.

When you're shopping for a portable music player, you can choose from three types of storage: flash memory (64MB–1GB capacity), microdrives (1.5GB–4GB capacity), and larger 1.8" hard drives (10GB–40GB). Flash devices are small, are lightweight, are inexpensive, and won't skip if you're jogging; microdrive devices

offer a good compromise between size and capacity; and the 1.8" hard drive devices, though physically larger, offer the most storage—enough space in many cases to double as file and digital photo storage devices.

The other thing you need to think about is where you're going to get your songs from. If you're ripping songs from CDs, any of these players will do; they're all compatible with the ubiquitous MP3 format. But if you plan on downloading music from an online music store, choose your player carefully. The Apple iTunes Music Store downloads files in the not-so-ubiquitous AAC format; Apple's iPods are compatible with this format, but most other players aren't. Other online stores and services, including Napster and BuyMusic, download files in Microsoft's WMA format. Almost all music players—except the iPod—are compatible with this format. So, if you want an iPod, you're stuck with the iTunes Music Store; if you want to download from another site, you'll have to pass on the iPod.

That said, the best of these players have a definite cool factor. Whether you go for small size or big storage capacity, these gadgets are as pleasing to the eye as they are to the ear—and they feel good sitting in your palm, as well!

  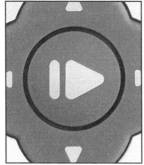 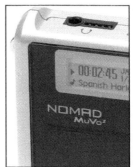 

Apple iPod

Imitators come and imitators go, but the coolest portable music player remains Apple's trendsetting iPod. The iPod is that rare gadget that's both stylish and popular with the masses; it's the best-selling portable music player in history, with more than three million units sold to-date.

Apple now makes three models of iPod; the difference is the size of the hard disk. Opt for the 40GB model and you can store up to 10,000 songs. You can also use the iPod to store regular computer data, including digital photos and the like.

Even though the iPod is Apple's baby (and the styling definitely reminds you of the family connection), it's that rare Apple product that's compatible with both Apple and Windows computers. It stores and plays back music in the AAC, MP3, WAV, and AIFF formats.

Cool features (besides the trendy looks) include the handy click-wheel navigator, high-resolution backlist display, dual USB 2.0 and FireWire compatibility, and the seamless interface to Apple's top-notch iTunes Music Store. And if you use the FireWire connection, you can recharge your iPod directly from your PC; FireWire doubles as a power connection for the portable device.

Weaknesses include a relatively short battery life (just 6 hours in typical use), no built-in FM radio or CompactFlash slot, and incompatibility with Microsoft's WMA file format. This last weakness is the biggest because you can't use your iPod to download songs from Napster, BuyMusic, or any non-Apple online music service.

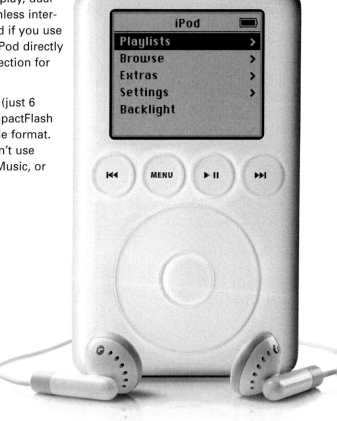

Model: iPod
Manufacturer: Apple (www.apple.com)
Storage type and capacity: 15GB/ 20GB/40GB hard drive
Dimensions: 2.4" × 4.1" × 0.62" (40GB model: 0.72" deep)
Weight: 5.6 oz. (40GB model: 6.2 oz.)
Price: $300 (15GB), $400 (20GB), $500 (40GB)

Apple iPod Mini

The iPod Mini delivers all the great features of the original iPod in a much smaller package. The Mini incorporates a fairly robust 4GB microdrive within its tough anodized-aluminum casing and is available in five cool colors. (I like the blue, myself.) Like the bigger iPod, it connects to your PC via either FireWire or USB 2.0 and syncs easily with Apple's iTunes Music Store.

What's not to like about the Mini? Well, it would be nice if Apple threw in a docking cradle, and the Mini would be a much better value at $50 less. All in all, though, the iPod Mini is ideal for trendsetters who want a small form-factor portable music player—or just a smaller version of their beloved iPod.

Model: iPod Mini
Manufacturer: Apple (www.apple.com)
Storage type and capacity: 4GB microdrive
Dimensions: 2" × 3.6" × 0.5"
Weight: 3.6 oz.
Price: $250

Creative Nomad MuVo^2

The MuVo^2 is a decent alternative to the iPod Mini. It's small and stylishly squarish, the controls are easy to operate, and it costs less than an iPod Mini. Best of all, it stores and plays WMA-format files (as well as MP3s), something the iPod Mini doesn't do. This means, of course, that you can use it with Napster and other non-iTunes services.

Inside, the MuVo^2 has either 1.5GB or 4GB of microdrive storage, depending on the model—enough to store either 50 or 128 hours of WMA-format music. Connection to your PC is via USB 2.0.

Model: MuVo^2
Manufacturer: Creative (www.creative.com)
Storage type and capacity: 1.5GB/4GB microdrive
Dimensions: 2.6" × 2.6" × 0.8"
Weight: 3.2 oz.
Price: $119.99 (1.5GB), $199.99 (4GB)

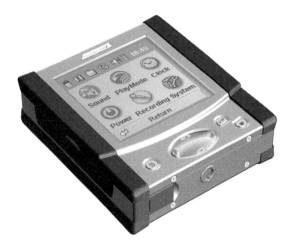

Archos Gmini 220

What you get with the Gmini 220 is maximum storage in minimum space. The Gmini features a huge 20GB hard drive in a very compact 6-oz. package and offers long battery life (10 hours), to boot.

The Gmini includes a PDA-like interface and the ability to store files in folders, which makes it particularly powerful as a file-storage device. Also cool is the CompactFlash slot, which lets you easily back up your digital photos to Gmini's hard drive, and the built-in photo viewer software.

Model: Gmini 220
Manufacturer: Archos (www.archos.com)
Storage type and capacity: 20GB hard drive
Dimensions: 2.7" × 3" × 0.9"
Weight: 6 oz.
Price: $350

SoniqCast Aireo

The Aireo is the first portable music player to incorporate Wi-Fi wireless technology. This lets you download music and data files directly from your PC, no cables necessary. You can configure the Aireo to download files on demand or on a predefined schedule. Future versions of the Aireo software promise content download from Wi-Fi hotspots and peer-to-peer file transfers from one Aireo player to another.

The Aireo offers a 1.5GB microdrive and includes a built-in FM transmitter, so you can wirelessly transmit music directly from the Aireo to a car stereo. It also features an SD card slot for transferring photos from your digital camera.

Model: Aireo
Manufacturer: SoniqCast (www.soniqcast.com)
Storage type and capacity: 1.5GB micro-drive
Dimensions: 2.8" × 4.5" × 0.9"
Weight: 6.8 oz.
Price: $300

iRiver iFP-390T

If you're willing to trade off storage capacity for a smaller and lighter player, consider the iRiver iFP-390T, the latest upgrade to one of my all-time favorite flash memory players. It's a slick package, with a neat little joystick-based navigational system; it's small enough to fit in even the tightest of pockets.

What makes the iFP-390T especially useful is the integrated FM radio and voice recorder and its ability to record directly from the audio line-in jack. You can record up to 8 hours of MP3-format audio from the radio or line-in jack or 72 hours of mono audio from the built-in microphone. Battery life is an exceptional 24 hours.

Model: iFP-390T
Manufacturer: iRiver
(www.iriveramerica.com)
Storage type and capacity: 256MB flash memory
Dimensions: 1.4" × 3.6" × 1.1"
Weight: 1.2 oz.
Price: $200

Creative Nomad MuVo TX

The MuVo TX is a miniature music player that incorporates a built-in USB 2.0 flash drive. Slide the player out of the battery module and plug it in to your PC's USB drive to transfer files; the USB connector is on the end of the player module. The player itself is extremely small, like a keychain USB drive.

The music player has a built-in microphone, an LCD display, and a scroller button to select your favorite tunes and playlists. MuVo TX models are available in 128MB, 256MB, and 512MB versions.

Model: MuVo TX
Manufacturer: Creative (www.Creative.com)
Storage type and capacity: 128MB/256MB/512MB flash memory
Dimensions: 1.4" × 2.9" × 0.6"
Weight: 1.5 oz.
Price: $119.99 (128MB), $179.99 (256MB), $249.99 (512MB)

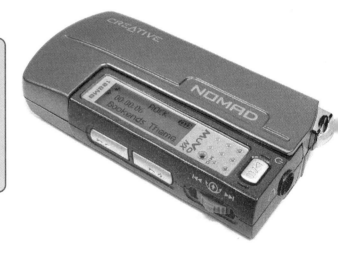

iPod Accessories

With more than three million units sold, the Apple iPod is the single most popular portable music player—and one of the most popular consumer electronics devices, period. The iPod is so popular that a large market has sprung up for iPod accessories, from cases to connectors and more.

What types of accessories are we talking about? A short list includes cables and docking units, FM transmitters, car kits, media readers, voice recorders, remote controls, external speakers, and cases of all sorts and colors. You should also consider upgrading from the standard iPod headphones; check out my recommended third-party earbuds and headphones, starting on p. 80.

A number of companies, including Belkin (www.belkin.com) and Griffin Technology (www.griffintechnology.com), manufacture a variety of iPod accessories. Belkin in particular has a large number of useful and stylish iPod accessories available; its catalog is definitely worth checking out.

Of course, because the iPod is Apple's baby, you can find a ton of iPod accessories on the Apple site (www.apple.com/ipod/accessories.html). Also good are sites such as We Love Macs (www.welovemacs.com) and XtremeMac (www.xtrememac.com), which offer accessories from a variety of manufacturers.

  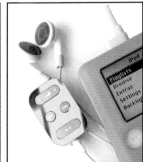 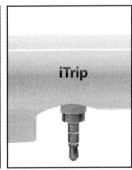 

Altec Lansing inMotion Portable Audio System

This is my pick for best iPod accessory on the market today. The inMotion is an audio system designed around the iPod; insert your iPod and the sound is amplified and fed through right and left speakers. Not only does this let you share your iPod music with others, but it also delivers a big room-filling sound at a relatively low price.

The entire system is battery powered, so there aren't any power cables to bother with. The base of the unit incorporates a highly efficient Class D power amplifier; just slip the iPod into the dock to start rocking. An auxiliary input jack on the back lets you connect a CD player or other device, and Altec Lansing offers a free adapter that lets the unit work with an iPod Mini.

The inMotion is built around two speakers, each with two 1" full-range microdrivers. Despite their small size (and no accompanying subwoofer), they deliver a decent bass response, thanks to Altec Lansing's MaxxBass technology. Dynamic range is 60Hz–10KHz, with a 75 dB signal-to-noise ratio.

This big sound comes from an extremely small footprint, just 8" wide and 5.4" deep. It folds up for easy portability and weighs just 15 oz. With an iPod/inMotion combo, you won't need a separate desktop audio system!

Model: inMotion
Manufacturer: Altec Lansing (www.alteclansing.com)
Price: $149.95

naviPod Wireless Remote Control

It might seem silly to have a remote control for a portable device you hang on a belt clip, but this gadget won me over. With the naviPod, you don't have to keep your iPod close; you can control it from across the desk or across the room.

The naviPod is a two-part device. The receiver unit attaches to the top of your iPod and includes a stereo plug you can use to connect headphones or auxiliary speakers. The palm-sized remote control unit is a cool-looking circular device that includes play/pause, fast forward, reverse, and volume up/down buttons. You also get a chrome stand that holds the iPod upright on a desk.

The remote is an infrared model, just like most of today's television remotes. The transmitter has a good range, so it should work in even the largest rooms. And the remote control feels good in your hand; the rubberized push buttons are laid out logically and have good tactile feedback.

TEN Technology also manufactures the naviPlay, which is a Bluetooth (RF instead of IR) wireless remote. The naviPlay remote isn't quite as cool as the naviPod, but it does include a headphone jack for private listening.

Model: naviPod
Manufacturer: TEN Technology (www.tentechnology.com)
Price: $49.95

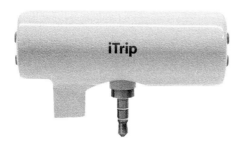

Griffin iTrip FM Transmitter

Listen to your iPod music through any FM radio—in your car, in your home, wherever. The iTrip is a miniature FM station that transmits music from your iPod to any nearby FM radio; just tune in the radio to listen to your iPod tunes. It differs from other FM transmitters in that you can choose any radio station on the dial to transmit by entering special station codes directly from the iPod.

The iTrip—which is a cool-looking white canister that fits on top of your iPod—doesn't need batteries; it receives its power from the iPod itself. It turns on automatically when you plug it in and turns off after 60 seconds of silence.

> **Model:** iTrip
> **Manufacturer:** Griffin Technology
> (www.griffintechnology.com)
> **Price:** $35

Monster iCarPlay FM Transmitter

Here's another gadget that transmits your iPod music to any FM radio. The iCarPlay is specially designed for in-car use and includes a Smart Digital Charger that plugs in to your car's DC/lighter jack. The Smart Digital Charger not only powers the iCarPlay, but also recharges your iPod.

The iCarPlay plugs in to any iPod with a Dock Connector, including the iPod Mini. It transmits over any one of eight preset FM frequencies.

> **Model:** iCarPlay
> **Manufacturer:** Monster Cable
> (www.monstercable.com)
> **Price:** $69.95

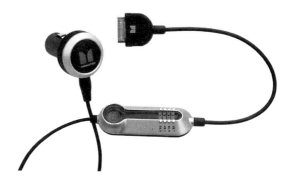

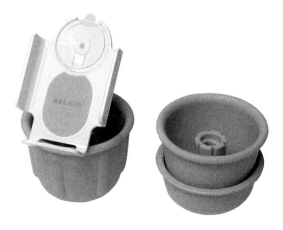

Belkin Digital Camera Link

Your iPod has a decent-sized hard disk, and you can use any excess disk space to store more than just music files. With Belkin's Digital Camera Link, you can use your iPod to store hundreds of digital photos, transferred directly from your digital camera.

All you have to do is connect your digital camera (via USB) to the Digital Camera Link and then connect the Digital Camera Link to your iPod. Transfer the pictures from your camera to your iPod; later, when you dock your iPod to your PC, you can download the pictures to your computer's hard disk. It's a great way to free up space in your digital camera without having to lug your PC around!

Belkin TuneDok Car Holder

If you want to listen to your iPod in the car, where do you stash the darned thing? That's where Belkin's TuneDok comes in. It's a cup holder-like iPod holder; slide your iPod into the TuneDok and fasten it anywhere on your dash via the AirGrip suction cup.

Fine-tune the iPod's position via the ratcheting neck feature, and use the cable-management clip to tidy up any dangling cords. It beats tossing the iPod on the passenger seat—or on the floor!

Model: F8E477
Manufacturer: Belkin (www.belkin.com)
Price: $89.99

Model: F8E467
Manufacturer: Belkin (www.belkin.com)
Price: $29.99

Belkin iPod Media Reader

Want to transfer digital photos and other files you have stored on a digital media card to your iPod? Then plug in Belkin's Media Reader and start transferring.

The Media Reader connects directly to your iPod and reads the following digital media formats: CompactFlash I, CompactFlash II, SmartMedia, Secure Digital, Memory Stick, and MultiMediaCard. Use the software built in to your iPod to transfer the files, and store them on the iPod's hard disk.

Model: F8E461
Manufacturer: Belkin (www.belkin.com)
Price: $109.99

Belkin iPod Voice Recorder

Belkin makes a lot of great iPod accessories, and here's another one. The Voice Recorder lets your iPod double as a digital audio recorder. It features a built-in microphone and plugs directly in to your iPod. You can record hundreds of hours of conversations in mono WAV format. The Voice Recorder even has a built-in speaker, so you can listen to what you've recorded without headphones.

And here's something extra neat—thanks to the built-in speaker, you can use the Voice Recorder as a travel alarm clock!

Model: F8E462
Manufacturer: Belkin (www.belkin.com)
Price: $59.99

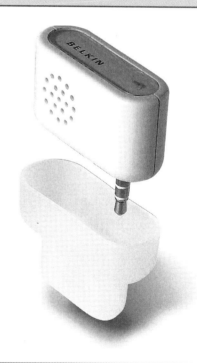

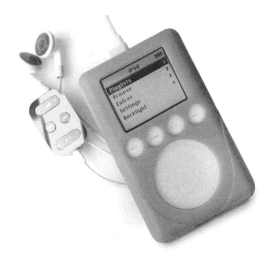

SportSuit Runabout Case

The SportSuit Runabout is an iPod Mini case for music lovers on the run. It's a neoprene case that straps around your wrist. The iPod slips snugly into the case, allowing full view of the screen and access to the headphone jack. Cord management straps keep the headphone cable from getting in the way while you jog; judicious use of Velcro keeps everything else in place.

The SportSuit Runabout only fits the iPod Mini, but Marware makes other SportSuit cases (complete with armbands) for the regular iPod.

Model: SportSuit Runabout
Manufacturer: Marware, Inc. (www.marware.com)
Price: $29.95

iSkin eVo iPod Protector

One of the most popular types of iPod accessory is the carrying case, and one of the coolest carrying cases is the iSkin eVo. The iSkin eVo is a snug-fitting molded silicone case, complete with clear screen protector and beveled button cutouts.

The iSkin eVo comes with a RevoClip belt clip that features a rotary click-lock movement that lets you rotate the iPod 180°. It's available in a variety of trendy colors, from Arctic and Blush to glow-in-the-dark Lava and Wasabi; iSkin also makes versions for the iPod Mini.

Model: iSkin eVo
Manufacturer: iSkin, Inc. (www.iskin.com)
Price: $29.99

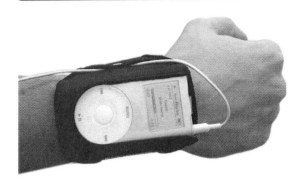

iPod Armor

When you want hardcore protection for your iPod, check out the iPod Armor aluminum hard case with foam padding interior. This is an extremely rugged case that absorbs just about any abuse you can throw at it. Slip the iPod inside, close it, and your iPod's protected. Best of all, the iPod Armor allows full access to all iPod controls, so you can listen while it's tucked away. Purchase the optional Armor Clip to attach the iPod Armor to your belt.

> **Model:** iPod Armor
> **Manufacturer:** Matias Corporation (www.ipodarmor.com)
> **Price:** $49.95

Groove Speaker Purse

Carry your iPod in real style—along with its own portable speakers. Felicidade's Groove Purse is a fashionable oversized tote purse in crisp white synthetic leather. Slide your iPod into the outside compartment, and it automatically connects the two built-in powered speakers. You end up with a groovy-looking iPod boom box, with plenty of room inside for anything else you need to carry around.

The Groove Purse is both stylish and functional, which is a rarity these days. Many fashion mavens regard this as the ultimate iPod accessory!

> **Model:** Groove Purse Tote
> **Manufacturer:** Felicidade (www.drbott.com)
> **Price:** $144.95

Headphones

The headphones or earbuds that come with most portable music players are the weakest link in the chain. Most of these phones are adequate at best, and some just plain suck. The very first thing I do when I buy a new portable player is throw away the stock headphones and replace them with something that sounds a lot better.

You'd be surprised at the difference a good set of headphones can make. Most portable music players deliver pretty good sound, but you need a good set of phones to hear it. And, naturally, you need really good headphones to appreciate the compact discs you play on your home audio system.

Headphones come in two types—open-air and closed-ear. And don't forget earbuds, which fit inside your ear. (I discuss earbuds in the next section, so read ahead if you're interested.)

Open-air headphones sit lightly on top of your ears. This type of phone is lightweight and very comfortable to wear, even for extended periods. The downside—which might not be a downside, depending—is that they're not well isolated from ambient noise. That is, you can still hear what's going on around you. So you'll hear your music, but still know if the telephone is ringing.

Closed-ear headphones are often called *sealed* phones because the heavily padded ear cups completely cover your ears. This results in excellent sound quality and good isolation from external noises. The downside is that these phones are heavy and cumbersome and become uncomfortable in long listening sessions. They're better for use in your living room (or in the recording studio) than with a portable device.

When you're shopping for headphones, evaluate both sound and comfort. Look for a unit that delivers a clear sound with no distortion; a deep and controlled bass without a lot of boominess; a smooth, even frequency response without bright or tinny highs; and good positioning of the sound image between the right and left channels. And be sure you like the way the phones fit and feel. Imagine using the phones for a couple of hours and determine how you'll like them after that kind of use. You definitely want an adjustable headband and for the ear cups to fit comfortably on or over your ears.

Grado SR60

Leo's Pick

What can I say about Grado's SR60 headphones—other than they sound terrific? What more do you need to know?

Well, how about the fact that the SR60 has won numerous product of the year honors from a variety of respected audiophile magazines? Or the fact that reviewers continually vote the SR60 at the top of what is a very lively pack of products?

There has to be a reason for all this acclaim, and in the case of the SR60s, it's the sound, pure and simple. This model has been around since 1999, and there's no real reason for Grado to change it. Once you get something right, don't mess with it.

The SR60 uses a relatively lightweight open-air design, which means they sit on your ears instead of over them and let you hear what's going on around you. That makes them perfect for use with portable music players, where you don't want heavy, isolated phones. And, all things considered, they're relatively inexpensive—especially when compared to the high-priced phones typically used by audiophile listeners.

If you still don't understand what all the fuss is about, just give them a listen. The SR60s sound so much better than what you're used to; you'll never go back to those wimpy portable phones and buds. These are the real deal.

Model: SR60
Manufacturer: Grado Labs (www.gradolabs.com)
Price: $69.99

Koss PORTAPRO
Portable

Koss has always made great headphones, and the PORTAPRO Portable is the latest in a long line of high-quality, lightweight performers. What's unique about the PORTAPRO Portable are the Comfort Zone pads that fit against your temporal regions, just above the ears. This, combined with the light weight, makes for surprising comfort.

The PORTAPRO Portable collapses for easy packing when you're on the go, and you get a carrying case, too. These are extremely comfortable phones, with a much better sound than you're probably used to.

> **Model:** PORTAPRO Portable
> **Manufacturer:** Koss (www.koss.com)
> **Price:** $49.99

Sennheiser PX 100

Here's another set of lightweight, affordable, great-sounding headphones. The PX 100s are perfect for home audio listening or for use with portable music players. They're fairly small, are extremely lightweight, and deliver terrific sound.

For portable use, I appreciate the fold-and-flip design; they fold up into a somewhat manageable package. And they're sturdy little buggers, so don't worry about giving them a good workout.

> **Model:** PX 100
> **Manufacturer:** Sennheiser
> (www.sennheiser.com)
> **Price:** $49.99

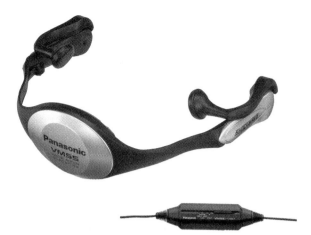

Panasonic Shockwave Brain Shaker Extreme Headphones

If you're tired of portable headphones that deliver wimpy bass, the Panasonic Brain Shaker Extreme is the phone for you. These headphones deliver the most powerful bass of any headphones I've heard, courtesy of what Panasonic calls the Virtual Motion Sound System (VMSS). This is a subwoofer-type device that wraps around the back of your neck; the VMSS delivers bass vibrations through your spine, which compliments the normal stereo sound that comes from the wraparound earplugs.

Of course, spine-throbbing bass can be a real pain in the neck after long listening sessions. And the around-the-neck design tends to pull the buds out of your ears. But for super booming bass, these are the phones to get!

Model: RP-HS900
Manufacturer: Panasonic
(www.panasonic.com)
Price: $39.95

Sony Infrared Cordless Digital Surround Headphone System

And now for something completely different. The MDR-DS8000 is a cordless headset designed for use with surround-sound home theater systems. Not only do you get digital infrared wireless listening, but you also get a set of phones that delivers a full six-speaker surround-sound field. It's amazing, actually; sit anywhere in the room and get the perfect surround-sound experience, without disturbing anyone else.

This system is compatible with all existing surround-sound technologies—Dolby Digital EX, DTS ES, Dolby Pro Logic II, you name it. The gyro head tracking system provides realistic positioning when you move your head around; the effective range is 33 feet.

Model: MDR-DS8000
Manufacturer: Sony (www.sonystyle.com)
Price: $799.99

Earbuds

Earbuds are like headphones without the phones. Instead of bulky foam cups that enclose your entire ear, earbuds are tiny earphones that fit inside your ear. The advantage of in-ear devices is that they do a better job of blocking background noise than standard over-the-ear headphones. Plus, they're small and light, perfect for portable use.

You might think that earbuds, because of their small size, wouldn't sound as good as full-size headphones. You'd be wrong. Most earbuds sound very good, and the best deliver even better sound than similarly priced headphones. That's because the tiny transducers fit right inside your ear, with nothing to interfere with the sound; the better the fit, the better the sound quality. Earbuds also deliver good isolation from external sounds. Again, the better the fit, the better the isolation. And the better the isolation, the better the sound you hear.

If there's any defining characteristic of the "earbud sound," it's that the bass is a little weak and the treble a little high. You can easily fix this by adjusting the tone or equalization controls on your portable player.

Interestingly, most earbuds sound better after a little use than straight out of the box. That's because the buds have to be broken in a bit to "loosen" the transducers; they might sound a little rough initially but will smooth out after a few weeks of listening.

You'll also improve the sound by letting the earbuds shape themselves to the contour of your ears. To that end, many high-end earbuds come with a number of tips or sleeves, typically in different sizes. You'll need to experiment with different sleeves to find the one that fits you best. The sleeves also improve the bass response, so they're definitely worth using.

One variation on the common earbud is the canal phone, which looks like an earbud but fits deeper into the ear canal, rather than just resting in the outer ear. This provides an air-tight seal and super-good sound isolation. Canal phones are at the high-end of the price spectrum but are good if you want professional sound reproduction. (These are what most pro musicians use on stage.) For the best sound, you can purchase custom-fitted canal stems that are made from molds of your ears.

Shure E3c Sound Isolating Earphones

The Shure E3c earphones—actually canal phones—provide a true audiophile listening experience. These are high-end earphones with high-end performance, priced at the high end of the scale.

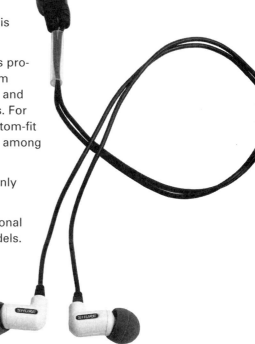

Why spend this amount of money for a set of earphones? Simple—for the sound. The E3c delivers the type of studio-quality sound you expect from Shure products. The unit's high-energy micro-speakers are made of studio-grade components (hence the unit's high price) and deliver an extended frequency response. The result is heavenly.

The E3c's earbuds fit securely in your ears, and flexible sleeves produce great sound isolation. You get one pair of disposable foam sleeves, three pairs (small, medium, and large) of flex sleeves, and three pairs (small, medium, and large) of ultra-soft flex sleeves. For the best fit, however, consider having an audiologist make custom-fit ear molds; it'll cost you but will give you huge bragging rights among your friends.

Whichever earbud you use, the E3c weighs next to nothing—only 0.9 oz. It comes with its own carrying case, natch.

Bottom line, if you want the same earphones used by professional musicians, buy the E3c. You'll never go back to traditional models.

Model: E3c
Manufacturer: Shure (www.shure.com)
Price: $179.99

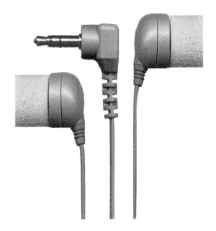

Etymotic Research ER-6 Isolator

All earbuds are quiet, but the ER-6 gets my vote for the quietest earbud model, short of those offering active noise cancellation (which we'll discuss in a few pages). Like the Shure and Future Sonics models, these deliver pro-quality results—truly tremendous sound. (Use the foam eartips for best bass.) You get all sorts of eartips and filters as included accessories, as well as a nice zippered pouch to carry it all around in. You can also fit the ER-6 with a special Musicians Earplug (optional, extra) for an even tighter fit.

> **Model:** ER-6
> **Manufacturer:** Etymotic Research
> (www.etymotic.com)
> **Price:** $139

Future Sonics Ears EM3

Here's another set of pro-level earbuds. The Future Sonics Ears cost a tad less than the Shure E3c, but they deliver comparable sound quality. You get a good fit with the standard sleeves, although custom sleeves are available—for a cost, of course. They're light, they sound great, and they're extremely durable. (And if you want even better sound quality, move up to the Future Sonics MG4 Ear Monitors, custom-molded in-ear monitors used by musicians worldwide.)

> **Model:** Ears EM3
> **Manufacturer:** Future Sonics
> (www.futuresonics.com)
> **Price:** $159

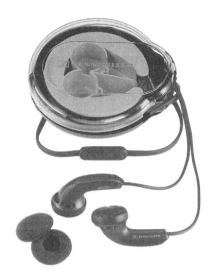

Sennheiser MX 500

If ultra-high-priced earbuds aren't your cup of tea, consider these affordable Sennheiser buds. The sound's pretty good, the buds are lightweight and comfortable, and you get an in-line volume control that also functions as a retractable cord case.

You won't confuse these with the Shure or Etymotic models, but they're a pretty good deal for the price—and much better-sounding than the standard phones that come with today's portable music players. The buds themselves are a cool blue metallic, which adds a bit of style to things.

> **Model:** MX 500
> **Manufacturer:** Sennheiser
> (www.sennheiser.com)
> **Price:** $19.99

Sony Sports Series Fontopia Ear-Bud Headphones

Here's another set of affordable earbuds, also with in-line volume control/cord case. The gimmick here is that these are "sports" phones, which means they come in a traffic-stopping yellow color and are a little sturdier than the standard-issue buds. They're also water-resistant, so feel free to sweat all you want, or take a quick dunk in the pool. They'll stand up to it.

> **Model:** MDR-E827G
> **Manufacturer:** Sony (www.sonystyle.com)
> **Price:** $19.99

Noise-Canceling Headphones

If you like your music without all the background noise, check out a set of noise-canceling headphones. Even if you use headphones a lot, you might not be aware of just how much background noise gets through to your ears and how that noise affects what you hear. Everyday life has a lot of ambient noise, from air conditioners to passing cars, crying babies, and the like. And if you travel a lot, you know how noisy it gets onboard an airplane; the constant engine noise can really wear you down.

So-called *active noise-canceling headphones* have built-in microphones that sample ambient noise and electronic circuitry to remove the noise. The phones synthesize sound waves that are equal and opposite to the low frequency the microphone picks up; the result is that low-frequency noise is cancelled out. Most consumer-oriented noise-canceling phones can attenuate (cut) ambient noise by 10 decibels or so—an effective 70% reduction.

The biggest effect comes with low-frequency sounds, like the hum you get in a crowded airplane. Turn on the noise-canceling phones and listen to that annoying background hum disappear. Most noise-canceling phones come with normal stereo connectors, as well as connectors to use with in-flight entertainment systems, so you can use them to listen to music and movies on the plane.

People with some degree of hearing loss also find noise-canceling phones useful. If you have trouble distinguishing conversation in a noisy room, try listening with a set of noise-canceling phones turned on. (But no music playing, of course!) The distracting ambient noise gets softer, making conversations easier to hear.

Which brings up the point that you don't have to use noise-canceling headphones just for music. The noise-canceling circuits work whether you're connected to a music player or audio system. When you turn on the phones, the noise cancellation kicks in, even if you're not listening to anything. I like wearing my noise-canceling phones on long plane flights just to block out the ambient noise, with no music playing. The relative quiet is soothing.

Don't confuse active noise-canceling headphones with *passive* noise-canceling phones. Passive canceling headphones are simply normal phones with big ear cups that fit completely over your ears. This closed-ear design blocks out some outside noise, but it doesn't cancel it out completely. These types of phones can also be heavy and uncomfortable to wear for extended periods of time.

  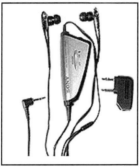  

Bose QuietComfort 2

The Bose QuietComfort 2s are, without a doubt, the quietest headphones on the market today. These phones set the standard for noise-canceling performance.

Bose's Accoustic Noise Canceling technology electronically identifies and then reduces unwanted noise. You don't even have to listen to music to use these phones; just put them on, turn them on, and hear virtually all background noise disappear. (The audio cable is even removable.) The phones come with a hi/lo switch, so you can pick the amount of noise reduction that suits your taste.

When you do listen to music, active equalization circuits automatically fine-tune the frequency response for best performance. The sound is pretty good, although not as good as the best standard headphones, like the Grado SR60. (That's true of all noise-canceling phones; cutting ambient noise effects the frequency response to some degree.)

These are also the bulkiest phones on the market, but that's the price you pay for near-total quiet. You won't want to wear them when you're jogging, but they're just fine for wearing on a long plane trip. The ear cushions are quite comfortable.

The QuietComfort 2 comes with a standard mini-plug for use with portable devices, a 1/4" adapter for home audio equipment, and a dual plug adapter to use when flying. You also get a compact carrying case for the phones and all the accessories.

Model: QuietComfort 2
Manufacturer: Bose (www.bose.com)
Price: $299

Panasonic RP-HC70

Here's what I like about Panasonic's noise-canceling headphones: the price. The Panasonic RP-HC70 delivers more than acceptable performance at a fraction of what you'd pay for the Bose QuietComfort 2 phones.

These headphones are a little smaller and lighter than the Bose models; the open-air design makes them comfortable to wear for extended periods. They fold up for easy packing, of course, and have an in-line volume control. And they do a pretty good job of canceling background noise—not as good as the Bose model, but definitely helpful when you're traveling on a long trip!

Model: RP-HC70
Manufacturer: Panasonic
(www.panasonic.com)
Price: $49.95

Sony MDR-NC11

The Sony MDR-NC11 is unique among noise-canceling headsets because it uses in-the-ear earbuds instead of the typical over-the-ear headphone configuration. Earbuds filter out a lot of noise naturally; when you add active noise-cancellation circuitry, you get an extremely quiet combination. Plus they're small, light, and (if you like earbuds) comfortable. Just pop the buds in your ears, turn on the noise canceller, and settle back for some genuine peace and quiet.

Model: MDR-NC11
Manufacturer: Sony (www.sonystyle.com)
Price: $149.99

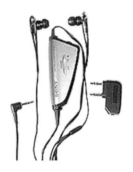

Portable Video Players

You know all about portable audio players. But how about portable *video* players? Well, there's nothing surprising or complex here; a portable video player is a portable device that plays back video (as well as audio) files on a built-in screen.

That said, this is a relatively new consumer electronics category, and there aren't a lot of devices on the market yet. That will change, of course, as more and more consumers discover the benefits of watching movies on a handheld device that looks like a portable game machine.

Don't confuse portable video players with portable DVD players (which I discuss next). Portable video players don't play back DVDs; instead, they play digital video programming recorded to their built-in hard disks, the same way portable audio players play back digital music.

Most portable video players have at least a 20GB hard disk. Movies are recorded in MPEG-4 format, which is the visual equivalent of audio MP3 files; you get 4 hours of programming per gigabyte. Picture quality is typically around 300 × 225 pixels, which is okay for watching on a small screen. Most units play back movies using Microsoft's Windows Media Center software.

All portable video players also function as portable music players, so you don't have to carry two devices around. Some also let you view digital photographs on the built-in screen.

Getting movies onto the portable device can be a bit of a challenge, considering that Hollywood insists on strong copy protection. Some players, like the Archos AV300 series, ignore the copy protection and let you record video from your VCR or DVD player. Other players, like the RCA Lyra A/V Jukebox, enable the copy protection, which limits what you can copy to and watch on the portable device. Before you buy, find out the type of programming you can copy to the portable device, and how.

 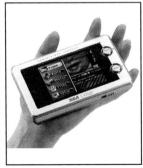   

Archos AV300 Series

The Archos AV300 series was the first portable video player to hit the market, and until something better comes along, it remains my pick in this category.

Size- and shape-wise, it's a lot like other video players—that is, it feels like an overgrown digital audio player. You view programming on the 3.8" color LCD screen, which takes up most of the 4.5" × 3.75" faceplate. You can also hook the unit up to a television or computer to view movies on a bigger screen.

To fill up the AV300, you record directly from any VCR or DVD player—no PC necessary. Archos manufactures 20GB, 40GB, and 80GB versions; the big one can store up to 320 hours of video in MPEG-4 format. You can also use the AV300 to store and view digital photos and play digital music.

The AV300 comes with a wireless remote control, which seems a little odd to me, but there it is. You can also purchase a digital camera add-on to turn the thing into a bulky and low-performance digicam. My recommendation is to use it for what it is—a really cool portable movie player.

Model: AV300 series
Manufacturer: Archos (www.archos.com)
Price: $499.95 (AV320, 20GB), $599.95 (AV340, 40GB), $799.95 (AV380, 80GB)

RCA Lyra A/V Jukebox

RCA's Lyra A/V Jukebox is a credible competitor to the Archos AV300 series units. It's not quite as good a performer, unfortunately, although it does cost about a hundred bucks less.

The screen on the Lyra is a little smaller than the Archos, at just 3.5". It uses a 20GB hard disk, which holds up to 80 hours of programming. But the real drawback is that, unlike the Archos, you can't record copyrighted VHS and DVD content—which significantly limits what you can view. Try before you buy.

Model: Lyra RD2780
Manufacturer: RCA (www.rca.com)
Price: $399.99

Creative Zen Portable Media Center

The portable video player I'm really looking forward to is Creative's Zen Portable Media Center. This neat-looking little unit won the 2004 Best of CES Award and should turn a lot of heads.

As I write this, Creative hasn't finalized the form factor, although it looks like it will include a 3.8" color LCD and a 20GB or bigger hard drive. It should be available by the time you read this and be worth your attention.

Model: Zen Portable Media Center
Manufacturer: Creative (www.creative.com)
Price: TBA

Portable DVD Players

If you don't mind carrying a slightly larger unit, you can skip all the fuss and muss that comes with using a portable video player by watching movies straight from DVD on a portable DVD player. These battery-operated devices let you insert a DVD and watch a movie on the built-in screen.

All portable DVD players work in pretty much the same fashion. The big differences between the units are screen size, overall size and weight, and battery life. The bigger the screen, the heavier the unit—and the lower the battery life. The smaller the screen, the more "personal" it is—you won't find a crowd of people gathered around to watch *The Matrix* on a tiny 5" screen.

The most popular units have either 7" or 9" diagonal color LCD screens. Most screens are in the 16:9 format, ideal for watching widescreen movies. The screens are just like the ones used in notebook PCs, with plenty of brightness and resolution.

These are battery-operated units, so you can watch movies on-the-go. Most batteries last 2.5–3 hours on a charge, more than long enough to watch an average movie. Just make sure your flight is long enough to get the whole movie in.

Although these gadgets have built-in speakers, you'll probably want to listen with headphones, instead—unless you want to share your movie with your fellow travelers. This might be fine in a car, but passengers on an airplane might object.

If you do use a portable DVD player in a car, make sure it's in the backseat. Drivers shouldn't be distracted by a movie playing in the seat beside them—and several states outlaw front-seat video operation, anyway.

You can also use a portable DVD player in the home; audio/video output jacks let you hook the player up to any home TV and audio system. For example, my brother used to use his portable player as a bedroom DVD player when he wasn't traveling. He just hooked it up to his bedroom TV, kept the screen flipped down, and got good double-duty out of his unit.

Of course, an alternative to carrying around a portable DVD player is to watch movies on your notebook PC. If your notebook has a DVD drive—and if your battery will last two hours or so—you don't need a separate movie player. Plus, you can check your email when the movie's over!

Toshiba SD-P5000

What makes Toshiba's SD-P5000 so cool is its huge honkin' screen. Believe it or not, this portable DVD player has a gargantuan 15" screen, twice the size as the average portable player. The screen is mounted on a double hinge, so you can fold it completely parallel with the base and mount the whole thing on your wall. This also makes it great for use in the backseat of your car during long trips.

Leo's Pick

The SD-P5000 does double duty as a DVD player and television set, thanks to its built-in TV tuner. You can also use it to play back digital audio files, view digital photos, and play back video from a camcorder.

Operation can be either AC or DC, for home or auto use. If you want true portability, you have to purchase the optional battery pack, which promises 2.5 hours of cord-free operation.

Drawbacks? Unlike other portable players, this unit has a non-widescreen 4:3 ratio screen. And did I mention that it's big and heavy? This is not an easy unit to schlep around.

All that said, there's no other portable DVD player like this one. There's absolutely nothing like sitting on a plane and watching a movie on a notebook-size screen. Sometimes size does matter.

Model: SD-P5000
Manufacturer: Toshiba (www.toshiba.com)
Screen: 15" 4:3
Price: $799.99

Sony DVP-FX700

There's nothing overly special about this Sony DVD player, other than it does what it's supposed to do and it does it very well. It offers a good compromise between screen size and portability, with a 7" widescreen LCD in a 7.5" × 6" unit. Even better, it's just an inch thick—small enough to carry in a briefcase or backpack.

Picture quality is about what you'd expect, and you get three hours on a battery charge. You can even use it to play back tapes from your camcorder; the AV outputs can be switched and used as inputs.

Model: DVP-FX700
Manufacturer: Sony (www.sonystyle.com)
Screen: 7" 16:9
Price: $499.99

Audiovox D1500A

This is an ultra-compact DVD player, weighing just 5 pounds. Of course, to get the unit this small, you sacrifice something—in this case, screen size. Instead of a big 16:9 screen, the D1500A has a small 5" non-widescreen (4:3) LCD. That's a small price to pay for handheld portability, which this unit definitely delivers. It's the smallest portable DVD player on the market today—a terrific source for travel entertainment.

Model: D1500A
Manufacturer: Audiovox
(www.audiovox.com)
Screen: 5" 4:3
Price: $399.99

Panasonic DVD-LX9

Here's another unit from Panasonic, similar to the DVD-LX8 but with a docking cradle and external speakers. The DVD player fits into the top of the docking station, creating a neat little desktop DVD system. The two auxiliary speakers provide a bigger sound, and you get a wireless remote control to work everything from across the room.

Bottom line, if you want a DVD player that does double-duty as a portable and a desktop unit, the DVD-LX9 does the job.

Model: DVD-LX9
Manufacturer: Panasonic
(www.panasonic.com)
Screen: 9" 16:9
Price: $899.99

Panasonic DVD-LX8

Panasonic's DVD-LX8 is priced the same as the Sony unit but offers a larger screen. What I like about this one is the design that places the 9" LCD screen on an adjustable arm. Twist and turn the screen to find the best viewing angle.

Of course, the larger screen makes for a larger unit overall, so if size is an issue, get the Sony instead. But if you want a cool-looking unit with a swivel display, this is the model for you.

Model: DVD-LX8
Manufacturer: Panasonic
(www.panasonic.com)
Screen: 9" 16:9
Price: $699.99

Digital Voice Recorders

In the old days, if you wanted to make a voice recording you had to use a tape recorder, using tiny microcassette tapes that held only an hour or so worth of recording. Today, however, you can make voice recordings digitally, recording directly to flash memory. This provides larger recording capacity and the capability of transferring your recordings to your computer's hard disk.

Today's digital voice recorders can hold up to 44 hours of recording, depending on the amount of memory included. That's more than enough to record a semester's worth of lectures, a long meeting, or an interview with somebody particularly long and windy. You can even use these voice recordings as personal memo devices or high-tech Dictaphones.

What's particularly cool is the fact that you can transfer all your voice recordings to PC, typically via USB cable. Then you can use special voice-to-text software to convert the recordings to text files and edit those files in your word processor. Or you can use the audio files in voice email messages or post them to a website.

Most digital voice recorders let you record at two different speeds. (*Speed* is a bit of a misnomer, a holdover from when you could vary tape speed; today, you just record at different digital bit rates.) SP delivers better sound quality but takes up more storage space; LP lets you store twice as much data but with a drop off in sound quality. Recording is typically in mono, but some recorders have a stereo mode that takes up twice as much storage space.

The big players in this market are Olympus and Sony, both of which offer a variety of models at all price points. All the units function similarly, letting you organize your recordings in different folders in the device's memory.

When shopping for a digital voice recorder, there are several things to look for. First is recording capacity; more is typically better, although you might not need to record 44 hours worth of anything at a time. Second, consider how the recordings are stored; some units have flash memory built in, but others use removable media cards for storage. Third, make sure you're comfortable with the look and feel of the unit; some are more portable than others. Fourth, consider how the thing operates; are the controls logical and well laid-out? Finally, look at any extra features, such as the ability to function as a digital music player.

Olympus DM-1

Now this is one neat digital voice recorder. It looks cool, has a big capacity, and is quite flexible.

Leo's Pick

What I particularly like about the DM-1 is that it records directly to SmartMedia cards; you can get up to 22 hours of recording on a 64MB card or 44 hours on a 128MB card. Use multiple cards to extend the recording time and organize your recordings.

Speaking of organization, the DM-1 lets you store your recordings in one of three folders; each folder can store up to 199 messages. You can record in either SP or LP mode, depending on the voice quality you need. It has a built-in microphone, of course, as well as voice activation mode for hands-free recording.

It's USB-compatible, which makes it easy to download your audio recordings to your PC—or transfer digital audio files to the DM-1. That's right, you also use the DM-1 as a digital music player, which is a nice case of double duty. To top it all off, in a category that's a little old school, the DM-1 is particularly stylish. The case is bright blue plastic, which will look right at home with all your other cool gadgets.

Model: DM-1
Manufacturer: Olympus
(www.olympusamerica.com)
Price: $249.99

Sony ICD-ST25VTP

This Sony voice digital recorder comes with Dragon Naturally Speaking voice-to-print software, so you can convert your recordings to text and download them directly to your PC. You can even use the ICD-ST25VTP to send voice emails with attached files.

Recording time (in LP mode) is 696 minutes—a little more than 11 hours. The Voice-Up Function automatically increases the volume of the person speaking when recorded at a distance.

Model: ICD-ST25VTP
Manufacturer: Sony (www.sonystyle.com)
Price: $199.99

Olympus VN-240PC

If you don't need quite that much recording time, check out Olympus's VN-240PC. This compact unit offers up to 4 hours of recording time (in LP mode) at an affordable price. Transfer recordings to your PC via USB and view what's happening on the big LCD screen. And if you want to save some time, play back your recordings in the fast mode—30% faster than real time.

Model: VN-240PC
Manufacturer: Olympus
(www.olympusamerica.com)
Price: $79.99

Handheld GPS Devices

GPS stands for global positioning system, which is a way to determine location based on signals beamed from a network of 24 satellites positioned in six geosynchronized orbital paths around the Earth. A GPS unit measures the speed of each satellite and compares it relative to the unit's location, thus determining the unit's latitude, longitude, and altitude.

It's rather complicated technology, originally developed for military use, which has now filtered down to the consumer level. You can purchase a handheld GPS unit for $200 or so and get the same type of performance that our soldiers do in the field.

You use a GPS unit not only to tell you where you are, but also to show you where you're going. You punch in a location, and the GPS software maps out a route and displays it on an onscreen roadmap. Your current position is marked on the map, and the map scrolls as you travel. Most units provide turn-by-turn directions; some even use a synthesized voice to tell you what to do next.

GPS units are great for when you're traveling or for when you're hiking, biking, or boating outdoors. If you do plan on outdoor use, look for a unit that's rugged enough to hold up under bad conditions and is water resistant. (The latter is especially important if you use it while boating.)

When you're shopping, here are some features to compare. First, determine how many satellites a unit uses for navigation (sometimes described as the number of *channels*); most utilize 12 satellites, but others use more for higher accuracy. Second, examine the base maps that come with the unit; make sure your home area is fully covered. Third, see how many routes the unit can store in memory. Fourth, find out how many *waypoints* it can store. (A waypoint is a place or attraction along a route—like a gas station or restaurant.) Fifth, look for the largest number of *track points*, which are locations you manually add to your route. Finally, examine the GPS-to-PC connection and the mapping software that comes with the unit.

If you're really into this GPS thing, take a look at the TomTom Navigator (p. 64) that turns your PDA into a handheld GPS device and the Timex GPS Watch (p. 106) that calculates running time and distance. Also check out the many car GPS devices, starting on p. 240; although you can use a handheld device in your car, a dedicated dashtop unit might be a better choice.

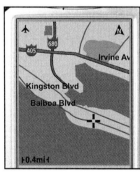

Magellan SporTrak Color

The SporTrak Color is one full-featured GPS device. First, it features a big 240 × 160 pixel color display, which makes delineating points on the map easy. It includes a base map of North America, plus you can upload other maps from your PC as necessary.

Your location is tracked via 12 GPS satellites; it's accurate to within 3 meters, which is pretty darned close. You can store up to 20 routes and 500 waypoints, as well as 2,000 track points. Transfer saved routes to your PC with the optional MapSend software.

In addition to the standard GPS functionality, the SporTrak Color includes a built-in barometer and three-axis compass. It also shows you when the sun will rise and set, as well as the phase of the moon—and there's even a built-in fish and game calculator, so you'll know what's biting when, wherever you are.

This is truly a gizmo you can take with you anywhere. Even though it's compact and lightweight, it's extremely rugged. And, even better, it's waterproof—so don't worry about dumping it overboard when you're fishing!

Model: SporTrak Color
Manufacturer: Magellan (www.magellangps.com)
Price: $349.99

Cobra GPS 500

Cobra's GPS 500 is a low-cost, high-performance handheld GPS unit. It features a built-in U.S./Canada base map, 2MB of memory, and the ability to continually track up to 18 GPS satellites—6 more than competing models. Track your travel with up to 20 routes and 500 waypoints with names and symbols.

Cobra keeps the price low by using a grayscale, rather than a color, display. The GPS 500 also includes a built-in compass, altimeter, and clock. Connect to your PC to exchange data with various mapping programs.

Model: GPS 500
Manufacturer: Cobra (www.cobra.com)
Price: $139.95

Lowrance iFinder Pro

The iFinder Pro is a pocket-size unit with a built-in base map featuring highways, interstate exits, and other details from southern Canada to northern Mexico. It features a 3" backlit grayscale display, good for both nighttime and daytime viewing—even in direct sunlight.

The iFinder Pro tracks up to 12 GPS satellites and lets you log up to 100 routes and 1,000 waypoints. Create your own maps and save them to a MultiMediaCard or SD card; MapCreate software for your PC is included.

Model: iFinder Pro
Manufacturer: Lowrance (www.lowrance.com)
Price: $199.95

Garmin iQue 3600

The iQue 3600 is a Palm OS PDA with built-in GPS technology and mapping software. It features a flip-up patch antenna for best reception, and a speaker for turn-by-turn voice commands. The unit's 32MB of memory lets it incorporate base maps for North America, South America, Europe, and the Pacific Rim, making this the GPS unit of choice for international travelers. Plus, by integrating GPS and PDA functions, you only have to carry one gadget with you when you travel.

The iQue 3600 lets you track 50 routes with 50 waypoints per route. It finds its way by tracking 12 GPS satellites and connects to your PC via USB.

Model: iQue 3600
Manufacturer: Garmin (www.garmin.com)
Price: $590

Garmin Rino 130

The Rino 130 is a two-way radio with built-in GPS technology. Not only can you use it as a walkie-talkie, but you can also transmit your exact location with the press of a button. You can also request GPS information from other units.

The two-way radio works up to 5 miles using the GMRS band. The GPS function includes a base map of North America and tracks 12 GPS satellites. The Rino 130 also includes a NOAA weather radio and barometric pressure sensor, so you'll have advance notice before it starts to rain.

Model: Rino 130
Manufacturer: Garmin (www.garmin.com)
Price: $375

High-tech Watches

A watch is a watch is a watch, right? Wrong. High-tech watches today do more than just tell time (though they do that, too—often by receiving highly accurate atomic signals); they utilize state-of-the-art technology to deliver functions formerly reserved for dedicated devices.

What kind of functionality can you find in a high-tech watch? Here's a sampling:

- Calculate speed and distance using GPS technology—great for runners and joggers

- Deliver news and weather reports—and instant messages—via a wireless Internet connection

- Transfer computer files via built-in flash memory

- Display current temperature, barometric pressure, and other weather data

- Let you talk to friends and family via two-way radio

- Let you take pictures with a built-in digital camera

- Let you operate your TV and VCR via remote control

All this sound a little science fiction-y? Well, it's not. All these operations are built in to affordably priced watches on the market today, sold by brand-name watch manufacturers—Timex, Casio, and the like. It's somewhat amazing what they can pack into the body of a wristwatch, but technology lets them miniaturize just about anything.

Me, I'm waiting for a single watch that does all these things and plays back videos, too. I'm betting some company will have one on the market within three years.

Timex GPS Watch

Our previous gadget category covered handheld GPS devices, so it's only natural to lead off this category with a GPS-enabled wrist watch. This double-duty gizmo uses GPS technology to help you calculate speed and distance data when running or jogging.

Leo's Pick

The GPS Watch is only half the package. In addition to the watch, you get an armband- or belt-mounted GPS transceiver (supplied by Garmin) that calculates speed and distance data, triangulated from a network of GPS satellites. The transceiver unit wirelessly transmits the data to the watch, where you view it on the watch's LCD display.

The GPS Watch lets you track average speed or pace, maximum speed or best pace, and accumulated distance. It includes a continuous odometer and has a 100-lap memory recall. You can set alarms for both target distance and target speed.

The watch itself features an Indiglo night light and a special Night-Mode feature for when you're running in the dark—not that I'd recommend it, all things considered. It's fairly rugged and water resistant to 50 meters.

I think this Timex unit offers a fairly cool use of GPS technology. It's a must-have for fitness-oriented gadget hounds.

Model: 58681
Manufacturer: Timex (www.timex.com)
Price: $199.95

Meritline RIST Memory Watch

Back on p. 34 I listed a half-dozen or so keychain flash memory devices. Well, here's a variation on the theme, a flash memory device built in to a high-tech wrist watch.

The RIST Memory Watch contains 128MB of flash memory to store all manner of digital files. You connect the watch to your PC via the supplied USB cable and transfer files as you would with any other USB drive. The watch part, of course, works just like a normal watch.

Model: ML1390B
Manufacturer: Meritline
(www.meritline.com)
Price: $109

Abacus Wrist Net Internet Watch

For those of you who can't bear to leave the Internet behind, take it with you with Abacus's Wrist Net Internet Watch. This watch employs Microsoft's MSN Direct service to deliver all the information you need, relayed from the Internet via FM signals.

The Wrist Net Watch and MSN Direct deliver news, weather, sports, and stock information, as well as instant messages from your online buddies. You also get an online calendar and appointment scheduler—and Internet-accurate time. Of course, you have to subscribe to the MSN Direct service, which costs $9.99 per month. But then you'll be connected continuously—the ultimate wireless wired guy.

Model: Wrist Net
Manufacturer: Abacus
(www.abacuswatches.com)
Price: $129

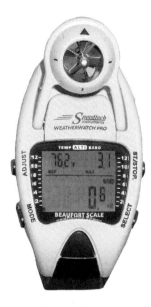

Xact Wristlinx 2-Way Radio Watch

Now here's something cool—an honest-to-goodness, real-world *Dick Tracy* wrist-radio. The Wristlinx functions like any other two-way radio unit, but it fits on your wrist. The microphone and speaker are located just below the LCD display.

You can use the Wristlinx to talk to other Wristlinx users or to anyone with a standard two-way radio. Just hold the watch up to your face and start talking; it's voice activated.

> **Model:** Wristlinx
> **Manufacturer:** Xact
> (www.xactcommunication.com)
> **Price:** $49.99

SpeedtechWeather Watch Pro

Here's a high-tech watch that functions like a portable weather station. The WeatherWatch Pro tracks and displays temperature, wind chill, wind speed, barometric pressure (with nine-hour history graph), altitude, and date. It also includes a chronograph, a yacht racing timer, and an alarm.

The WeatherWatch Pro measures the wind speed with a built-in impeller. One of the impeller fins is magnetized, is highlighted in green, and always points north. This contributes to its somewhat bulky size; if it's too big for your wrist, you can detach it from the wrist strap and wear it on a lanyard around your neck.

> **Model:** WW-1
> **Manufacturer:** Speedtech Instruments
> (www.speedtech.com)
> **Price:** $150

Casio Color Wrist Camera Watch

This high-tech watch is part of Casio's innovative Technowear line. You get a fancy watch that doubles as a digital camera. The watch face is actually a color LCD screen that lets you preview and view the pictures you shoot.

The built-in camera has a 2X digital zoom and shoots 176 × 144 pixel JPG pictures. It uses infrared technology to transfer the pictures you shoot to your PC. The watch stores up to 100 images in its 1MB of memory.

Model: WQV10D-2
Manufacturer: Casio (www.casio.com)
Price: $329.95

Casio TV Remote Control Watch

Here's a high-tech watch for extreme couch potatoes. If you're too lazy to reach over and pick up the remote control, just use the buttons on this Casio Technowear watch to change channels.

That's right, this wicked little gizmo functions as a remote control for your television, cable box, or VCR. Several very small buttons let you control power on/off, volume up/down, and channel up/down for the TV, and play, stop, rewind, and fast forward for your VCR. For some unknown reason, it also has a built-in stopwatch, as if anyone using this watch will ever need to time themselves in the 100-yard dash.

Model: CMD30B-1T
Manufacturer: Casio (www.casio.com)
Price: $79.95

Battery-Related Gadgets

To be portable, a portable electronic device must get its power from batteries. It's not surprising, then, that a variety of battery-related gadgets is available out there—devices that either recharge or replace the batteries that come with your favorite portable devices.

The most common battery-related gadget is the battery charger. If you keep feeding traditional alkaline batteries into your portable devices, you'll quickly go broke; they last for a few hours and then you throw them away. A better approach is to use batteries you can recharge. When they wear down, just pop them in the charger until they're nice and fresh; then use them again.

Of course, you have to invest in both the rechargeable batteries and a battery charger, but that won't set you back a lot. Even the best battery chargers cost less than $50, and you'll typically pay $10 or so for a four-pack of rechargeable AA batteries. You'll spend that much on alkalines in a month, easily.

A lot of battery chargers are on the market today. One is pretty much the same as the next,

unless you want a unit that both charges and conditions your batteries, like the Powerex and Ansmann units. The typical charger can recharge a set of batteries in an hour or two; the fastest unit—Rayovac's I-C3—can recharge four AAs in just 15 minutes.

By the way, you should preemptively recharge any batteries that have been sitting in a device unused for awhile. That's because all rechargeable batteries *self-discharge* over time—that is, they lose power when they just sit around. If you know you're going to be using a device you haven't used for awhile, take out the batteries and recharge them the night before. It's good insurance.

Other battery-related gadgets offer other ways to recharge or replace batteries. Case in point is the iSun Solar Charger, which recharges batteries from solar power rather than AC power. Also of interest are power inverters, which transform DC power (such as from a car battery) into AC power that any device can use.

  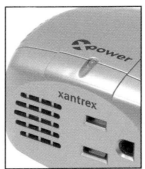  

iSun Solar Charger

Leo's Pick

You don't have to be a slave to the power companies—or the battery manufacturers. With the iSun Solar Charger, all you need to recharge your portable device is a nice sunny day.

The iSun is a personal solar panel that can supply power to any small electronic device—PDAs, portable audio players, cell phones, and so on. It's a great accessory when you run out of juice too far away from the nearest power outlet.

Here's how you use it. Unfold the iSun, position it toward the sun, and then plug in your portable device. That's it; the sun's rays do the rest. And if you need to charge a more power-hungry device, such as a notebook PC or small television set, you can daisy-chain up to five iSun units together.

The only drawback to the iSun is that the sun needs to be out. It won't work at night and delivers considerably less power than normal on cloudy days. On the upside, this is the ultimate eco-friendly power device—and it will get you going when all other power is out.

Model: iSun
Manufacturer: ICP Solar Technologies
(www.icpsolar.com)
Price: $79.95

Rayovac I-C3 15-Minute Battery Charger

Most battery chargers take at least an hour to recharge a set of batteries. Rayovac's I-C3 does the job in just 15 minutes. That ultra-fast recharge is made possible by Rayovac's In-Cell Charge Control technology and special I-C3 batteries; ordinary NiMH and NiCd batteries still take a few hours to charge.

Zapping batteries this fast takes a lot of power, and power generates heat. To keep your batteries from getting blistering hot, the I-C3 features a built-in cooling fan. The batteries still come out warm to the touch, but that's a small price to pay for this kind of recharging speed.

Model: I-C3
Manufacturer: Rayovac
(www.rayovac.com)
Price: $39.95

Powerex Intelligent Battery Charger and Conditioner Kit

With so many portable devices using rechargeable batteries, you need a decent battery charger to keep everything recharged. The Powerex Charger/Conditioner isn't like other "dumb" chargers; it features a built-in microprocessor controller with trickle charge for intelligent battery cycling. It even rejuvenates old batteries by subjecting them to an automatic discharge/charge cycle.

Even better, the Powerex unit includes two independent battery banks, which let you charge two unique sets of batteries simultaneously. For example, you can put two NiMH AA batteries in one bank and two NiCD AAAs in the other. It's like having two separate chargers—both of them fast and smart!

Model: MH-C204F
Manufacturer: Meritline
(www.meritline.com)
Price: $39.99

Ansmann Energy 16 Battery Charger/Conditioner

Ansmann's Energy 16 is the Rolls Royce of battery chargers. It's extremely flexible; you can charge 12 AA or AAA batteries or 6 C or D cells, plus 4 9V cells, all at the same time. It can charge both NiMH and older NiCd batteries simultaneously and analyzes the batteries before charging to identify bad cells.

Insert a battery, and the Energy 16 performs a capacity quick test and displays the charge state. The Energy 16 conditions each battery before it recharges it; charging stops when the cell is fully replenished.

Model: Energy 16
Manufacturer: Ansmann Energy
(www.ansmann.us)
Price: $139.99

XPower Micro Inverter 175

A power inverter is a device that converts DC power to AC power, so you can use corded devices anywhere there's a DC power outlet. The XPower Micro Inverter converts 175 watts of 12-volt DC power to 115-volt AC power, perfect for powering notebook PCs, videogame consoles, camcorders, and small televisions.

All you have to do is plug any AC-powered device in to the Micro Inverter and then plug the Micro Inverter in to a DC power source, like a car's lighter socket. The Micro Inverter is compact and lightweight, which makes it easy to take with you on any trip.

Model: XPower Micro Inverter 175
Manufacturer: Xantrex Technology, Inc.
(www.xantrex.com)
Price: $44.99

Cases and Bags

Just because you have a portable device doesn't mean it's easy to carry around. After all, do you really want to tuck an unprotected notebook PC under your arm or stuff a bare PDA into your back pocket?

Of course not, which is why there's a big market for all sorts of portable cases and bags. You can find cases for PDAs, notebook PCs, portable music players, cellular phones, and other hand-held gizmos made from a variety of materials—cloth, leather, vinyl, aluminum, you name it. You can find cases that open from the top or fold from the side; cases that zip closed or use Velcro fasteners; and cases that clip on your belt or roll along on heavy-duty wheels.

These cases are made by dozens, maybe hundreds, of companies, in all manner of stylings and colors. There's lots of basic black, of course, but if you look hard you'll also find cases in day-glo orange and leopard-skin prints.

The big case company is Targus, and it makes cases for just about everything. Belt cases, briefcases, backpacks, rolling cases—you name the style, Targus has it. It's always my first stop when I'm case shopping.

You shouldn't rule out the smaller companies, though. I listed some of these companies back on p. 78, when I discussed the iPod cases. Other companies worth checking out are Bellagio Designs (for PDA cases) and Tune Belt (for music player cases). Also deserving of attention are the extremely rugged aluminum cases from Star Case and the James Bondian e-Holster.

Just make sure you buy a case for its functionality and not (just) its stylishness. Whichever case or bag you use really should protect your portable device and be easy to use and carry. Looking cool is one thing, but you'll have to use this thing every day—so you better like it!

Targus Notebook PC and PDA Cases

In my opinion—and this is my book, so my opinion counts—Targus makes the best cases on the market today. This company certainly makes the most different types of cases, for all major models of notebook PCs and PDAs.

Targus cases come in a variety of styles, from classic briefcase-type cases to rolling cases and backpacks. I use a Targus backpack notebook case myself, and it has lasted me 5 years so far with no major signs of wear. It has enough pockets to hold all my papers and accessories, and it's well-padded to withstand all manner of daily abuse.

Also cool are Targus's rolling cases, which add a set of wheels on the bottom and a pull-up handle on top. They're great for the heavy road warrior, or if you like to carry the entire contents of your office around with you.

The best protection comes from Targus's Air Protection System cases. These cases are extra padded to provide up to four times more shock protection than the standard case.

Whatever type of case you're looking for, chances are Targus has it. See its website for more models and information.

Model: Various
Manufacturer: Targus (www.targus.com)
Price: $10–$150

Star Case Hard-Sided PC and PDA Cases

For the ultimate in protection, slide your notebook PC or PDA into a rugged aluminum case from Star Case. These cases will protect your portable device from anything short of a mortar attack.

Inside, your device is protected by custom-cut foam or leather padding. Outside, it's deep-drawn aluminum all the way; you can add optional locks and casters, if you like. Star Case has a variety of stock models and also custom-designs cases for any piece of equipment you can think of.

> **Model:** Various
> **Manufacturer:** Star Case
> (www.starcase.com)
> **Price:** $200+

Tune Belt MP3 Armband Carrier

If you have a small portable music player, you're probably used to clipping it on your belt when you walk or jog. The Tune Belt provides an even better solution by letting you strap your player around your upper arm.

The Tune Belt holds most sizes and shapes of small digital music players in its 3" wide × 3.5" deep pocket. The player is held firm—and protected against bumps and perspiration—by two neoprene layers. The armband is easily resizable up to 20" biceps.

> **Model:** AB3
> **Manufacturer:** Tune Belt
> (www.tunebelt.com)
> **Price:** $12.95

Bellagio Leather PDA Cases

If you want a truly fashionable case for your PDA, check out Bellagio's line of leather cases. These are really beautiful cases, made from top-notch Italian leather, that hold and display your PDA in style. Some cases flip open from the top; others fold closed into a book-like form factor. You can even have Bellagio emboss your name or initials for a small additional fee.

Bellagio makes a wide range of elegant and practical cases for all popular PDA models. See their website for ordering information.

Model: Various
Manufacturer: Bellagio Designs
(www.bellagiodesigns.com)
Price: $35–$45

e-Holster PDA/Phone Cases

The cool thing about e-Holster cases is that they make you feel like James Bond, carrying a Walther PPK in a shoulder holster. In fact, e-Holsters *are* shoulder holsters, which you can wear over your jacket or under it. What might seem impractical at first is actually a fairly comfortable way to carry your portable device; it's always at the ready, and nobody's going to lift it from you in a crowd.

e-Holsters are available in vinyl, ballistic nylon, and leather for all types of PDAs, cell phones, and small digital cameras. See the e-Holster website for more information.

Model: e-Holster
Manufacturer: Personal Electronics Concealment, LLC (www.eholster.com)
Price: $60–$100

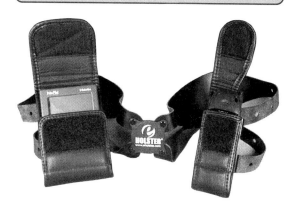

Other Cool Portable Gadgets

Now we come to the fun category. Here's where I get to talk about all the cool portable gadgets that don't easily fit in any other category—the gadget hound's junk pile.

What sorts of gadgets am I talking about? It's an odd list—robot vacuum cleaners and robot dogs, wearable video screens and wearable camcorders, truly useful emergency radios and virtually useless compressed-air guns. The only thing these gizmos have in common is that they're relatively portable, at least to the degree that you can carry them around if you really want to.

These gadgets come from a variety of companies, from big multinationals like Sony and Grundig to smaller companies that only make a single product. I have to admit, I have a soft spot for these one-product companies. Real entrepreneurs, these guys are, worth rooting for.

The more practical among you might question why anyone would need any of these products. Fair question. But that's the fun of gadgets—of course you don't need them, but they're so neat you want to have them. Of course, you might not use them every day; you might not use them at all after the novelty wears off, but who cares? They're neat and you can play with them if you want to. They're cool toys for the technology age.

Now you'll have to excuse me. I have to go find out if my robot dog will play with my robot vacuum cleaner—and if so, why they need me around at all.

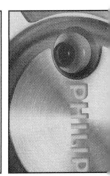

Grundig Emergency Radio

This is the perfect radio to have on hand for emergencies, big and small. The Grundig Emergency Radio receives AM, FM, and short-wave signals—so you can listen in on broadcasts from around the world. It runs on AC, DC, or battery power. Or, in case of a major emergency, you can power it with the hand crank. Two turns per second for 90 seconds provides 40–60 minutes of operation.

It's a rugged little gizmo and includes a built-in emergency light—which can also be hand-powered by the crank. It comes in blue, yellow, sand, metallic red, metallic bronze, and metallic pearl white.

> **Model:** FR200
> **Manufacturer:** Elton Corporation
> (www.grundigradio.com)
> **Price:** $39.95

Skymaster Weathermaster Portable Weather Station

The Skymaster Weathermaster is a portable weather station in the body of a small pocket knife. It provides all sorts of weather info—temperature, wind chill, heat index, wind speed, relatively humidity, dew point, barometric pressure (with 16-hour history graph), and altitude.

On top of all that, the Skymaster Weathermaster is water resistant, and it floats—which makes it perfect for outdoor activities. Carry it in your pocket or around your neck on the supplied lanyard.

> **Model:** SM-28 Skymaster
> **Manufacturer:** Speedtech Instruments
> (www.speedtech.com)
> **Price:** $175

Photon Freedom Micro Keychain LED Flashlight

You wouldn't think a flashlight would be particularly cool, but then you haven't seen the Photon Freedom Micro yet. This little gizmo has a high-powered LED bulb that provides an extremely bright light in a really small package.

Squeeze the thumb-sized button once for full illumination, or press and hold the button to vary the brightness level. You can also access for safety strobe functions (fast, medium, slow, and SOS); plus there's an additional "signaling" mode. It's available with eight colored LEDs, as well as ultraviolet and infrared models. There's even a "covert" version that minimizes side-light visibility—great for viewing a program in a darkened theater!

> **Model:** Photon Freedom Micro
> **Manufacturer:** Laughing Rabbit, Inc.
> (www.photonlight.com)
> **Price:** $19.95

Bar Master Deluxe Pocket Bartender

This is the gadget you need before you host your next party. The Bar Master Deluxe is a handheld drinks guide—like a PDA for bartenders. It lets you call up drink recipes by name, type of drink, kind of alcohol, occasion, or type of glass used.

The Bar Master Deluxe includes more than 1,000 recipes and lists ingredients for each drink. It also provides cocktail basics, a glossary of bartending terms, key measurements, and a collection of drinking games. And it fits in your shirt pocket!

> **Model:** Bar Master Deluxe
> **Manufacturer:** Excalibur Electronics
> (www.thebarmaster.com)
> **Price:** $24.95

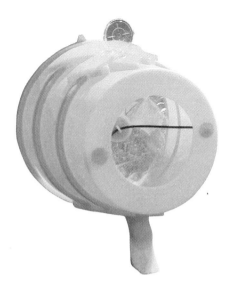

AirZooka Air Gun

Okay, there's nothing really high-tech about this gadget, but it's kind of fun anyway. The AirZooka is a small gun that shoots a ball of compressed air up to 40 feet. Just pull back and then release the plastic air launcher; then watch the fun begin.

The AirZooka is manually powered, so you don't have to worry about cords or batteries. Because it's just air, it's safe for all ages. And it comes in a variety of cool colors, from Outrageous Orange to Passion Pink.

Model: AirZooka
Manufacturer: Unrealtoys
(www.airzooka.net)
Price: $14.95

Sony AIBO Entertainment Robot

Our final portable gadget is so portable it walks around by itself! This is one of my favorite gadgets, period—the Sony AIBO robot. It's shaped like a little robot dog and even acts like one—short of leaving little piles of batteries behind.

Owners really love their AIBOs and treat them like real pets. That's not surprising; you can program the AIBO to follow you around the house and play with balls and pet toys. They even develop a bit of a personality and respond to more than 100 words and phrases. Each AIBO exhibits autonomous behaviors based on recognition of the owner's face and voice.

Sci-fi scary, or cute and lovable? You be the judge!

Model: ERS-7
Manufacturer: Sony (www.sonystyle.com)
Price: $1,799

Digital Photography Gadgets

3

Point-and-Shoot Digital Cameras

Almost a third of U.S. households own a digital camera, and within the next four years or so sales of digital cameras will have nearly replaced sales of 35mm film cameras.

The biggest part of the digital camera market is the low end, consisting of reasonably priced point-and-shoot cameras. These cameras are ideal for people who value simplicity, and they produce good enough quality pictures for a variety of situations—snapshots, websites, emailing to family, and the like.

Although point-and-shoot cameras tend to take the guesswork out of picture taking, that doesn't mean they lack features and functions. If you're in the market for a point-and-shoot camera, here are some of the things to look for:

- **Picture resolution**—This is measured in megapixels. The more megapixels, the sharper your pictures will be. Most decent point-and-shoot cameras today have a resolution in the range of 3–5 megapixels.

- **Zoom lens**—This helps you get up close to distant subjects. Ignore the digital zoom specs (that's an electronic zooming effect that creates blocky-looking results) and focus on the optical zoom. Most low-end cameras have a 3X zoom; again, more is better.

- **Size and weight**—Many of these cameras are little bigger than a credit card and weigh less than half a pound. The smaller and lighter, the easier it is to carry around in your pocket.

- **Ability to shoot short video+sound movies**—Although most people don't use this feature.

- **Speed**—That is, how long it takes to power up and to shoot a picture after you've pressed the auto focus button. Many low-end cameras have a noticeable shutter lag that makes it difficult to take pictures of fast-moving subjects—like kids at sporting events.

There are a lot of good cameras in this category, most priced well under $500. (The list prices for these cameras are fairly useless; most $500 cameras end up selling for $300 or less.) Shop carefully to find the camera you like best and get the lowest price.

Canon PowerShot S500

Leo's Pick

Canon's PowerShot S500 is one of the best-selling digital cameras today, and for good reason. It delivers the most megapixels for the price—a really good bang for the buck.

With 5-megapixel resolution, the PowerShot S500 takes some of the sharpest pictures of any camera in this price range. You also get a 3X optical zoom (36–108mm) and a solid auto focus system that works from 2" to infinity.

Canon's DIGIC image processor results in faster display and write times for each picture, as well as lower power consumption—which translates into faster operation and longer battery life. The camera's continuous burst mode captures up to 2.2 frames per second. Naturally, it has a built-in flash, as well as automatic red eye reduction.

Where this camera really shines is in printing and transferring pictures to PC. The Print/Share button enables one-button direct printing to any Canon Direct Photo Printer or any third-party printer that supports the PictBridge standard. The same button also enables one-touch image transfer to most Windows computers.

Canon also adds some cool direct print options, such as the ability to do in-camera image cropping, using the camera's 1.5" LCD monitor. You can also use the ID Photo Print feature to automatically generate passport-style prints on select Canon printers.

To top it all off, this is a very easy camera to carry around. It measures just 3.4" × 2.2" × 1" and weighs in at 6.5 oz. It's tough to ask for any more at this price point.

Model: PowerShot S500
Manufacturer: Canon (www.powershot.com)
Resolution: 5 megapixels
Zoom: 3X
Price: $499

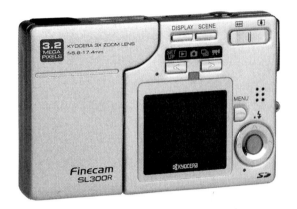

Minolta DiMAGE Xt

Minolta's DiMAGE Xt might be the slimmest digital camera on today's market, thanks to a unique nonextended zoom lens. It's slim enough to fit in any pocket or bag and weighs only 4 oz.

The camera shoots in both JPEG and TIFF formats and incorporates a 1.5" LCD monitor. Resolution is 3.2 megapixels, and it accepts both SD and MMC cards.

Model: DiMAGE Xt
Manufacturer: Minolta
(www.dimage.minolta.com)
Resolution: 3.2 megapixels
Zoom: 3X
Price: $399

Kyocera Finecam SL300R

The Kyocera Finecam SL300R is one weird-looking little camera—but the odd design belies a unique functionality. The camera's swivel design lets it fold flat to fit in your pocket; twist it open to shoot. It's pretty neat, once you get used to it.

The camera features a rugged all-metal exterior, a 1.5" LCD display, 3.2-megapixel resolution, and a 3X optical zoom lens. It's compatible with both SD and MMC cards.

Model: SL300R
Manufacturer: Kyocera Imaging
(www.kyoceraimaging.com)
Resolution: 3.2 megapixels
Zoom: 3X
Price: $399.99

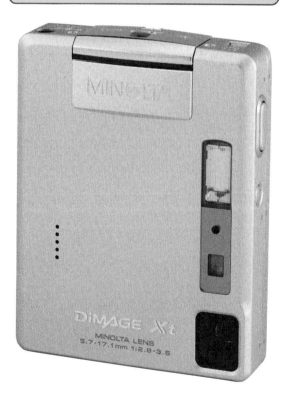

Sony Cyber-shot DSC-T1

This Sony is another "back pocket" digital camera—with a huge 2.5" LCD color monitor. Like all Sony Cyber-shot cameras, the DSC-T1 features a high-quality Carl Zeiss lens for really sharp pictures. Resolution is 5.1 megapixels, and it includes a 3X optical zoom (38–114mm).

Like the Casio Exilim, this Sony comes with a handy USB docking/recharging cradle. It saves pictures to Memory Stick media and has a cool slide-aside lens cover. Bottom line—excellent performance in a small, convenient package.

Model: DSC-T1
Manufacturer: Sony (www.sonystyle.com)
Resolution: 5.1 megapixels
Zoom: 3X
Price: $499.95

Casio Exilim EX-Z4U

This is a small camera with a big screen—a whopping 2" color LCD. In spite of the big screen, it's just 0.9" deep, about the same height and width of a credit card (2" × 3"), and weighs just 2.5 oz. Resolution is a very good 4 megapixels.

Even neater, the EX-Z4U comes with its own USB cradle; insert the camera in the cradle, connect the cradle to your PC's USB port, and automatically transfer pictures from your camera to your PC. Interestingly, the camera includes a built-in speaker for playback of audio snapshots, which lets you add comments or other audio to your still images. It's also a quick shooter, with a shutter release lag of just 0.01 seconds.

Model: EX-Z4U
Manufacturer: Casio (www.exilim.casio.com)
Resolution: 4 megapixels
Zoom: 3X
Price: $399.99

High-end Digital Cameras

If you want more than a simple point-and-shoot camera, better take out the high-limit credit card. There's a new wave of digital camera on the market, targeted at the so-called *prosumer* photographer, that offers a raft of advanced features and high-resolution 8-megapixel performance.

Why do you need more megapixels? It's simple, really. If you want to create large-size prints, you have to fill up all that space with picture information. The more pixels, the more picture information—and the bigger the prints you can make. With an 8-megapixel camera, you should be able to make prints up to 14" × 17"; lower-resolution point-and-shoot cameras can only make prints half that size.

Most cameras in this prosumer category sport similar high-end features—long zoom lenses; metal bodies; electronic viewfinders (as well as the standard large LCD monitor on the back); and intelligent hot shoes to which you can attach external flashes, strobe lights, and the like. Many of these cameras also let you save photos in the RAW file format, which is more versatile that JPEG or TIFF when it comes to post-photo processing in Adobe Photoshop or some similar program.

As you'll soon see, any one of these cameras costs around $1,000—which is also about what you'd pay for a digital SLR camera, like the Nikon D70 I discuss on p. 135. Given the choice, some serious photographers will step up to the D-SLR models. But the prosumer cameras are a better choice for the casual photographer. Operation isn't much more complex than with a point-and-shoot model, and that 8-megapixel resolution delivers the best possible picture quality today. In short, these are relatively easy-to-use cameras that produce extremely sharp prints. What's not to like?

Sony Cyber-shot DSC-828

Leo's Pick

My favorite of the new 8-megapixel camera is the Sony Cyber-shot DSC-828. Why? For me, it's the lens. Sony uses a Carl Zeiss Vario Sonnar lens with T* coating, which translates into an extremely sharp picture under even the most demanding conditions. Sony's cameras are known for their fine lenses, and this one sets a new standard of quality. (It's a 7X zoom, the equivalent of a 28–200mm traditional zoom.)

Here's something else neat about this camera—it can shoot in the dark. Sony's NightShot system captures infrared images in total darkness, up to 10 feet away. I dare you to find another consumer-level camera that does that!

I also like the color this camera delivers. That's because of a unique four-color filter CCD. That extra color (RGB + Emerald) produces photo colors that are closer to human color perception, especially with blue, blue-green, and red hues.

What else do you get on this puppy? Well, a Real Imaging Processor delivers increased speed with lower power consumption; you also get the ability to shoot in automatic, aperture priority, shutter priority, or manual mode; manual zoom and manual focus rings; the expected eye-level electronic viewfinder and 1.8" LCD monitor; the ability to save in JPEG, TIFF, or RAW format; and the ability to write to Memory Stick, Memory Stick PRO, CompactFlash I and II, or IBM Microdrive media.

All these features add up, however; this is a big camera, weighing in at a hefty 2.1 pounds. So, buy yourself a strong strap!

Model: DSC-F828
Manufacturer: Sony (www.sonystyle.com)
Resolution: 8 megapixels
Zoom: 7X
Price: $999.95

Olympus C-8080 Wide Zoom

I've always liked Olympus's digital cameras, especially their zoom lenses. The new C-8080 Wide Zoom has a 5X wide-angle zoom (28–40mm) which, while good, isn't quite as long as some of the other prosumer cameras. Oh well; I still like this camera.

It's a fast camera, thanks to the TruePic TURBO image processor. This technology decreases the camera's start-up and camera lag time and lets you shoot 1.6 frames per second. You can save your pictures in JPEG or TIFF formats and to xD or CompactFlash cards.

Model: C-8080 Wide Zoom
Manufacturer: Olympus
(www.olympusamerica.com)
Resolution: 8 megapixels
Zoom: 5X
Price: $999.95

Minolta DiMAGE A2

Minolta's DiMAGE A2 has two unique things going for it. First, its proprietary anti-shake technology results in better stability, especially when using the zoom. Second, a tiltable LCD monitor (up by 90° or down by 20°) provides positioning flexibility.

Beyond those features, the DiMAGE A2 has the expected 8-megapixel resolution, the expected 7X zoom lens (28–200mm), and all the other expected bells and whistles. It's a solid performer, no matter how you look at it.

Model: DiMage A2
Manufacturer: Minolta
(www.dimage.minolta.com)
Resolution: 8 megapixels
Zoom: 7X
Price: $999.95

Nikon CoolPix 8700

This is a nice, solid-feeling camera, thanks to the magnesium alloy body and a sturdy construction. I particularly like the 1.8" LCD on a snap-out, tilting connector; this lets you shoot at just about any angle.

Performance-wise, the CoolPix 8700 has an 8X Nikkor lens (35–280mm) and 8-megapixel resolution. A special noise reduction mode minimizes digital artifacts in long nighttime exposures. You can save to RAW or JPEG format and to CompactFlash or Microdrive media.

Model: CoolPix 8700
Manufacturer: Nikon (www.nikonusa.com)
Resolution: 8 megapixels
Zoom: 8X
Price: $999.95

Canon PowerShot Pro1

Our final prosumer camera comes in a professional black finish and features a large 2" LCD monitor. You get 8-megapixel resolution (of course) and a 7X zoom lens. The Pro1 features 12 EOS-based shooting modes—Portrait, Landscape, Night Scene, and so on. There's also an enhanced Super Macro mode for really close-up photography.

Like other Canon cameras, you get a Direct Print mode for one-button printing to select Canon printers, as well as one-touch file transfer to your Windows PC. It's a good mix of D-SLR-like features with point-and-shoot–like operation.

Model: PowerShot Pro1
Manufacturer: Canon (www.powershot.com)
Resolution: 8 megapixels
Zoom: 7X
Price: $999

Digital SLRs

Now we come to my favorite camera category—digital single lens reflex (D-SLR) cameras.

D-SLRs look, feel, and work like good 35mm film cameras. They differ significantly from point-and-shoot and prosumer digital cameras in both operation and performance.

Let's take the typical point-and-shoot or prosumer digital camera. These cameras have their lenses permanently attached and require you to view what you're shooting via either an electronic viewfinder or LCD monitor screen. They typically have small image sensors (less than an inch across) that produce good, but not great, pictures, and they don't offer a lot of operating flexibility.

D-SLR cameras use a reflex mirror apparatus so that, when you look through the optical viewfinder, you're actually viewing through the lens itself. You also get the ability to use interchangeable lenses and larger image sensors, often as big as 35mm film, which provide better results in low-light conditions. In addition, these cameras are usually designed by the companies' 35mm camera divisions (instead of their consumer electronics divisions) and provide all the operating flexibility you need to make great photos, fast.

D-SLR cameras have been around since the early 1990s, when they used to cost $20,000 or more. Fortunately for us, the price has come down over the years; today's most affordable D-SLRs cost around the same price as high-end prosumer cameras.

Bottom line, a D-SLR camera delivers a better picture (no matter what the megapixel rating), lets you use interchangeable lenses, and has more operating flexibility. So, if all you want to do is take quick snapshots, stick with a point-and-shoot or prosumer digital camera. But if you want pro-level performance and flexibility, check out a D-SLR. You'll notice the difference as soon as you pick it up; a D-SLR just *feels* like a real camera.

In case you're wondering, I only list two D-SLRs here because I limited myself to cameras you could buy for around $1,000. There are lots of other capable D-SLRs, but only the Nikon D70 and Canon Digital Rebel come in at that magic $1,000 price point; other cameras by Fuji, Olympus, and Pentax cost two to three times as much but don't deliver that much additional performance.

Nikon D70

Nikon's D70 is my favorite digital camera, period. For what it's worth, this is the model I purchased for my own personal use.

With the D70, you get high-end D-SLR performance at a relatively affordable price. This camera is fast (operation is instant-on, and you can shoot up to 3 frames per second), rugged (black metal case), and versatile. You can shoot in a variety of preprogrammed modes, as well as aperture priority, shutter priority, or manual mode; you can also override the auto focus just by touching the manual focus ring on the lens.

Speaking of versatility, this camera gives you three types of auto focus: single area AF, dynamic area AF, and closest subject priority dynamic area AF. It shoots in either JPEG or RAW (NEF) format, with ISO settings of 200–1600. Buy a big CompactFlash card (I or II) to hold all those big images!

Image-wise, the D70's performance is exemplary. Images are sharp and clean, with a remarkable depth of field. (Resolution is 6.1 megapixels.) Of course, some of that depends on which lens you use, and the D70 works with any Nikkor lens—even those you use with your 35mm camera. You can buy the D70 body-only or in a package with an 18–70mm zoom lens; I recommend the package, which is surprisingly affordable.

Model: D70
Manufacturer: Nikon (www.nikonusa.com)
Resolution: 6.1 megapixels
Price: $1,000 (body only),
$1,299 (with 18–70mm lens)

Canon EOS Digital Rebel

Leo's Pick

The D70's chief competitor is the Canon EOS Digital Rebel. The Digital Rebel actually beat the D70 to market by about six months; it was the first D-SLR priced under $1,000.

Like the D70, the Digital Rebel comes in either body-only or with-lens versions. Again, the lens kit is the best deal, only $100 more than the body-only version. And if you want to buy additional lenses, the Digital Rebel is compatible with more than 50 of Canon's EF lenses.

This camera's performance is everything you'd expect from a D-SLR. Resolution is 6.3 megapixels, you can shoot at ISO speeds from 100 to 1600, and it has a continuous shooting mode that fires off a burst of four shots at 2.5 frames/second.

Let's compare the Digital Rebel to the D70. First, and most important, both image quality and operation are similar. Less important, the D70 has a faster flash and a cooler black case. (The Digital Rebel's metal case is a cheesy fake chrome color.) If you get the standard lens kits, the Digital Rebel's 18–55mm zoom isn't quite as long as the D70's 18–70mm zoom, but the Digital Rebel costs $300 less. It's a toss-up.

Bottom line? You can't go wrong with either the Canon EOS Digital Rebel or the Nikon D70. You get terrific performance and SLR operation at a consumer-level price. Cool!

Model: EOS Digital Rebel
Manufacturer: Canon (www.canoneos.com)
Resolution: 6.3 megapixel
Price: $899 (body only),
$999 (with 18–55mm lens)

Specialty Digital Cameras

For most folks, some sort of point-and-shoot digital camera is all you'll ever need. But every now and then, you run into a special situation where a normal digital camera doesn't quite do the job; something a little different is called for.

Several companies make specialty digital cameras that shine at particular tasks. For example, if you like to snorkel or scuba dive, you know you can't take your standard-issue digital camera underwater with you; it'll fritz out at the first good dunk. But some cameras are designed especially for underwater use and hold up under all sorts of wet conditions. These are the cameras you need when you want to shoot in the water.

When you have a special need, you need a special camera. In addition to underwater cameras, you can find cameras that take 3D pictures, cameras built in to binoculars, and cameras designed for covert use. You won't want to use these cameras for all your pictures, but they have their place.

Read on to learn more about some of these specialty digital cameras. Who knows? You might want to invest in a second camera for some special situations.

JB1 007 Digital Spy Camera

Leo's Pick

When it comes to cool, who's cooler than James Bond?

The JB1 is the kind of gadget you'd expect Agent 007 to carry. In fact, this is an official licensed James Bond 007 camera, made in the U.K. (I don't think Q was involved, but you never know.)

With the JB1, you get a digital camera built in to a cigarette lighter case. It's small enough to fit in any pocket and inconspicuous enough not to draw attention if Blofeld's around.

The camera's a quick shot—flip the top, click the button, and close the top again. There's no switching on required. Just flip and click, as if you were playing with the lighter. No one will know you just took a picture.

Even cooler, the camera offers a surveillance mode that lets you record images at preset time intervals of up to 90 minutes. Just set the camera on a table and come back for it later; your pictures will be waiting. Built-in LiteSync technology automatically takes full depth-of-field pictures with normal fluorescent lighting, no flash required. You can even record short video clips with sound, as well as up to 12 minutes of straight audio.

The JB1 operates on a single AAA battery and connects to your PC via USB. It takes pictures at either 640 × 480 or 320 × 240 resolution; the internal memory holds up to 150 of the higher-resolution pictures. The pictures aren't great, but the whole setup is sexier than Pussy Galore and Plenty O'Toole combined!

Model: JB1
Manufacturer: Digital Dream (www.jbcamera.com)
Price: $99.99

Sony Cyber-shot DSC-U60 Waterproof Digital Camera

If you're into snorkeling, you know that lots of cool stuff is just under the surface to photograph. So, the next time you hit the water, take the DSC-U60 with you. This camera features a rugged, waterproof design designed for what Sony calls the "sports utility lifestyle."

The DSC-U60 can take pictures up to 5 feet underwater, and the unique vertical design is perfect for one-handed operation. It features 2-megapixel resolution and has a 1" LCD monitor. There's even an MPEG video mode (no audio) for taking short movies while you're underwater.

> **Model:** DSC-U60
> **Manufacturer:** Sony (www.sonystyle.com)
> **Price:** $249.95

Sealife ReefMaster DC300 Underwater Digital Camera

For serious underwater photography, you need something more substantial than the Sony Cyber-shot. Designed for scuba-diving photographers, SeaLife's ReefMaster digital camera is depth-tested up to 200 feet—it'll withstand the pressure of the ocean depths.

The ReefMaster has a rubber-armored body with soft grips and pop-up manual viewfinder, as well as a 1.6" LCD color monitor. The one-button operation makes it easy to use when you're diving, and you'll appreciate the high-quality 3.3-megapixel pictures. Your photos are saved on SD cards.

> **Model:** ReefMaster DC300
> **Manufacturer:** Sealife
> (www.sealife-cameras.com)
> **Price:** $399.95

Ezonics EZBinoCam LX

Into bird watching? Like to get up close at sporting events? Wouldn't it be great to capture photographically what you see through your binoculars?

The EZBinoCam LX builds a small digital camera into a pair of high-quality binoculars and lets you take 2-megapixel photos at 8X magnification. What's great about the EZBinoCam is that anybody can use it, thanks to automatic exposure and focus-free settings. Just zero in on what you want to shoot and snap the picture. It connects to your PC via USB and writes your photos to SD or MMC cards.

> **Model:** EZBinoCam LX
> **Manufacturer:** Ezonics
> (www.shopezonics.com)
> **Price:** $199.99

Photo3-D 303 Kit

Remember 3D movies? Now you can take 3D pictures from any digital camera, thanks to the Photo3-D 303 Kit. Attach your camera to the handheld Photo3-D device and snap a picture; then slide the camera to the second position and take a second picture. This creates a *stereo pair* of images; use the included Photo3-D Mixer software to combine the images into a single 3D image, which you can view with special 3D glasses.

The kit includes everything you need to shoot and create your own 3D photos, including several pair of special 3D glasses. You might look geeky wearing the glasses, but your pictures will look cool!

> **Model:** Photo3-D 303 Kit
> **Manufacturer:** Photo3-D (www.photo3-d.com)
> **Price:** $129

Digital Camera Accessories

To get the most use out of your digital camera, it pays to fill up your camera bag with a variety of useful accessories. This is maybe less true if you have a low-price point-and-shoot camera, but accessorizing is definitely a good idea if you've spent north of five bills for a more fully featured model.

How will camera accessories help you take better pictures? Here are some examples:

- **Lens filters**—Reduce glare and improve color rendition in all your photos

- **External flash kits**—Provide better fill lighting for both indoor and outdoor shots

- **Lighting kits**—Help you shoot more detailed portraits and indoor still-life photos

- **Light meters**—Help you determine the right exposure levels for your photos

- **Tripod**—Holds your camera steady and helps eliminate blurry shots, especially when you're shooting in low light

- **LCD hood**—Makes it easier to view your camera's monitor, especially in bright sunlight

- **Cleaning kit**—Helps you keep your camera free of dust and dirt and extend its working life

Professional photographers spend a lot of money on accessories like these, and for good reason. When it comes to taking good pictures, they appreciate all the help they can get—as should you. It's amazing how a small investment in an accessory or two can make your life so much easier.

And here's something else to keep in mind. Most of the accessories I list aren't specific to digital cameras. That is, you can use most film camera accessories with your digital camera; you don't have to buy special digital accessories. A tripod is a tripod, no matter what kind of camera you put on top. So, head down to your local camera store and see what they have to offer!

Tiffen Digital Camera Lens Filters

Leo's Pick

You'd be surprised how big a difference a little filter can make on the pictures you take. For example, I leave my polarizing filter mounted on my Nikon D70 24/7; there's no instance where it detracts from what I'm shooting, and more often than not it results in slightly more intense colors with less glare and flare.

Most mid-priced and up cameras can accept external lens filters, which screw onto the end of the camera lens; read your camera's instruction manual to be sure. If your camera accepts lens filters, check out Tiffen's offerings. Tiffen manufactures a wide range of filters for use on both consumer and pro-level digital cameras.

Tiffen's most popular filters include

- Ultraviolet (UV), sky, and haze filters for absorbing UV light and reflections
- Polarizing filters for deepening color intensity
- Light balancing filters for eliminating washed-out images
- Color graduated filters that produce half-color, half-clear images
- Color conversion filters for correcting various type of indoor lighting
- Color compensating filters for balancing excessive green casts
- Color filters for black-and-white photography
- Warm and enhancing filters for improving skin tones
- Special effects filters, including soft/portrait, center spot, mist, diffusion, ultra contrast, star, fog, and sepia filters

Tiffin also makes a number of adapter rings and other camera accessories. See the company's website for the full range of products.

> **Model:** Various
> **Manufacturer:** Tiffen (www.tiffen.com)
> **Price:** $25–$150

Metz Mecablitz Digital Flash Kits

Almost all consumer digital cameras come with some sort of built-in flash, which works okay but often leaves a lot to be desired. Using an external flash produces much better results because the light is generally more powerful and offset slightly to the side of the camera, which reduces both glare and red eye.

When it comes to external flash kits, check out the Metz Mecablitz line. Metz produces dozens of models for different uses. Most flashes attach to your camera's hot shoe; if your digital camera doesn't have a hot shoe, try Metz's 34-CS-2 Digital model, which incorporates a slave trigger unit and automatic flash mode.

Model: Various
Manufacturer: Metz (www.metz.de)
Price: $50–$400

Smith-Victor KT500 Lighting Kit

If you shoot a lot of formal indoor shots—including product shots for eBay—it's worth your while to invest in photo flood lights. I particularly like Smith-Victor's KT500 kit; even though it's a few steps below what the pros use, it's both easy to use and quite affordable.

The KT500 is a two-light kit for a total of 500 watts of lighting. The kit includes two 10" reflectors, two sockets and cords, two 6' telescoping stands, and two 250-watt photoflood bulbs. Just set them up and turn them on, and see for yourself how much better your photos look.

Model: KT500
Manufacturer: Smith-Victor Corporation (www.smithvictor.com)
Price: $135

VidPro TT-800 Tripod

If you shoot a lot of indoor shots or a lot of low-light photos, you know how hard it is to hold your camera perfectly still for the length of an extended exposure. For that reason, every serious photographer needs a tripod for her camera.

VidPro makes a full line of camera tripods, and my favorite is the TT-800. It extends to 55" in height and has a three-way pan head with a large quick-release platform. For even steadier pictures, it has a built-in center column stabilizer and lock, along with flip-lock legs with rubber nonskid feet.

Model: TT-800
Manufacturer: VidPro
(www.vidprousa.com)
Price: $49.99

Minolta Auto Meter VF

If your camera has a manual mode, you can manually set the exposure and aperture settings to produce great-looking photos under various lighting conditions. Of course, you need to know all there is to know about the available light, which is where a handheld light meter is useful.

Minolta's Auto Meter VF is a multifunction meter with simple operation and exceptional accuracy. It has a large, easy-to-read LCD display; recommended shutter speed appears on the left, aperture on the right. It even has an analyze function, which displays the flash/ambient lighting ratio. Hold it out, press a button, and let it tell you what settings to use.

Model: Auto Meter VF
Manufacturer: Minolta
(www.minoltausa.com)
Price: $229.99

Hoodman LCD Hoods

Ever have trouble seeing your camera's LCD screen? It's a particular problem outdoors on a sunny day, which is why you might want to consider using an LCD hood. Hoodman sells a variety of rubber hoods that fit over any LCD screen and turn your open-to-the-elements monitor into a hooded viewfinder.

Each Hoodman hood incorporates a 2X magnifier to allow close focus on the LCD screen and provides glare-free viewing. Models are available for 1.5"–1.8", 2", 3", and 3.5"–4" screens; they're also good for use with camcorders.

> **Model:** Various
> **Manufacturer:** Hoodman
> (www.hoodmanusa.com)
> **Price:** $9.95–$19.95

Norazza Digital Cleaning Kits

A clean digital camera takes better pictures (no dust on the lens) and lasts longer—and cleaning is easier with a kit designed just for that purpose. Norazza's cleaning kits contain everything you need to keep your camera's body, lens, and monitor clean and free of dust and dirt.

Each kit includes one microfibre cleaning cloth, a nylon brush, five cotton swabs, five wet/dry wipes, a carrying case, and an instruction booklet. The kits also come with two cleaning cards for cleaning inside your camera's media card slot; separate kits are sold for CompactFlash, Memory Stick, SD/MMC, SmartMedia, and xD Picture Card products.

> **Model:** Digital Cleaning Kits
> **Manufacturer:** Norazza (www.norazza.com)
> **Price:** $19.99

Other Cool Digital Photography Gadgets

There's more to digital photography than cameras and lenses. After you take your photos, how will you view them?

Yes, you can view your pictures on your computer screen. Yes, you can print them on a photo printer or take them to a professional photo processor. But what other ways are there to share your digital photos?

Over the next two pages, I discuss a handful of products that will revolutionize the way you share your digital photos. You'll read about products that let you

- View digital photos in a picture frame you can set on any table top.
- View digital photos on any television set.
- View 360° walkthroughs of any room in your house, on any PC.

Think about it; a digital photo is just like any other computer file, nothing more than a collection of bits and bytes. Why shouldn't you be able to beam those bits and bytes into a variety of devices?

I particularly like the idea of viewing digital photos on a big-screen TV; it seems like such a natural activity. It's actually quite enjoyable to sit back with friends and family, put on some good music, and watch a photo slideshow on the family TV set. The SanDisk Digital Photo Viewer discussed here is a relatively simple, low-cost way to do this. Also good are some of the digital media hubs I discuss on p. 172, such as the Roku Digital Media Player. These two devices take much different approaches to the issue at hand; check them both out to see which you prefer.

CEIVA 2 Digital Photo Frame

The CEIVA 2 Digital Photo Receiver is, as its name implies, a frame for digital photos. The frame itself is approximately 8" × 10"; photos are displayed on a 5" × 7" high-resolution LCD screen.

The Digital Photo Receiver works by receiving photos from an online photo service and then displaying them in a digital slide show, no computer necessary. Your friends and family upload their pictures to the CEIVA.com website, at no charge; they can even customize their pictures with captions, messages, and the like. Then, each night, the CEIVA unit dials a local phone number and downloads any pictures that have been sent to it—up to 30 pictures each day. You can configure the slideshow to change pictures from every 5 seconds up to 3 hours.

If you see a picture you like, CEIVA lets you order prints by mail at the touch of a button. You can even configure the CEIVA to display local weather information, news headlines, TV listings, horoscopes, and other similar information.

Of course, to use the CEIVA system, you have to subscribe to the CEIVA Network. This will set you back at least $9.95, depending on which services you want.

This is a great gift for parents and other family members who might not otherwise be able to view your digital photos. Buy them the Digital Photo Receiver, subscribe them to the CEVIA service, and start uploading your pictures to the CEVIA.com website. Every morning they'll look forward to seeing what new pictures you've sent them!

> **Model:** CEIVA 2
> **Manufacturer:** CEIVA (www.ceiva.com)
> **Price:** $149.95

SanDisk Digital Photo Viewer

Want to view your digital photos on your big TV screen without messing around with your computer? Then you want SanDisk's Digital Photo Viewer, a small box you connect directly to your television set via composite video or S-Video cables. Insert a digital media card, and see your digital pictures onscreen.

The Digital Photo Viewer supports a variety of media card formats, including CompactFlash I, CompactFlash II, SmartMedia, Secure Digital (SD), Memory Stick, and MultiMediaCard, and reads JPEG files up to 6 megapixels in size. It comes with its own wireless remote control, which lets you control the slideshow presentation from your easy chair.

> **Model:** Digital Photo Viewer
> **Manufacturer:** SanDisk (www.sandisk.com)
> **Price:** $69.99

EGG Photo 360° Pack First

The EGG Photo 360° system lets you create your own virtual tours of any room in your house—even the inside of your car. This is the tool realtors use to create interactive home walk-throughs. The photo you take is processed through a special lens that sees a full 360° view; a viewer can then use his mouse to pan around the entire room.

To create a 360° picture, all you have to do is attach the EGG 360° lens to your digital camera and press the camera's shutter release. When you transfer the resulting picture to your computer, you use the special EGG software to create an interactive 360° picture file.

> **Model:** Photo 360° Pack First
> **Manufacturer:** EGG Solution
> (www.eggsolution.com)
> **Price:** $1,495

Home Movie Gadgets

Basic Camcorders

Digital video recording lets you use your PC as a movie editing studio to create sophisticated home movies you can distribute on DVDs. The key to successful digital movie making—whether you're making independent films or movies of your kids' birthday parties—is to start with a digital camcorder.

You don't have to spend a lot of money to get a digital camcorder. Now that analog VHS camcorders have been relegated to the garbage bin (or to eBay—kind of the same thing), virtually every camcorder sold today records in a digital format. But which format is the right one for you?

Here's a short list of the digital camcorder formats you'll find in today's camcorders:

- **MiniDV**—This is the most popular and most common digital camcorder format. It records broadcast-quality video (500+ lines of resolution) on small, low-priced cassettes, about 1/12 the size of a standard VHS tape. Use MiniDV for optimal compatibility with video editing programs and other equipment.
- **MicroMV**—This is a newer and smaller digital format, somewhat proprietary to Sony

camcorders. MicroMV tapes are 70% smaller than MiniDV tapes and record in the MPEG-2 format rather than the more universal DV format. As a result, MicroMV tapes are incompatible with most video editing software. This format does enable the smallest camcorders on the market, however.

- **DVD**—DVD camcorders don't use tape at all; they record directly to DVDs, in either DVD-RAM or DVD-R/RW format. You can get up to 120 minutes on a blank DVD.
- **Digital8**—This is an older, and generally lower-priced, digital format. For compatibility with older analog recorders, Digital8 camcorders can view 8mm or Hi-8 tapes. Digital8 camcorders tend to be a bit larger in size and weight than MiniDV models.

Most budget camcorders are in the MiniDV format, although some low-priced Digital8 models are still floating around. MiniDV camcorders are also the most affordable models to operate; a 60-minute MiniDV tape costs $5 or less. Look for a model that feels good in your hand, offers a wide zoom range, and delivers a good picture under all lighting conditions.

Canon ZR60 MiniDV Camcorder

For amateur filmmakers on a budget, Canon's ZR60 is a great camcorder for the price. You get MiniDV operation with 540 lines of horizontal resolution, an 18X optical zoom lens, and an image stabilization system that provides fairly impressive results. There's also a Wide Attachment you can affix to the lens for wide angle or panoramic shots.

The ZR60 provides a number of preprogrammed recording modes, including Auto, Sports, Portrait, Spotlight, Sand & Snow, Low Light, and Night. You also have the option of using manual focus, exposure, white balance, and shutter speed controls, if that's your cup of tea.

You can do a lot of editing right in the camera, thanks to a variety of digital fade (wipe, flip, puzzle, and the like) and special effects (black and white, mosaic, ball, wave, and so on). You also have the option of doing AV inserts and video dubbing, and there's a built-in speaker for on-the-go playback. The 2.5" LCD view screen is on a swivel mount.

My only gripe about the ZR60 is that it's not that great in low-light conditions. This makes it better for daylight than night-time shooting. Still, it's a lot of camcorder for the price and well worth your consideration.

Model: ZR60
Manufacturer: Canon (www.canondv.com)
Format: MiniDV
Price: $449.95

Canon ZR85 MiniDV Camcorder

Canon's ZR85 is a logical step up to the lower-priced ZR60. The DIGIC DV system produces slightly better color than the ZR60, plus you get a longer 80X optical zoom lens and better low-light shooting with the new Night mode.

Even cooler is this system's size and ergonomics. The ZR85 fits snugly in your hand, and there's a nifty little thumb rest beside the record button. This, along with the low weight, contributes to the good overall balance and intuitive feel. This might be the most comfortable camcorder I've ever used.

Model: ZR85
Manufacturer: Canon (www.canondv.com)
Format: MiniDV
Price: $599

Panasonic PV-GS55 MiniDV Digital Palmcorder

Here's another small, lightweight camcorder. The PV-GS55 weighs in at a paltry 0.79 pounds and measures just 3 1/8" × 2 5/8" × 4". Packed into this compact package is a 10X optical zoom, 2.5" color LCD monitor, and Panasonic's MagicPix low-light shooting system.

The PV-GS55 comes with a zoom microphone and wireless remote control and can record in 16:9 widescreen mode. It includes a bunch of digital effects, including digital zoom, digital mirror, strobe, mosaic, stretch, monotone, and so on. You can also use it as a Webcam, via USB connection to your PC.

Model: PV-GS55
Manufacturer: Panasonic
(www.panasonic.com)
Format: MiniDV **Price:** $599.95

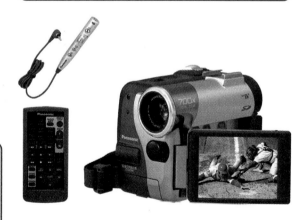

Sony DCR-PC109 MiniDV Handycam Camcorder

Sony's DCR-PC109 compact camcorder costs a little more than the Canon and Panasonic models but offers a bit more for your money. First, you get Sony's NightShot Plus infrared recording system, which lets you shoot in the dead of night. And when you're shooting during the day, you'll appreciate the high-quality Carl Zeiss Vario-Tessar lens (with 10X optical zoom) and the Super SteadyShot image stabilization system.

The DCR-PC109 comes with the Handycam Station, a docking station that provides quick connection to your TV or PC. The camcorder can also double as a digital still camera, recording to Memory Stick media.

Model: DCR-PC109
Manufacturer: Sony (www.sonystyle.com)
Format: MiniDV
Price: $899.99

Sony DCR-TRV260 Digital8 Handycam Camcorder

If you're on a tight budget, consider this Sony camcorder that uses the older Digital8 format. For three and a half bills, you get a camcorder with a 20X optical zoom lens, NightShot Plus infrared recording, 2.5" color LCD, a bevy of fade and special effects, and a fairly compact design, all things considered.

Even better, you can use this camcorder as a full-featured Webcam. Connect it to your PC via USB and send streaming video in real time.

Model: DCR-TRV260
Manufacturer: Sony (www.sonystyle.com)
Format: Digital8
Price: $349.99

High-end Camcorders

At the high end of the digital camcorder market you get one of three things: smallness (thanks to the compact MicroMV cassette format), ease of use (thanks to direct-to-DVD recording), or pro-level performance. And when I say pro-level performance, I mean pro-level performance; the very best consumer camcorders deliver digital pictures good enough for television or film use.

These pro-level camcorders look, feel, and perform just like the type of camcorder you see TV news crews or independent filmmakers lugging around. They're big and bulky, often let you use interchangeable lenses, and shoot in the 16:9 widescreen format. More important, they come with a bevy of automatic recording modes and manual adjustments that let you custom-tailor your movies to a variety of shooting styles and situations. Plus, picture quality is second to none, especially under difficult lighting conditions. Lots of technospeak, I know, but it all translates into lots of flexibility to deliver eye-popping widescreen pictures.

Even if you don't pop for one of these big-bucks pro-level camcorders, you should still expect pro-level performance and features. Any camcorder selling in the high three figures should have a good-quality zoom lens, an image stabilization system (to keep your pictures steady even if your hands aren't), a variety of automatic exposure modes, and some sort of video editing built in. This last feature lets you perform in-camera edits between scenes, including audio dubbing, fade in and out, and other special effects.

If you are in the mood for a pro-level camcorder, pay particular attention to the image sensing system. Look for a 3-CCD system that splits the image optically and feeds color-filtered versions of the scene to three CCD sensors, one for each color—red, green, and blue. (All TV and film production is done with 3-CCD cameras.) The bigger the CCDs, the better; 1/3" CCDs are better than 1/6" ones. Also look for progressive scan technology and true 16:9 framing for film-like results. Expect to spend two grand—or more.

Sony DCR-VX2100 MiniDV Handycam Camcorder

Sony's DCR-VX2100 looks like a professional video camcorder and performs like one, too. This camcorder delivers the best picture of any Sony Handycam and provides a host of operating features that will appeal to burgeoning filmmakers everywhere.

This MiniDV model uses HAD progressive-scan CCD technology that delivers superior low-light performance and a sharper picture under any lighting condition. It's a 3-CCD imaging system; each 1/3" CCD has 380,000 pixels for brilliant digital picture quality. Expect 530 lines of horizontal resolution.

Lens-wise, this Sony has a 58mm aspherical lens that minimizes distortion and compensates for varying lighting situations. The lens has a 12X optical zoom. Recording is in the 16:9 widescreen format, with sound in 16-bit digital PCM stereo.

There are lots of cool operating features, from a built-in color bar generator to manual focus and zoom rings, to manual shutter speed and exposure controls. An intelligent accessory shoe provides power on/off and other operational commands to a variety of "intelligent" accessories. And Sony's Super SteadyShot optical stabilization system uses motion sensors and an optical active prism stabilization system to deliver super-steady pictures under a variety of conditions.

I could go on and on, but you get the picture. This is a true pro-level camcorder, and you actually get what you pay for—in terms of both picture quality and operating flexibility.

Model: DCR-VX2100
Manufacturer: Sony (www.sonystyle.com)
Format: MiniDV
Price: $2,999.99

Panasonic PV-DV953 MiniDV Digital Palmcorder

Here's a 3-CCD camcorder at a slightly more affordable price. The Panasonic PV-DV953 comes with a really good seven-element multi-coated Leica Dicomar lens (10X optical zoom), along with Panasonic's Mega optical image stabilization and MagicPix low-light recording systems.

It's easy to see what you're recording, thanks to the big 3.5" color LCD. You can also use the PV-DV953 as a really nice Webcam (with USB connection) or overpriced digital still camera (recording to SD card).

Model: PV-DV953
Manufacturer: Panasonic (www.panasonic.com)
Format: MiniDV
Price: $1,499.95

Canon XL1S MiniDV Camcorder

The Canon XL1S is, if anything, even higher-end than the Sony DCR-VX2100. This is the camera of choice for many independent filmmakers; what the pros especially like is the interchangeable lens system that lets you use any of Canon's XL and EF 35mm camera lenses. (The XL1S comes with a 16X image-stabilized zoom lens, but you'll want to assemble a library of different lenses for different shooting situations.)

The XL1S incorporates professional styling and rugged magnesium body, uses a 3-CCD imaging system, and shoots in the 16:9 widescreen ratio. Canon uses special pixel-shift technology to deliver a wider dynamic range, reduced vertical smearing, and brighter video in low light. This camera must be seen to be believed!

Model: XL1S
Manufacturer: Canon (www.canondv.com)
Format: MiniDV
Price: $4,499

Panasonic VDR-M70 DVD Palmcorder

If you ultimately want to save your home movies on DVDs, why not record to DVD (instead of tape) in the first place? That's the thinking behind this Panasonic Palmcorder, which lets you record directly to DVD-RAM or DVD-R discs in MPEG-2 format. Just pop in a disc and start shooting; you get up to 120 minutes of recording time per disc.

The camcorder itself has a 10X optical zoom with digital electronic image stabilization. It also lets you do in-camera fade-in and fade-out, so you can edit as you go.

> **Model:** VDR-M70
> **Manufacturer:** Panasonic (www.panasonic.com)
> **Format:** DVD recorder
> **Price:** $899.95

Sony DCR-IP1 MicroMV Handycam Camcorder

If you care more about size than performance, check out Sony's DCR-IP1, the world's smallest and lightest camcorder. It uses the MicroMV format (70% smaller than MiniDV tapes), so the camcorder itself is only slightly larger than a deck of cards and weighs just 8 oz.

Even at this compact size, you get a lot of features, including 10X optical zoom, digital still mode, fade effects, and SteadyShot image stabilization. Just insert the camcorder into the Handycam Station docking station to connect to your PC or TV.

> **Model:** DCR-IP1
> **Manufacturer:** Sony (www.sonystyle.com)
> **Format:** MicroMV
> **Price:** $1,199.99

Camcorder Accessories

The well-equipped filmmaker has a variety of accessories at his disposal to help make better home movies. Spend a few bucks on the right accessories, and you end up with better-looking pictures and a better-sounding soundtrack.

What kinds of accessories are we talking about? Here's a short list:

- **Camera stabilizers**—These keep your camera steady no matter how much you move around—sort of like the Steadycam units that Hollywood cameramen use.

- **Robotic tabletop mounts**—For remote operation.

- **Video lights**—These brighten the room and provide more light when you shoot—absolutely necessary for getting great-looking pictures.

- **External microphones**—These pick up what everyone is saying in a scene. Take your pick from camera-top mics (some in stereo) or wireless mics that clip onto the subject's shirt.

Of course, you don't absolutely need every one of these accessories, but do you really *need* any gadget? Of course, you don't—which doesn't mean you don't *want* it. You can spend some really big bucks on moviemaking accessories, especially if your goal is to make your home movies look (and sound) more professional. Light the scene, mic the actors, and steady the camera; that's what the pros do. And you can do it, too, thanks to these cool accessories.

Read on to learn more.

   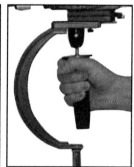 

FlowCam Handheld Camcorder Stabilizers

Embarrassed by shaky camera work? Tired of looking at movies that jump all over the place as the camera operator walks around the room? Then check out any one of VariZoom's FlowCam camera stabilizers, and be prepared for a huge improvement in the movies you shoot.

The basic FlowCam is an odd-looking device that attaches to and hangs off the bottom of your camcorder. The weighted base counterbalances any movement you make and stabilizes the camcorder as you move around. With a FlowCam stabilizer attached, you can walk, run, and even jump while shooting—the image stays stable because your camcorder stays stable.

VariZoom offers a number of different models for different types of camcorders, and for different uses. The low-priced FlowPod is a handheld device that also extends into a sturdy monopod, while the FlowCam Ultra Lite offers a locking gimbal handle that can rotate and tilt in any direction. There are even three pro-level models: The FlowCam GT adds a support vest for even more stability, the FlowCam Prolite is a vest-mounted system for bigger cameras, and the FlowCam Running Gig provides the same sort of functionality as the Steadycam rigs that Hollywood uses.

All FlowCam stabilizers are rugged devices, crafted from aircraft-grade aluminum. If you want a pro-quality shoot, how can you afford not to use one of these gadgets?

Model: FlowPod ($399); FlowCam Ultra Lite ($399); FlowCam GT ($3,400); FlowCam Prolite ($4,100); FlowCam Running Gig ($7,200)
Manufacturer: VariZoom (www.varizoom.com)

Sunpak Readylite 20 Video Light

The quickest way to improve the picture quality of your home movies is to better light the scenes you shoot. To that end, check out the Sunpak Readylite 20, a video light that can attach to any camcorder.

The Readylite 20 is cordless (with 17 minutes of operation on the rechargeable NiCd battery), so it doesn't even have to be attached to your camcorder; you can set it up to provide side lighting or back lighting, whatever is best. If you do mount it on your camera, it's compact enough not to get in the way while you're shooting.

> **Model:** Readylite 20
> **Manufacturer:** ToCAD (www.tocad.com)
> **Price:** $59.99

Eagletron PowerPod Robotic Mount

If you want to use your camcorder as a remote-controlled Webcam, check out the PowerPod robotic tripod. Attach your camcorder, connect the gizmo to your PC, and use your computer (and the included TrackerCam software) to pan, tilt, and zoom to your heart's content.

The PowerPod works with small camcorders that weigh under 3 pounds. It's also good if you want to use your camcorder for video conferences or remote surveillance.

> **Model:** PowerPod
> **Manufacturer:** Eagletron
> (www.trackercam.com)
> **Price:** $169.99

Sony ECM-S930C Stereo Camcorder Microphone

The built-in microphone in most camcorders is functional at best. If you want to pick up more and better sound when you're shooting, you need an auxiliary microphone, like Sony's ECM-S930C.

What's neat about this mic is that it's stereo. The ECM-S930C utilizes left- and right-side microphone capsules, as well as a directional switch, to record real-world stereo sound. And it's a high-quality microphone, as well, with a wide frequency response and low noise level. It's also very small and light, with a universal mount to fit on top of almost any camcorder.

Model: ECM-S930C
Manufacturer: Sony (www.sonystyle.com)
Price: $159.99

Sony WCS-999 Wireless Microphone System

When you're shooting someone from across a room, no camcorder-mounted microphone will do the job. For remote shooting, you need a remote microphone.

Case in point: Sony's WCS-999 wireless microphone system, which consists of a lavalier microphone, 900MHz FM transmitter, receiver, and monitoring earphone. The receiver connects to any camcorder, and the whole shebang has a range of up to 150 feet. This is the kind of small, unobtrusive microphone that TV studios use—and it's affordable for even casual home movie makers.

Model: WCS-999
Manufacturer: Sony (www.sonystyle.com)
Price: $149.99

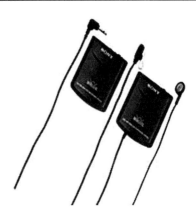

Video Capture Devices

If you have a digital camcorder, you can easily transfer movies to your PC—just connect your camcorder to your PC's FireWire port, and you're in business. But if you have an older VHS or 8mm camcorder, you don't have a FireWire connection. How do you get your old analog movies into your computer for digital editing?

To transfer analog videotapes to digital media, you need a video capture device. Such a device converts analog media to digital format, which you can then save and edit on your computer and ultimately output to DVD.

You connect the output of your analog camcorder or VCR to the input of the video capture device, using either composite or S-Video connections. (S-Video provides better quality.) The capture device is connected to your PC, of course, via either USB or FireWire. Launch the software that comes with the capture device,

and then press play on your camcorder or VCR. The capture device captures the video signal in real time and then encodes it to a digital file on your computer.

You can find video capture devices in both external and internal configurations. I list the best external ones here because they're easiest to work with. There are quite a few boxes in the $200 range, all of which deliver similar performance and features. My favorite model, though, is the semi-pro ADVC300 from Canopus, which has a slew of advanced features that do a much better job converting old and worn tapes to digital format. The other units deliver digital files that look pretty much like the original tapes; the Canopus unit makes your original movies look better than they did before—which is why the Canopus device costs three times as much as the others!

   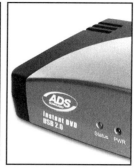 

Canopus ADVC300

If money is no object, this is the video capture device to get.

The Canopus ADVC300 is a high-end, high-quality capture/conversion unit. Its bidirectional operation easily converts analog videotapes to DV and back in one simple step. Even better, it can be used as a standalone converter, without needing a computer.

What's neat about the ADVC300 is how it filters and stabilizes poor analog source video prior to digital conversion. First, the included software lets you adjust brightness, contrast, saturation, hue, and sharpness for all the video you capture. Then the unit's digital 3D noise reduction eliminates noise in the signal. Special 3D Y/C separation circuitry separates brightness (Y) and chrominance (C) from the composite source signal by cross-referencing each frame with the frames immediately in front and behind to refine the overall image. Digital auto gain control (AGC) automatically adjusts the input video level for a clearer picture; digital line time base correction (LTBC) technology detects images with strong horizontal jitter and employs powerful correction methods for perfect frame synchronization.

Sound impressive? It is. In fact, this is similar technology to what you might find in a big-time television studio. It's made easy for consumer use, however. The ADVC300 connects to your PC via FireWire; you also get composite video, S-Video, and FireWire DV inputs, as well as composite, S-Video, FireWire, and (here's what makes this unit unique) *component* video outputs. That component video output lets you view your work on a high-end video monitor, if you want.

How cool is that?

Model: ADVC300
Manufacturer: Canopus (www.canopus.us)
Price: $599

AVerMedia DVD EZMaker Pro

Next up is a series of more traditional capture devices, starting with AVerMedia's DVD EZMaker Pro. What's neat about this unit is that it features a built-in hardware MPEG-2 encoder, which means your PC doesn't have to do the encoding. This frees up your PC for other uses while you're capturing video.

This unit captures both analog and digital video, which not all of these devices do. The DiscDirect features captures and burns direct to DVD, which is great for burning DVDs from MiniDV camcorders. In addition, this portable unit weighs less than one-quarter pound, so you can take it with you on vacation.

Model: DVD EZMaker Pro USB2.0
Manufacturer: AVerMedia (www.aver.com)
Price: $149.99

Dazzle Digital Video Creator 150

The Dazzle DVC 150 converts analog video from any camcorder, VCR, or TV. It connects to your PC via a fast USB 2.0 interface.

The unit itself has S-Video and composite video inputs/outputs, along with RCA stereo audio inputs/outputs. It comes with Pinnacle Studio QuickStart software for editing your movies and burning to DVD or Video CD.

Model: DVC 150
Manufacturer: Pinnacle Systems (www.pinnaclesys.com)
Price: $149.99

Plextor ConvertX PX-402U

This Plextor capture device captures video from any device with analog video outputs and converts it to a wide variety of digital formats: MPEG-1, MPEG-1, MPEG-4, and DivX. The included WinDVD Creator 2 software guides you step-by-step through the process and lets you edit the video, add special effects, and burn to DVD or Video CD. It connects to your PC via USB 2.0.

Model: PX-402U
Manufacturer: Plextor (www.plextor.com)
Price: $159

ADS Instant DVD 2.0

The ADS Instant DVD 2.0 does a little bit better job than the other $200 units when it comes to processing your analog recordings. It uses temporal and spatial video preprocessing filters to remove noise from old VHS tapes; it also includes a 9-bit video digitizer with 2X over-sampling and four-line comb filter.

This unit connects to your PC via USB 2.0. Use the included software to capture and burn directly to disc in one step.

Model: Instant DVD 2.0
Manufacturer: ADS Technologies (www.adstech.com)
Price: $199

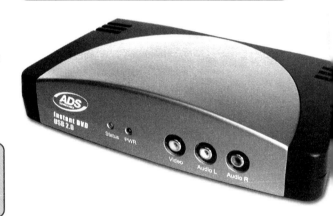

Tape-to-DVD Burners

To get full use out of a video capture device, of course, you need to have a DVD burner connected to your PC. If your intent is simply to transfer all your old videotapes to DVD, there's a better solution—a tape-to-DVD burner.

This type of device combines a video capture device and a DVD burner in one easy-to-use unit. Connect your VCR or camcorder to the unit, insert a blank DVD, and press a button or two. The tape-to-DVD burner captures the video from your VCR and then burns it directly to DVD. It's really that simple.

If you have a lot of old VHS tapes sitting around the house, this is the way to go. It's pretty much a one-step transfer process, from tape to DVD just like that. And even though these devices connect to your PC, there's not a lot of computer operation involved.

Of course, the capture and burning process takes some time. The capturing is done in real time as you play the tape from your VCR. Then it has to be burned to DVD, which takes a little less time but is still somewhat time-consuming. It's not like working with all-digital files, but it's a job that has to be done.

So, dust off all those videotapes and get ready to transfer them to DVD. When you're done, you can toss that VCR once and for all!

HP DVD Movie Writer dc4000

There are two major tape-to-DVD devices on the market today, and HP's dc4000 is the best-selling of the two. Essentially, it's an external DVD burner with built-in analog video capture. Just connect your VCR or camcorder to the dc4000, insert a blank DVD, and activate the Video Transfer Wizard for automated and unattended conversion of your home movies to DVD.

The dc4000 burns to both DVD+R/RW and DVD-R/RW discs. If you want, you can use the included software to edit your movies (on PC) before you burn them.

Model: dc4000
Manufacturer: Hewlett-Packard (www.hp.com)
Price: $299.99

Iomega Super DVD QuikTouch Video Burner

Iomega's Super DVD QuikTouch functions as an external CD/DVD burner for your PC or as a standalone DVD burner for your camcorder or VCR. The video capture card is integrated into the drive, which enables one-touch direct video capture and burning from any analog or digital device.

This unit writes to DVD-RAM, DVD-RW, DVD+RW, and CD-RW format discs and connects to your PC via USB 2.0. It also includes a full suite of video editing and DVD burning software.

Model: Super DVD QuikTouch 32900
Manufacturer: Iomega (www.iomega.com)
Price: $309.95

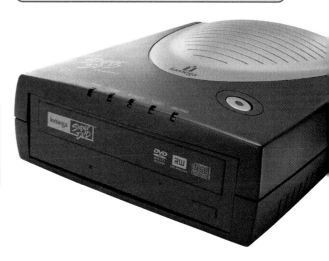

Other Cool Moviemaking Gadgets

There are still a few more moviemaking gadgets I want to talk about. These aren't necessarily must-have gadgets, but if you're serious about moviemaking, you might want to give them a look-see.

The first device is a standalone digital video mixer. Why would you need a separate mixer when you can do all the editing you want from your PC? Simple—this puppy does a lot more than any PC-based editing software can do. First, it lets you connect more than one input, so you can mix between different video sources. Second, you get a ton of built-in editing effects. And third, this unit lets you edit in real time, which makes it the only choice if you're mixing video for a live event. Think big business presentations or any happening with a fancy multimedia component.

The second gadget is a real-time video sketch device. This little device lets you do all sorts of big-time video production; you can use it for onscreen John Madden-type "chalk talks," to notate presentations or onscreen action, or to put yourself "in the picture" (for instance, in front of a weather map). That's a lot of cool uses, and there's a lot more if you put your mind to it. You can use it for real-time video or to annotate digital pictures on your PC.

Our final gadget isn't nearly as sexy, but it has its uses. It's a slide-to-video converter that fits on any camcorder lens and lets you add still pictures to your video productions. Not sexy, perhaps, but definitely functional, especially if you have a lot of old slides you want to transfer to DVD.

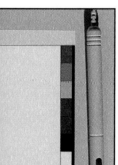

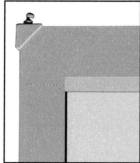

MXProDV Digital Video Mixer

When computer-based video editing isn't powerful enough for you—or when you need real-time editing capabilities—it's time to turn to a freestanding video mixer. The MXProDV is a real-time DV production tool, a switcher/mixer/editor for both digital and analog video. It produces digital effects in real time—no waiting for rendering—which makes it ideal for both post-production and live applications.

What do you get with this type of unit? First, you get a lot of input/ output flexibility. The MXProDV includes two FireWire DV audio/video inputs, four S-Video inputs, and four composite video inputs, as well as a full set of audio inputs. That lets you hook up a lot of video sources simultaneously—just like the big boys at the pro video production houses do.

You also get more than 500 manual or automatic video transitions. These include a variety of fades; sawtooth, curved-edge, and straight-edge wipes; slides; dissolves; zooms; and trailing effects and organic shapes. Other effects include soft edges, color borders, and drop shadows, as well as multiple pictures-in-picture.

Tech-wise, the MXProDV uses RGB color correction to compensate for lighting imperfections or color differences between sources. There are two freeze-frame buffers for still montages and single-source editing. There's also a built-in audio mixer with onscreen level meters.

Sound like overkill? It probably is, for most home moviemakers. But if you do a bit of pro or semi-pro work, you'll appreciate everything this unit has to offer. Plus, there are just a *ton* of knobs and switches to play with!

Model: MXProDV
Manufacturer: Focus Enhancements
(www.focusinfo.com)
Price: $3,295

Canon FP100 35mm Slide to Video Adapter

Okay, it's hard to get really enthused about this gadget, but it's still a useful addition to any serious moviemaking arsenal. The FP100 is an adapter that fits on the front of your camcorder lens and lets you capture 35mm slides to videotape or relay to an A/V-compatible PC. It's the best way I know to capture slides to digital files, which you can then import into your moviemaking software.

Model: FP100
Manufacturer: Canon (www.canon.com)
Price: $125

StudioSketch 2

The StudioSketch 2 is a digital tablet that lets you draw directly on your TV screen or capture your drawings to digital files or videotape. You can sketch over a live video input or on top of any 1 of 12 built-in backgrounds. It's great for play-by-play sports annotating, business presentations, and classroom projections.

Also cool is the digital Chroma Keyer feature, which lets you create your own weather map displays. Stand in front of a green background, wave your arms around, and "draw" on the virtual weather map, just like your local weather guy. Geeky cool!

Model: StudioSketch 2
Manufacturer: Boeckeler
(www.studiosketch.com)
Price: $1699

Home Audio/Video Gadgets

5

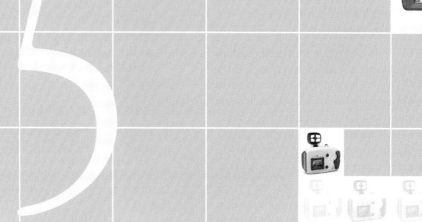

Digital Media Hubs

This is one gadget that didn't exist three years ago. A *digital media hub* is a device that lets you play digital audio files on your home audio system. You rip your favorite CDs to hard disk, and the media hub accesses the hard disk to play individual songs and playlists. It's a great space-saver (you don't need to keep all your physical CDs in view anymore) as well as a way to get instant access to every song in your collection—including all the MP3 and WMA files you've downloaded from the Internet.

There are two primary types of digital media hubs. The first type is a self-contained unit that has a built-in hard disk and CD drive. You insert a CD into the drive, burn it to the built-in hard disk, and then play songs from the hard disk. This type of unit typically looks like a regular consumer audio component and connects to your home audio system via digital or analog connections.

The second type of digital media hub doesn't have a built-in hard disk or CD drive. Instead, it connects to your home network, accesses the digital audio files stored on your computer's hard disk, and then streams the music through your home audio system. This type of hub is typically a small and relatively low-cost device that connects directly to your home audio

system; it plugs in to your home network via either wired or wireless connection.

When you're shopping for a digital media hub, take these points into consideration:

- If you get a self-contained unit, how big is its hard drive? (More hard disk space means you can store more CDs.)

- If you get a PC-based unit, does it connect via Ethernet or Wi-Fi? And if it's Wi-Fi, is it the slower 802.11b or the faster 802.11g (which you'll need to display videos and photos)?

- Can you connect multiple units to provide music to other rooms in your house?

- Does the unit have a built-in display or use your TV to display song information?

- Does it play audio only, or can it also stream videos or display digital photos and art-work?

- Can you control playback from the unit (or a remote control unit), or do you have to set everything up from your PC?

This might be a new type of gadget for you, but if you have a lot of CDs or digital music files, you'll wonder how you ever did without it!

Wurlitzer Digital Jukebox

This is one cool-looking device. The Wurlitzer Digital Jukebox is a free-standing digital media hub, with its own built-in hard disk. It comes in two configurations: the Freestanding jukebox with separate speakers and a Component unit that connects to your home audio system.

The Freestanding unit is the coolest of the bunch. It looks like a high-tech version of a classic jukebox, but a little smaller. Its 145-watt amplifier drives two auxiliary Klipsch speakers, each of which has two 3.5" mid-bass drivers and a 0.5" horn; the main unit has an integrated subwoofer for deep bass.

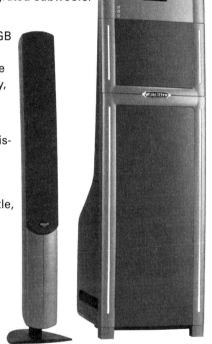

The main unit also hosts a CD player/burner and an 80GB hard drive that can hold 1,000 CDs (in WMA format). A wireless touch-screen remote control unit snaps into the main unit and features a 3.5" color touch-screen display, a scroll knob for rapid navigation, and dedicated transport buttons.

When you rip a CD to disk, the Jukebox retrieves and displays CD information (artist, album, songs, and genre), CD cover, and additional artist information from the Gracenote CDDB music recognition service. You can browse stored music by genre, artist, album, or song title, as well as create your own playlists. The Jukebox also receives digital Internet radio (when connected to your home network via Wi-Fi) and lets you export music to portable audio players. You can even send and control music to multiple locations throughout your house, via optional client units.

All this, and it looks cool standing in your living room, too!

Model: Wurlitzer Digital Jukebox
Manufacturer: Gibson Audio (www.gibsonaudio.com)
Price: $1,999 (Freestanding), $1,499 (Component)

Escient FireBall
DVDM-100

This is *the* system of choice for professional home theater installers, unusual in that it's based around both physical and digital media. FireBall manages, catalogs, and controls digital audio files, CDs, DVDs, Internet radio, you name it.

Connect up to three mega-disc CD/DVD changers and have instant access to up to 1,209 physical CDs or DVDs. Or connect one or more optional hard disk music managers to play digital music files. FireBall then taps into Escient's movie databases and Gracenote's CDDB service to retrieve information on more than 15,000 movies and 20 million songs; you can sort your movies and music by CD/DVD cover, category/genre, and more.

Model: DVDM-100
Manufacturer: Escient (www.escient.com)
Price: $1,995

Yamaha MusicCAST

Yamaha's MusicCAST is a media hub that functions as an audiophile-quality audio component. The MCX-1000 digital audio server serves as the base unit and has a built-in 80GB hard drive that can store up to 1,000 CDs (in MP3 format). Serve music to other rooms with one or more optional MCX-A10 client systems, which connect wirelessly.

The MusicCAST server lets you play music by artist, album, genre, or playlist and incorporates Gracenote's CDDB music database. There's a front panel display for song information; the obligatory wireless remote; and a full complement of analog, digital optical, and digital coaxial outputs.

Model: MCX-1000
Manufacturer: Yamaha (www.yamaha.com)
Price: $2,200

Turtle Beach AudioTron AT-100

The AudioTron AT-100 streams music to your home audio system from your PC's hard drive. It connects to your home network via a fast Ethernet connection (it's not wireless) and plays MP3, WMA, and WAV files—as well as Internet radio.

The AT-100 looks and feels like a regular audio component and has a built-in front panel display. It features both analog and digital coaxial audio outputs, and you can connect multiple units throughout your house. Unlike other hubs, it has no trouble playing music protected by rights-management schemes—with the notable exception of music purchased from iTunes. (Sorry.)

Model: AT-100
Manufacturer: Turtle Beach (www.turtlebeach.com)
Price: $299

Sound Blaster Wireless Music

Creative's Sound Blaster Wireless Music is a full-featured network music hub. There's no hard disk built in; it plays MP3 and WMA files stored on your computer's hard disk via an 802.11b or 802.11g Wi-Fi connection.

It's a small unit that can lay horizontal or (in the included holder) stand vertical. What's really neat is the wireless remote control, which has a built-in LCD screen that displays songs and playlists. Connect up to four Wireless Music units to send music to multiple rooms in your house.

Model: Sound Blaster Wireless Music
Manufacturer: Creative (www.creative.com)
Price: $199.99

NETGEAR MP101

The NETGEAR MP101 is the lowest-priced network music hub I've seen, and probably the simplest to set up and operate. It connects to your home network via wired Ethernet or wireless 802.11b or 802.11g Wi-Fi.

Connection-wise, all you have are analog RCA jacks—no digital connections. It does come with a wireless remote control, and you can connect multiple players to send music throughout your house. It's also good about searching your PC for existing Windows Media Player and MusicMatch playlists.

Slim Devices Squeezebox

Slim Devices' Squeezebox is unique in that it's a Linux-based network music hub. It's also capable of playing the widest variety of digital file formats: MP3, WMA, AAC, Apple Lossless, Ogg Vorbis, FLAC, WAV, and AIFF, as well as Shoutcast Internet radio.

The Squeezebox is a low-profile unit with built-in display. It connects to your PC via wireless Wi-Fi or wired Ethernet. You can synchronize multiple players for whole-house audio, and it even has a built-in alarm clock!

> **Model:** MP101
> **Manufacturer:** NETGEAR
> (www.netgear.com)
> **Price:** $139.99

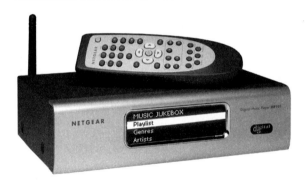

> **Model:** Squeezebox
> **Manufacturer:** Slim Devices
> (www.slimdevices.com)
> **Price:** $199

Roku SoundBridge

Roku's SoundBridge is a cool-looking network music hub, contained in a slim cylindrical aluminum tube. Its 12" built-in display can be read across the room.

The SoundBridge unit comes in two models (M1000 and M2000) and supports MP3, WMA, AAC, WAV, AIFF, FLAC, and Ogg Vorbis files; streams Internet radio; and has support for Apple's iTunes. It connects to your PC via wired Ethernet or wireless Wi-Fi connection (via an optional adapter). It comes with a wireless remote control and has a variety of audio outputs—analog RCA, digital optical, and digital coaxial.

> **Model:** SoundBridge M1000/M2000
> **Manufacturer:** Roku (www.rokulabs.com)
> **Price:** $249.99/$499.99

Roku HD1000

Roku's HD1000 is unique in that it's a hub for both music and pictures, designed especially for displaying digital photographs from your PC on your high-definition TV. The HD1000 connects to your home network or displays photos stored on digital media cards. (Roku even sells prepackaged Art Packs if you don't have enough photos of your own.)

If your normal video source is turned off, the HD1000 automatically kicks in and generates a changing screensaver. Picture quality is terrific; the HD1000 displays photos in true high-definition. It also plays digital music files, although it's not as versatile in this respect as Roku's SoundBridge.

> **Model:** HD1000
> **Manufacturer:** Roku (www.rokulabs.com)
> **Price:** $299.99

DVD Recorders

Toss out your VCR; the latest DVD recorders let you record just about anything to recordable DVD discs—television programming, old VHS tapes, even home movies from your DV camcorder. And you typically get terrific digital video and audio quality, to boot.

To record television or cable programming, make sure the DVD recorder has a built-in television tuner—and, ideally, some sort of electronic program guide. To record from your camcorder, look for a FireWire connection (sometimes labeled as a DV or i.LINK connection); the front panel is more convenient than the rear.

Some DVD recorders also function as personal video recorders (PVRs) thanks to a built-in hard disk. Hard disk recording is great for recording television programming (which you can later burn to DVD) and for pausing and rewinding "live" programming. My favorite unit, the Pioneer DVR-810H, adds a subscription to the TiVo service, which is the ultimate way to program your PVR.

For best playback, make sure your DVD recorder has progressive scan output, typically accompanied by component video and digital audio output jacks. Also look for units that have so-called "chasing playback;" this lets you watch the beginning of what you've already recorded before the complete recording is finished.

Note the five DVD recording formats: DVD-R, DVD-RW, DVD+R, DVD+RW, and DVD-RAM. Most home DVD recorders use the DVD-R/RW formats, although some units are also compatible with the DVD+R/RW formats. Use DVD-R for best compatibility with other players; use the rewriteable DVD-RW format when you want to record over and over again on the same disc.

Finally, if you have a lot of old VHS tapes you want to transfer to DVD, consider JVC's DR-MV1SUS. This is a combination DVD recorder/VCR that lets you make quick DVD recordings of VHS tapes. Just pop in the tape and a blank disc and press a button—it's that easy!

   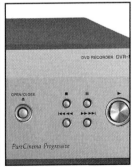 

Pioneer DVR-810H

Leo's Pick

Pioneer's DVR-810H is a combination DVD recorder and PVR. It incorporates an 80GB hard disk drive, with recording controlled via the TiVo service. You can even record content to the hard drive while dubbing different content from the hard drive to DVD.

For the purchase price, Pioneer throws in TiVo basic service free of charge—no monthly fees necessary. You can, however, upgrade to the more fully featured TiVo Plus service, on your dime.

The DVR-810H lets you burn to either DVD-R or DVD-RW discs. It features fast 18X DVD recording from the hard disc; you can dub a 1-hour program to DVD in a little over 3 minutes.

Being a rather high-end unit, the DVR-810H features progressive scan playback and all sorts of video niceties, including PureCinema 2:3 technology, a 9-bit/27MHz video digital/analog converter, and Faroudja Direction Correlation Deinterlacing (DCDi). Variable bit rate (VBR) recording provides gentle compression to fit slightly more material on each disc.

You get a bunch of outputs with this puppy, including two composite video, two S-Video, one component video, and both Dolby Digital and DTS Digital connections. In short, there's not much that this gizmo can't do—it's the ultimate DVD recorder for your home theater system!

Model: DVR-810H
Manufacturer: Pioneer
(www.pioneerelectronics.com)
Price: $1,199

Panasonic DMR-E85H

Panasonic's top-of-the-line DVD recorder incorporates a big 120GB hard drive and great editing capabilities. Record your program to the hard drive, edit out the commercials and add chapter stops, then burn to DVD.

This progressive scan unit features the TV Guide onscreen guide—not quite as versatile as TiVo, but it's free. You also get a Flexible Recording Mode that adjusts recording speed/quality to best fit a program on disk, as well as high-speed 32X dubbing from hard disk to DVD.

Model: DMR-E85H
Manufacturer: Panasonic
(www.toshiba.com)
Price: $699.95

Sony RDR-GX7

Sony's RDR-GX7 is a straight DVD recorder, no hard disk built in. Its claim to fame is all the formats it supports—DVD-R/RW and DVD+R/RW.

Naturally, you get progressive scan playback, as well as one-touch dubbing from DV camcorders, via FireWire. There's even a built-in television tuner for recording your favorite programs direct to DVD.

Model: RDR-GX7
Manufacturer: Sony (www.sonystyle.com)
Price: $699.99

Panasonic DMR-E55

The DMR-E55 gets my vote for best value. It's a good, solid DVD recorder, at an affordable price.

This unit features progressive scan playback and is compatible with DVD-R and DVD-RAM discs. It also has a built-in 181-channel TV tuner for off-air recording.

Model: DMR-E55
Manufacturer: Panasonic
(www.panasonic.com)
Price: $349.95

JVC DR-MV1SUS

Here's a unique unit, a combination DVD recorder/VCR that lets you easily dub your old VHS videotapes onto DVDs. This puppy offers lots of recording options: TV to DVD, VHS to DVD, DVD to VHS, and TV to VHS. You even get twin tuners for dual off-air recording.

The DVD recorder writes to DVD-R, DVD-RW, and DVD-RAM formats and offers progressive scan playback. The VCR is a four-head HiFi unit. You also get front-panel analog and digital (FireWire) A/V inputs for connecting your camcorder or other devices.

Model: DR-MV1SUS
Manufacturer: JVC (www.jvc.com)
Price: $799.95

Home Theater in a Box Systems

If you're setting up a new home theater system and are either confused by or don't want to be bothered with buying separate audio/video components, what you need is a single-purchase solution—a home theater in a box.

Home theater in a box (HTIB) systems give you everything you need for home theater surround sound playback in a single package. You get a single unit that contains a DVD/CD player and audio/video receiver/amplifier, along with matching front and rear speakers, all of which typically have color-coded cables for easy hookup. The only thing missing is the big-screen TV.

Home theater means surround sound, which means you can't just use the tinny little speakers built in to your television set. You need a full array of front and rear speakers, in what is called a *5.1 configuration*. The *5* refers to the bookshelf or floorstanding speakers that deliver the main sound: left front, center front, right front, right rear, and left rear. The *.1* is the sub-woofer, which delivers the deep bass punch you need to reproduce bone-shuddering explosions and the like.

All these speakers are driven by a multichannel amplifier built in to an audio/video receiver. The receiver also contains the surround sound decoding circuitry, as well as a switching circuit and (usually) an AM/FM tuner. You control the receiver with a multifunction remote control.

Three main surround sound formats are in use today. Most current movies use either Dolby Digital or DTS, both of which deliver six (5.1, remember) discrete channels of sound. Some older movies use the previous Dolby Pro Logic system, which matrixes the rear channels into the mix and results in a less effective channel separation. Don't worry; almost all of today's HTIB systems handle all three surround sound formats and automatically switch to the correct one when you insert a DVD for playback.

When it comes to choosing an HTIB system, look at the amount of amplifier power offered (more is better) and the size of the speakers. Actually, it's best to listen to the speakers because size alone won't tell you how they actually sound. And check out that remote control—you'll be using it a lot, so make sure it feels good to you!

Panasonic SC-HT920

Panasonic's SC-HT920 is a system that would look great surrounding a wall-mounted plasma television. All the components feature a modern mirror finish and super-thin design, so they look cool while being somewhat unobtrusive.

Leo's Pick

The front left and right Tall Boy speakers come on adjustable stands, so you can position them to match the height of your TV screen. The horizontal center channel speaker sits on your TV, of course, while the rear satellite speakers can be mounted on the wall or hung from the ceiling. The system also includes a stylish diamond-shaped subwoofer, a lot better than the typical boxy subwoofer you find with most other systems.

The receiver can handle all the major surround sound systems: Dolby Digital, DTS, and Dolby Pro Logic. The amplifier delivers 1000 watts total power—170W × 2 front, 260W center, 70W × 2 surround, and 260W sub. The controls are aligned across the top of the main unit, with a small display on the front. There's also a built-in AM/FM tuner, the ubiquitous remote control, and a nifty five-disc DVD/CD changer.

When style matters (and style *always* matters), this is the system to consider.

Model: SC-HT920
Manufacturer: Panasonic (www.panasonic.com)
Price: $499.95

Sony DAV-FC7 DVD Dream System

Sony's DAV-FC7 DVD Dream System provides surprisingly good performance at a very afford-able price—just a tad under $400. What you get for the money is fairly impressive—a five-disc progressive-scan DVD/CD/SACD changer, 600-watt amplifier (100W × 5 channels + 100W sub-woofer), four satellite speakers, a center front speaker, and a subwoofer. All controlled by remote, of course.

The main unit has the expected Dolby Digital, DTS, and Dolby Pro Logic II surround sound decoding. Color-coded speaker connections make it a snap to set up, and you get an onscreen display for fine adjustments.

Model: DAV-FC7
Manufacturer: Sony (www.sonystyle.com)
Price: $399.95

Samsung HT-DB390 Wireless Home Theater System

The great thing about this Samsung system is that you don't have to run any wires to the rear speakers—they're wireless! Sound for the rear speakers is beamed to a wireless receiver tower, using 2.4GHz digital technology; the rear speak-ers then connect to the tower.

The main unit provides 400 watts total power (60W × 5 channels + 100W subwoofer) and sup-ports Dolby Digital, DTS, and Dolby Pro Logic II. Naturally, it plays both DVDs and CDs, for your viewing—and listening—enjoyment.

Model: HT-DB390
Manufacturer: Samsung
(www.samsung.com)
Price: $499.99

Niro 1.1PRO

If two speakers are one too many for you, take a look at the Niro 1.1PRO. This puppy delivers the equivalent of five-channel surround sound with just *one* speaker, which you sit on top of your TV. Niro uses proprietary head-related transfer function (HRTF) and spatial filter network (SFN) technology to deliver a fairly decent surround sound simulation from the single speaker's five computer-controlled drivers. Bass comes from the obligatory (and separate) subwoofer. Naturally, you get DVD/CD playback from the separate receiver unit.

Model: 1.1PRO
Manufacturer: Nirotek America
(www.niro1.com)
Price: $799

Bose 3*2*1 DVD Home Entertainment System

Bose's 3*2*1 system is great when space is at a premium—and when you don't want to muck about running wires to rear speakers. That's because this system simulates the full surround sound spectrum from just two main speakers— front left and front right—plus a small sub- woofer.

The media center unit includes a DVD/CD player, an AM/FM tuner, and all the amplification for the speakers. The surround sound effect is surpris- ingly good, and you can't beat the ease of setup.

Model: 3*2*1
Manufacturer: Bose (www.bose.com)
Price: $999

Universal Remote Controls

If you're like me, you have a coffee table full of remotes. There's one for the TV, one for the A/V receiver, one for the DVD player, and one for the cable box or satellite dish. And that's before you start adding digital music hubs and the like.

How do you get rid of all those remotes?

The key is to combine all your operating functions into a single universal remote control unit. Most universal remotes have codes for the most popular audio/video components preprogrammed; other codes can be "learned" from the old remote. Once you have it programmed, the new remote can control four or more components, just by pressing the right buttons.

The best universal remotes feature some sort of LCD touch screen display. Typically, this display varies depending on which component you're trying to operate. Press the button for TV, and

the touch screen changes to display the television controls. Press the button for DVD, and the screen displays the DVD's controls. And so on.

The most programmable remotes are those in Philips's Pronto series. Pronto remotes have become a cult onto themselves, thanks to their almost-complete programmability. Use your PC to design your own custom screens; go online to find all sorts of custom screens and logos to use.

Of course, ultra-programmability is useless if you can't figure out how to use the darned thing. So, don't be seduced by too many whiz-bang features; make sure that the remote is simple enough for everyone in your household to use, without consulting an instruction manual every time they want to change channels.

    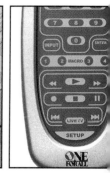

Philips iPronto

The hands-down winner for the most sophisticated consumer-grade remote control today (not counting big whole-house models sold by home theater installers) is the Philips iPronto. This funky unit combines a color touch screen remote control, a wireless Internet browser, and an electronic program guide into a unit that looks a little like a tablet PC.

This is one *big* remote control. The whole thing measures 9.4" × 7" × 0.9" and features a 6.4" color TFT VGA (640 × 480) touch screen display with a fully customizable user interface. You also get eight direct access buttons to navigate screen layouts and five programmable control buttons for volume up/down, channel up/down, and mute. Use the iProntoEdit PC editing software to add channel logos and other multimedia content you download from the Internet.

But the iPronto is more than a simple remote—it's also your own guide to what's playing. It uses Wi-Fi wireless technology (connected to any always-on broadband Internet connection) to acquire TV programming information for its built-in Electronic Program Guide. That Wi-Fi connection also lets you use the iPronto as a tablet web browser to surf the Internet and send and receive email. Also cool is the fact that the iPronto includes built-in stereo speakers, a microphone, and a headphone jack.

Naturally, the iPronto replaces all the other remotes in your house. It learns infrared codes from other remotes and has an MMC slot and a USB port for future upgrades. It's a power hog, as you might expect; good thing it uses a rechargeable lithium-ion battery and comes with its own external charger unit.

Model: TSi6400
Manufacturer: Philips (www.pronto.philips.com)
Price: $1,699.99

ProntoPro NG

Okay, the iPronto is probably overkill for most folks, but you gotta like the idea of a customizable color touch screen remote—which is what you get, for half the iPronto's price, from Philips's ProntoPro NG. This is a sleek unit with a high-resolution 3.8" color LCD touch screen display.

Like the iPronto, you use Philips' proprietary software to create your own screen layouts on your PC and then download them to the ProntoPro NG. And, so you don't have to worry about replacing batteries all the time, it comes with its own docking cradle/charger. Cool!

Model: TSU7000
Manufacturer: Philips
(www.pronto.philips.com)
Price: $899.99

Sony RM-AV3100

Admittedly, color remotes are a little pricey. If you want similar programmability and can settle for a monochrome LCD touch screen display, check out Sony's RM-AV3100. This unit lets you control up to 18 A/V components and is completely programmable.

Also neat is the ability to program macros so you can execute up to 44 consecutive operations at the touch of a button. It comes with a system on/off macro built in for centralized control of all Sony-brand devices.

Model: RM-AV3100
Manufacturer: Sony (www.sonystyle.com)
Price: $199.95

Harmony SST-659

Harmony's SST-659 differs from other remotes in that it isn't device-oriented—it's activity-oriented. Press a single activity button (such as Watch TV or Watch a Movie) and the SST-659 automatically turns on and switches to the appropriate components.

You set up the activity buttons specific to your home theater system through the online tools at the HarmonyRemote.com website; the remote connects to your PC via USB. You also can connect to the website every two weeks to download the electronic program guide, which is displayed on the remote's built-in interactive display.

> **Model:** SST-659
> **Manufacturer:** Intrigue Technologies (www.harmonyremote.com)
> **Price:** $199.99

One for All Kameleon 8-in-1 Remote

The Kameleon is one of the coolest-looking remotes on the market. The flexible touch screen display uses a combination of electro-luminescent backlighting and segmented LCDs that intelligently illuminates only the buttons necessary for the currently selected device; some of the buttons are animated.

As the name implies, this remote can control up to eight devices. It also includes a remote finder feature, which helps you locate the unit if you lose the remote. And, for all its coolness, the Kameleon is also a very affordable universal remote; you can find it in most stores for well under $100.

> **Model:** URC-9960
> **Manufacturer:** One for All/Universal Electronics, Inc. (www.uei.com)
> **Price:** $99.99

Satellite Radio

The latest big deal in automobile entertainment systems is satellite radio, where you get high-quality entertainment anywhere in the United States beamed down from a network of satellites. I'll talk more about auto satellite radio on p. 246, but what you probably didn't know is that you can also get satellite radio in your home. After all, why should you leave all that cool digital programming behind when you lock up your car?

There are two similar but competing satellite radio services: Sirius and XM. Both offer satellite radios for in-home listening and similar programming.

The Sirius satellite radio service has more than 100 streams of music and entertainment—60 commercial-free music streams, plus 40 sports, news, and entertainment streams. The monthly subscription fee is $12.95, and it's the official satellite radio partner of the NFL. Learn more at www.sirius.com.

XM satellite radio is a competing service that offers 120 channels of digital programming—68 commercial-free music channels, 32 news/talk/entertainment channels, and 21 channels of traffic and weather. The monthly subscription fee is $9.99 per month. Learn more at www.xmradio.com.

Which is the better service? As you can tell from the basic specs, they're both pretty similar. XM is a little more adventurous with its music programming; Sirius is a little more attuned to the news radio junkie. Bottom line: They both deliver much more high-fidelity entertainment than you're used to.

Of course, to listen to satellite radio in your home, you need to have a satellite antenna. Although this is a little bit of a bother, you can probably get by with mounting the antenna inside your house, rather than outside. The best location is often on or next to an outside wall. Make sure the antenna cable is long enough to reach to wherever you place the radio.

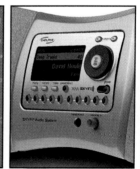

Delphi SKYFi XM Audio System

I tend to like the XM system a little better than Sirius (I like music more than talk), and I really like the SKYFi portable XM receiver. This little gizmo gives you satellite radio on the go—in your car or at home. Combine the receiver with the SKYFi Audio System, and for a little over $200, you have yourself at-home and in-car satellite listening.

Here's the deal: The SKYFi receiver is a palm-sized unit that receives the full range of XM satellite radio signals. In your car, it broadcasts XM signals over an unused FM frequency, so you can listen through your current auto audio system. When you get home, take the SKYFi receiver with you, insert it into the open slot on the front of the SKYFi Audio System, and continue listening to your XM programming through the device's built-in speakers.

Essentially, the SKYFi Audio System turns your SKYFi receiver into a boombox. It integrates a pair of high-quality speakers, a high-gain XM antenna (with a 22.5' cable), and a dock for the SKIFi XM receiver. You can place the antenna on your roof, on a table, or wherever works best; for portable use, the antenna attaches to the back of the boombox. The whole thing operates on six D-cell batteries or with the included AC adapter.

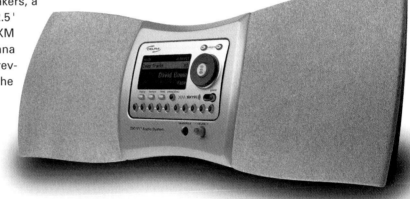

It's a great system for listening to satellite radio indoors or out!

Model: SKYFi Audio System
Manufacturer: Delphi (www.xmradio.com)
System: XM
Price: $99.99 (audio system); $129.99 (portable receiver)

Kenwood DT-7000S Sirius Tuner

Kenwood's DT-7000S lets you listen to Sirius satellite radio through your home audio system. It sits alongside your other audio components and connects to your receiver via a digital optical output.

The unit itself has a built-in four-line scrolling LCD display. And, like any good audio component, you also get a wireless remote control.

Model: DT-7000S
Manufacturer: Kenwood (www.kenwoodusa.com)
System: Sirius
Price: $300

Tivoli Model Sirius

If you prefer a standalone satellite radio, consider Tivoli's Model Sirius. This is a tabletop radio with an old-school look that can receive Sirius satellite radio signals. It's easy to use, with the big honkin' control dial that's typical of Tivoli's other popular table radios.

The Model Sirius features a classy all-wood cabinet and an easy-to-use digital interface. It also has an AM/FM analog tuner and a built-in alarm clock.

Model: Model Sirius
Manufacturer: Tivoli Audio (www.tivoliaudio.com)
System: Sirius
Price: TBA

Other Cool Audio/Video Gadgets

Our look at audio/video gadgets concludes with three gadgets that you've probably never thought about but that could be quite useful additions to your home theater setup.

The first of these gadgets, Terk's Volume Regulator, does just what its name implies—it regulates the volume level of your TV. It's great for equalizing the volume between channels or signal sources and for making sure that commercials don't get any louder than the surrounding program.

The second gadget, also from Terk, lets you transmit audio/video signals from one device to multiple televisions in your house. Have one set in the living room, one in the bedroom, and another in the kids' room? You don't have to buy separate DVD players or satellite receivers for each set; use the Terk Leapfrog to beam signals from a single device to all your TVs.

Finally, when you're faced with a multiplicity of video components connecting to a single television, you need some way of switching between them all. JVC's digital video switcher lets you connect up to 13 devices, using a variety of inputs (FireWire, composite video, S-Video, and component video) and outputs. You can even route the signals to a half-dozen TVs and switch between them all with the wireless remote. It's a state-of-the-art version of the simple push-button switchers of yesteryear.

Terk VR-1 TV Volume Regulator

Leo's Pick

I like this gadget. Terk's VR-1 TV volume regular delivers consistent audio levels throughout abnormally loud or quiet scenes in movie and television programs. It also helps to quiet loud commercials and keep the volume constant when you switch channels or when you switch between different inputs (cable, DVD, satellite, and so on).

The VR-1 uses advanced digital signal processing to automatically adjust the sound level without introducing additional noise. Built-in noise reduction circuitry minimizes audio hiss and provides cleaner, more audible sound from any source.

This gizmo does its job in real time by sampling the audio signal thousands of times per second. The VR-1 has a reaction time of only 0.002 seconds, so even sudden loud noises are automatically adjusted.

You connect the VR-1 between your TV and your home audio system using standard RCA cables. Turn it on and it operates automatically. You'll be amazed at the difference!

Model: VR-1
Manufacturer: Terk Technologies (www.terk.com)
Price: $49.99

Terk Leapfrog Wireless Audio/Video Transmitter/Receiver System

Here's a smart idea. Terk's Leapfrog system lets you transmit audio and video throughout your home from any source. It's great for sending DVD movies from your main home theater system to other rooms, for sharing satellite programming between multiple TVs, or for listening to your CD collection throughout the house.

The system transmits at 2.4GHz, with a range up to 150 feet. It's easy to connect and works with any TV, no matter how old. And it's surprisingly affordable—definitely cheaper than purchasing separate components for every TV in your house!

Model: LF-30S
Manufacturer: Terk (www.terk.com)
Price: $99.99

JVC Digital A/V Switcher

You can buy cheaper switchers, but they won't switch everything this baby does. This is the first A/V switcher with full digital video, component video, and digital audio connections. It's a professional-grade unit, using the highest-quality circuitry for zero signal loss.

Here's what you get. Inputs: eight composite/S-Video/audio, two component video, and two digital optical audio. Outputs: five composite/S-Video/audio, two component video, one digital optical audio. Plus, you get three FireWire DV input/output connections. You control them all via front-panel buttons or with the wireless remote control.

Model: JX-S777
Manufacturer: JVC (www.jvc.com)
Price: $799.95

Telephone Gadgets

6

Mobile Phones

When it comes to choosing a mobile phone, size and styling are important, but don't get seduced by every cool-looking phone that fits in your back pocket. It's more important to choose a phone that has the right feature set and operation.

You might think that all you'd use a phone for is making calls, right? Well, all phones are supposedly made for talking, but you can also find mobile phones that take digital pictures, store contact information, keep track of appointments, track your location using GPS technology, send and receive text or multimedia messages, send and receive email, surf the Web, download and play simple games, and play either FM radio or digital music. Determine which—if any—of these features you might use.

You also need to determine which modes and bands the phone works with. The *mode* refers to the type of network the phone works with— either analog (older) or digital (newer). *Dual-mode* phones work on both analog and digital networks, which is great when you're stuck in the boonies with no digital towers within reach.

The *band* refers to the frequency range that a digital phone receives. Code Division Multiple Access (CDMA) phones operate in either the 800MHz or 1900MHz frequency band; Global System for Mobile communications (GSM) phones operate in the 800MHz, 1800MHz, or 1900MHz frequency band. Know that CDMA is pretty much a U.S.-only standard, whereas GSM is the international standard in Europe, Australia, and much of Asia and Africa. You can find dual-band CDMA phones that work with both CDMA frequencies, dual-band GSM phones that work with two of the three GSM frequencies, and tri-band GSM phones that work with all three GSM frequencies.

That said, you probably don't have to worry about modes and bands if you stick with the phones offered by your chosen service provider. Sprint and Verizon are CDMA networks, whereas AT&T, Cingular, and T-Mobile are GSM networks. Obviously, not every phone listed here works on every network; in some cases, the same phone might be sold under different model numbers for different networks.

By the way, I haven't listed pricing for the phones in this section because pricing depends a lot on the service provider you sign up with and whatever specials the service might be offering at a given time. Some carriers might make you pay several hundred dollars for a particular phone—but other carriers might offer it for free!

Nokia 6800

My favorite basic cell phone is the Nokia 6800. The phone flips open to reveal a full QWERTY keyboard, which makes it great for SMS text messaging. Just turn the phone horizontal, open it, and start typing—with your thumbs, of course.

Typing is made even easier by the phone's concatenated messaging function, which lets you write longer messages without typing full words. There's also a Note feature for taking meeting minutes, writing to-do lists, or just jotting down whatever comes to mind.

In addition to text messaging, you get MMS multimedia messaging, which lets you send and receive messages with text, polyphonic tones, and images. The 6800 is also Internet-enabled, so you can send and receive email over the Internet. A built-in distribution list function lets you send a message to several people at a time.

Here's something else that's neat: The 6800 has a built-in stereo FM tuner, so you can listen to the radio when you're out and about. There's also a hands-free speaker phone for conference calls.

The display is 128 × 128 pixels, with 4,096 colors, which makes it just fine for playing simple downloadable games. It comes with the Triple Pop and Bounce games preinstalled.

Oh, and it works okay as a phone, too.

Model: 6800
Manufacturer: Nokia (www.nokia.com)
Operation: Dual-band GSM

Siemens SL56

The Siemens SL56 has a unique slider design; slide the top of the phone up to access the keypad. You can also make and receive calls without opening the phone by using one-touch buttons or voice commands.

The phone features a hands-free speaker phone and an okay 4,096-color display, which can also display images taken with the optional clip-on camera.

Model: SL56
Manufacturer: Siemens
(www.siemens-mobile.com)
Operation: Dual-band GSM

Kyocera SE44/SE47

Here's another cool slider phone, but with a more vivid 65,000-color display and more advanced features. This Kyocera model is Internet-enabled, and it also incorporates Enhanced Messaging Service (EMS) for two-way messaging using graphics, sounds, and fancy fonts.

It also has a built-in speaker phone and voice-activated dialing, as well as a scheduler, a calculator, an alarm clock, and a stopwatch. Finally, it incorporates a built-in GPS locator, in case you ever need Emergency 911 service.

Model: SE44/SE47
Manufacturer: Kyocera
(www.kyocera-wireless.com)
Operation: Tri-mode CDMA/PCS (SE44); dual-mode CDMA (SE47)

Samsung SPH-a460

The neat thing about this Samsung phone is the embedded GPS technology, which provides access to various location-based services—driving directions, traffic alerts, and so on. Even better, the GPS function helps 911 operators pinpoint your location in the event of an emergency.

The SPH-a460 is Internet-enabled, so you can browse the Web and send and receive emails. It also includes personal information manager tools for scheduling and to-do lists, as well as SMS text messaging. The display is a 128 × 128 pixel cool blue LCD screen.

Model: SPH-a460
Manufacturer: Samsung
(www.samsungusa.com)
Operation: Dual-band tri-mode CDMA/PCS

Motorola V70

Motorola's V70 features an innovative design with a unique rotating cover. Spin the cover open to reveal the phone's keypad, which otherwise is neatly hidden.

The V70's polished metal case and round display screen makes it look kind of like a big wrist watch. It's small for a phone, though, at just 3.3" × 1.7" × 0.8". It displays white text on a blue background, and the translucent keypad is illuminated in cool electroluminescent blue.

Model: V70
Manufacturer: Motorola
(www.motorola.com)
Operation: Single-band GSM

Camera Phones

Whether you want it or not, today's state-of-the-art cell phones come with built-in digital cameras. That's right—you can use your phone as a miniature camera to take digital photos.

Why would you want a camera in your cell phone? How about if you're out and about and see something you want to document visually but don't have your digital camera with you? Or maybe you're shopping and want to send a snapshot of what you're looking at to your spouse at home. Or maybe you're at a concert and want to share the moment with your friends back home. Or maybe you're in the locker room and want to take a few candid shots of...okay, that last one's a little creepy, but still.... The point is, adding a camera to a cell phone lets you take pictures just about anywhere and send them (via email or over the phone's messaging service) to just about anyone.

Of course, you can't expect a cell phone to deliver the quality of picture you get with a real digital camera. Most camera phones take extremely low-resolution photos, definitely not print quality. But it's not the quality of the photo that matters in this instance; it's the immediacy.

Also, many camera phones not only let you take still photos, but also let you take short (typically 15-second or less) video movies. Again, you're not going to use your cell phone to shoot a wedding video, but you might use it to capture something short and sweet and totally spur of the moment.

If nothing else, most of these phones let you attach photos to names in your address book. So, when your sister calls, instead of seeing the standard caller ID information, the phone puts her picture on the display—which is a pretty neat, if somewhat useless, application of the technology.

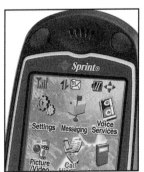

Sanyo SCP-5500/VM4500

Leo's Pick

I like the SCP-5500 not so much because of its built-in digital camera, but rather because you can use it as a walkie talkie. That's right, this camera phone is also a two-way radio, compatible with the Ready Link nation-wide network.

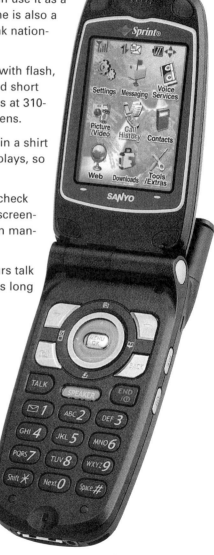

Of course, the SCP-5500 does feature a built-in camera complete with flash, as well as a built-in voice recorder. It can take both still photos and short (15-second) video clips, with or without sound. The camera shoots at 310-pixel VGA resolution and has a three-position (1X/4X/16X) zoom lens.

The SCP-5500 is a lightweight, compact flip phone that easily fits in a shirt pocket. There are both internal and external 65,000-color LCD displays, so you can see who's calling without opening the phone.

It's an Internet-enabled phone, so feel free to browse the Web or check your email. You can also use it to download games, ringers, and screen-savers from the Internet. There's also built-in personal information manager software for calendars, appointments, and to-do lists.

Best of all, this little phone has terrific battery life—up to 3.25 hours talk time and 10 days standby time. So feel free to talk—and shoot—as long as you like!

Model: SCP-5500/VM4500
Manufacturer: Sanyo (www.sanyo.com)
Operation: Dual-band tri-mode CDMA/PCS

Motorola V600

Motorola's V600 is a true world phone, with quad-band GSM global roaming. It has a built-in digital camera, of course, and it also features integrated Bluetooth wireless capability.

You can use the V600 to play back video clips and send MMS multimedia messages. You can even program the phone to glow a different color depending on who's calling—a cool color-coded type of caller ID!

Model: V600
Manufacturer: Motorola
(www.motorola.com)
Operation: Quad-band GSM

Sony Ericsson T610

The Sony Ericsson T610 is a nice-looking camera phone, with color aluminum panels (red, blue, or "haze") and a large 128 × 160 pixel high-resolution 65,000-color screen.

In addition to the built-in camera, the T610 is Bluetooth-enabled, so you can use it with any Bluetooth headset or connect the optional Stereo FM Radio Handsfree to listen to FM radio broadcasts. The unique mini-joystick makes it easy to play mobile games. And it's Internet-enabled, of course.

Model: T610
Manufacturer: Sony Ericsson
(www.sonyericsson.com)
Operation: Tri-band GSM

LG VX6000

The LG VX6000 is a small flip phone with a built-in camera. The internal display is 120 × 160 pixels, and there's a small external display for caller ID.

It's an Internet-enabled phone, plus you get voice-activated dialing and MMS multimedia messaging. All in all, it's a nice array of useful features in a very small package.

Model: VX6000
Manufacturer: LG Electronics (us.lge.com)
Operation: Dual-band CDMA

Nokia 3650

Nokia's 3650 is a good basic camera phone in an attractive package. It has a nice shape and feel and an excellent—if somewhat unique—circular button layout.

The built-in camera lets you capture still images and short videos at 640 × 480 resolution. Plus, you get MMS multimedia messaging, built-in Bluetooth wireless, voice dialing and a built-in voice recorder, and integrated speaker phone. The 4,096-color display is a nice 176 × 208 pixel size.

Model: 3650
Manufacturer: Nokia (www.nokia.com)
Operation: Tri-band GMS

Smart Phones

A *smart phone* is a mobile phone that adds PDA functionality. That is, it's a cell phone you can use like a PDA—or a PDA you can use like a phone.

A full-featured smart phone is somewhat larger than a typical mobile phone, shaped and sized more like a PDA. This makes for a somewhat awkward phone, but if you think of it as a PDA plus, then you're okay. The most popular PDA/phone is the Handspring Treo 600, which is a bit of a brick to haul around, but it's extremely functional, with its built-in QWERTY keyboard. It uses the popular Palm OS operating system for all of its PDA functions.

Other smart phones look and feel like traditional cell phones but add some degree of PDA functionality. Most of these type of smart phones use Microsoft's Windows Mobile operating system, which you'll either love or hate—or love to hate, as the case may be. These smart phones are easier to carry around than the larger PDA/phones but more difficult to use, PDA-wise.

You typically have a smaller screen and no keyboard, which makes entering data challenging, at best.

Why would you want a smart phone? Well, if you carry both a PDA and a mobile phone, a smart phone lets you cut your number of portable gadgets by half—that's if you don't mind the compromises inherent in such a combo device, of course.

On the other hand, maybe you just want a phone that can do a little bit more. In this instance, the scheduling and calendar functions of the Microsoft-enabled smart phones make a lot of sense; you probably don't need to get a bulky PDA/phone device.

In any case, make sure you give it a full try-out before you purchase any smart phone. Make sure it does everything you need it to do, in a way that's intuitive and comfortable to you. And definitely be sure you like the size and heft; whichever model you choose, you'll be using it a lot!

Handspring Treo 600

The nice thing about the Handspring Treo 600, unlike many other smart phones, is that it does both things well. It's a good phone *and* a good Palm OS PDA, no compromises on either side.

Older models went the flip phone route, where you could use it like a PDA with the flip closed but had to flip it open to use it like a phone. But now you can have access to all its functions without having to flip.

As if all that wasn't enough, the Treo 600 has a built-in camera, complete with picture caller ID on the big touch-screen display. You can also use the touch-screen to display an onscreen dial pad for push-button dialing.

And there's more. The Treo 600 has an integrated speaker phone, a built-in MP3 player, and an SD/MMC expansion slot. You also get all the applications that come with the Palm OS operating system, as well as Internet email, SMS text messaging, and MMS multi-media messaging. It's Internet-enabled with a color web browser.

Model: Treo 600
Manufacturer: palmOne
(www.palmOne.com)
Operation: Quad-mode GSM or dual-mode CDMA

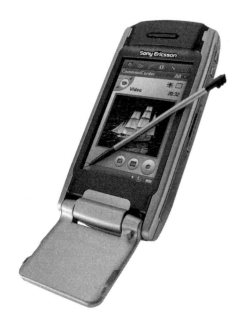

BlackBerry 7230 Wireless Handheld

Here's another big honkin' PDA/phone from the folks who make those cool little BlackBerry email/pager devices. This gadget comes with a 240 × 160 pixel, 65,000-color touchscreen display, as well as a mini-QWERTY keyboard, in a non-flip form factor.

The 7230 comes with all manner of personal information manager applications, including calendar, address book, memo pad, and task list. It's also Internet-enabled, so you can send both wireless email and SMS text messages—and surf the Web, of course.

Model: 7230
Manufacturer: Research In Motion (www.blackberry.com)
Operation: Tri-band GSM

Sony Ericsson P900

The Sony Ericsson P900 is a cell phone that's also a PDA that's also a mobile game machine. When closed, the flip portion contains the dialing keypad. Open or remove the flip and you get access to the full 208 × 320 pixel, 65,000-color touchscreen display. Turn the unit sideways to play games, including the preinstalled V-Rally racing game.

You also get a digital still/video camera and the ability to save photos and video clips to Memory Stick media. The P900 is Internet-enabled and Bluetooth-enabled, can send MMS multimedia messages, and can function as a digital audio and video player. It comes with built-in calendar and phonebook applications.

Model: P900
Manufacturer: Sony Ericsson (www.sonyericsson.com)
Operation: Tri-band GSM

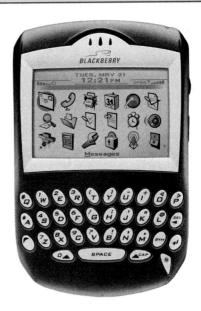

Samsung SPH-i700

Samsung's SPH-i700 is a legitimate competitor to the PalmOne Treo, but on the Pocket PC side of the fence. It uses the Microsoft Pocket PC 2002 Phone Edition operating system and offers a big color touchscreen display, speaker phone, and the like.

The SPH-i700 comes with pocket versions of Word, Excel, Outlook, Internet Explorer, and Windows Media Player. That means it can function as a digital music player, which is pretty cool. There's also the obligatory digital camera for pictures and such.

> **Model:** SPH-i700
> **Manufacturer:** Samsung
> (www.samsungusa.com)
> **Operation:** Dual-band CDMA

Motorola MPx200

Microsoft's Pocket PC Phone Edition is for larger PDA/phones; for regular-sized mobile phones, Microsoft offers the Windows Mobile operating system, which is what drives this Motorola smart phone.

The MPx200 lets you synch to your PC, stream digital music, and surf the Internet. You browse the Web via the Pocket Internet Explorer browser and send and receive email with Pocket Outlook. You can also play digital music files with Pocket Windows Media Player and send text-based instant messages via pocket MSN Messenger.

> **Model:** MPx200
> **Manufacturer:** Motorola
> (www.motorola.com)
> **Operation:** Dual-band GSM

Headsets

If you use your cell phone for extended periods at a time, you know how uncomfortable it can get. That's why many people use some sort of headset, so they don't have to hold the handset to the side of their heads all the time.

Mobile phone headsets include an earphone for listening and a microphone for talking. They're very popular among people who work all day on the phone, such as call center professionals. They're also great for using a cell phone in the car, which you really shouldn't be doing anyway, although I know you do.

Until recently, most headsets attached to the phone via a long cord—easy to connect, if somewhat inconvenient. Today, many new headsets attach cordlessly, thanks to Bluetooth wireless technology. If your phone is already Bluetooth-enabled, just synch a Bluetooth headset with your phone and you're ready to go. If you don't have a Bluetooth phone, you'll have to attach a Bluetooth adapter to it to use a wireless headset.

The two biggest headset companies are Logitech and Plantronics, both of which offer a variety of corded and cordless models. My favorite headset, however, comes from Shure, which makes a very effective noise-canceling model that's definitely worth checking out.

When you're shopping for a headset, the main thing to look for is comfort. Do you like the way it hangs on your ear? You should also check the performance; those mini-mics don't always work that well, especially if you're a quiet speaker. You might have to evaluate several models to find one you really like.

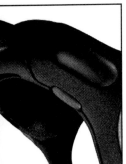  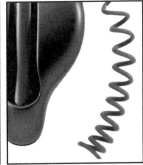  

Shure QuietSpot Headset

Leo's Pick

Shure's QuietSpot is a corded model that delivers the best sound of any headset on the market today.

First, you get a NoiseBlocker earphone with studio-quality speaker that delivers ultra-clear sound. Its lightweight in-ear design blocks ambient noise and stays securely and comfortably in your ear, even during long conversations. Shure claims that this earphone reduces outside noise by 80%, and I believe them.

The noise-canceling microphone (with foam windscreen) delivers very clear vocals. There's no shouting necessary, even in noisy rooms; the directional microphone picks up your normal speaking voice clearly while blocking 70% of extraneous noise. There's even an adjustable mic boom so you can position the microphone closer to your mouth.

As far as comfort, the QuietSpot delivers a snug fit, with flexible ear support. The included personal fit kit includes small, medium, and large soft foam and flexible silicone sleeves; pick the sleeve that gives you the best fit.

Model: QSH-3/QSH-4
Manufacturer: Shure (www.shure.com)
Type: Corded
Price: $49.99

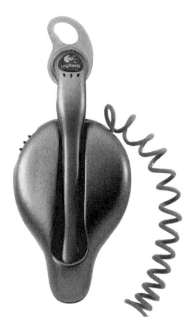

Logitech Mobile Earbud Miniboom

Logitech's Mobile Earbud Miniboom is a corded headset with a noise-canceling boom microphone, which does a good job of filtering out unwanted sounds when you're talking. Adjustable earbuds fit comfortably inside your ear for better isolation, and four FlexLoop cushions let you choose the right fit for your ear.

The cord is retractable for convenience. Operation is via a multifunction button, which lets you answer, end, or activate voice commands with a single click.

Model: Mobile Earbud Miniboom
Manufacturer: Logitech (www.logitech.com)
Type: Corded
Price: $39.95

Cardo allways Headset

Here's another lightweight headset with noise canceling microphone. What's cool about the allways is that it can fit around your ear, like a normal headset, or clip to a pair of eyeglasses or sunglasses, which is great for extended wear.

The allways is also quite fashionable, with exchangeable designer panels and a durable carrying case. There's also an optional Bluetooth adapter for wireless operation.

Model: allways
Manufacturer: Cardo (www.allways1.com)
Type: Corded
Price: $99.99 ($159.99 with optional Bluetooth adapter)

Logitech Mobile Bluetooth Headset

If you prefer to go the wireless route, check out Logitech's Mobile Bluetooth Headset. It connects cordlessly to any Bluetooth-enabled cell phone and has a long 7-hour battery life.

This unit has a flexible, soft-touch headset for comfortable fit on either ear. The microphone is of the noise-canceling type, and it comes with a convenient carrying case that doubles as a charging station.

Model: Mobile Bluetooth Headset
Manufacturer: Logitech
(www.logitech.com)
Type: Bluetooth wireless
Price: $99.95

Plantronics M3500 Bluetooth Headset

The Pantronics M3500 is another high-quality wireless headset that works with any Bluetooth-enabled phone. It lets you roam up to 30 feet from your phone while you're talking.

Plantronics's Audio IQ technology improves what you hear in noisy environments. The headset also includes active noise cancellation and an integrated digital signal processor (DSP), which work to reduce background noise and ensure clearer voice transmissions.

Model: M3500
Manufacturer: Plantronics
(www.plantronics.com)
Type: Bluetooth wireless
Price: $169.95

Cases and Holders

Even with a small pocket-sized phone, it pays to invest in some sort of case or holder—not only to protect your phone, but also to make it easier to access.

You don't have to spend a lot of money on a cell phone holder; you can pick up a belt-clip pouch or holster at any consumer electronics store for less than $10. But if you want something a little more stylish, check out the cases I talk about on the following pages. These are true designer cases that are made of quality materials and are quite functional.

And, while you're looking, don't forget the e-Holster (www.eholster.com), which I talked about back on p. 117. This is a case that you wear like a shoulder holster, which lets you do a cool quick draw when you have to answer your phone. It's a high-security way to carry an expensive portable device—and, when combined with a wireless headset/microphone, lets you look like a Secret Service agent on a mission for the President!

DIGITS

Leo's Pick

DIGITS is a line of cool-looking bags for cell phones and other portable devices. Each DIGITS case comes with both a belt loop and a shoulder strap, as well as a battery loop, "for warming your power supplies." Inside, it's extremely well-padded with a soft microfibre lining; outside, there's an easy-access front pocket and a see-through mesh pocket for extra gadgets. The case is made of a strong, waterproof fabric, and a protective seal keeps dust and dirt away from the merchandise.

The best thing about DIGITS, however, is the company's website. The promotional copy is…well, beyond mere description. Here's a sampling:

"Complete Sporty Guy Range for cruisers not losers. Here's the Sporty Guy. He's more than one. He's a whole range. In his pull-up socks and slippery shorts, his head-band and shuttlebuscock, he's where it gets digital. Do ya didjit."

I don't pretend to understand what any of that means, but I'm pretty sure it's groovy, man. Even better are the product photos, which show a spikey-haired naked hippy chick modeling each of the cases. (The site points out that she's 5'8" tall, in case that matters.) You gotta see it to believe it.

Crumpler makes DIGIT cases for a variety of cell phones, PDAs, digital cameras, and other portable devices. You get your choice of gray/black, blue/orange, and brown/tan color combinations. And, since you're a cruiser, not a loser, you'll probably like what you see.

> **Model:** DIGITS
> **Manufacturer:** Crumpler (www.crumplerusa.com)
> **Price:** $20–$60

AccuCase Cell Phone Cases

Bianchi makes the AccuCase line of sturdy, practical fabric cell phone cases. They use an open design (the phone slides in from the top), so you have easy access to your phone. A zippered closure keeps your phone secure, and the case clips to your belt.

The company makes three sizes of cases, for different sized-phones. Cases come in black, titanium, and burgundy colors.

Model: AccuCase
Manufacturer: Bianchi
(www.accucase.com)
Price: $20

FastDraw Cases

FastDraw cases are different from other cases in that they don't clip onto your belt or have a shoulder holster. Instead, they slip comfortably inside your waistband—or slip over the sun visor in your car.

The company obviously got its idea from the type of badge/ID holders popular with law enforcement officers. (They also sell this type of badge wallet, if you're interested.) The cases are made of lamb skin and are fully lined and reinforced.

Model: Original FastDraw
Manufacturer: FastDraw Products
(www.fastdrawproducts.com)
Price: $44.95

Chargers/Batteries

If you talk a lot on your mobile phone, you know how easy it is to run down the phone's battery. Then you have to hunt for your charging cable, track down the nearest AC power outlet, and wait for the thing to recharge.

Or not.

Several companies make gadgets that give you more options when it comes to recharging your cellular phone. These are particularly useful gadgets if you don't have your normal charging cable with you, of if you're not in easy reach of a power outlet.

Perhaps the most unusual charging option is the SideWinder. As the name implies, you get your power by winding it up, with the side-mounted crank. When your phone runs out of power, wherever you are, just attach it to the SideWinder and start cranking. It's great for emergencies.

Also cool—and less work—is Cellboost, a disposable external battery that attaches to the bottom of most any cell phone. Just plug the Cellboost into your phone and get an extra hour's talk time or charge. If you're smart, you'll carry a couple of these around in your purse or briefcase, just in case.

Finally, if you have your laptop PC with you, you can use ZIP-LINQ's ZIP-CELL cables to recharge your cell phone from your laptop. Just connect one end of the ZIP-CELL cable to your cell phone and the other to your PC's USB port; recharging commences automatically.

SideWinder Emergency Charger

Leo's Pick

The SideWinder is the emergency charger to take with you when you're camping or otherwise away from normal AC power. It's small and lightweight (just 2.5 oz.), but it puts out more power than a typical plug-in charger.

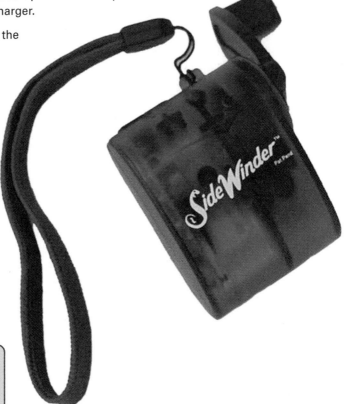

More accurately, it lets *you* put out the power. That's because it generates power when you rotate the SideWinder's side-mounted crank. Just 2 minutes of cranking gives you more than 6 minutes of talk time. To talk longer, just crank some more. It also contains an emergency LED flashlight that runs for 5 minutes with just 30 seconds of cranking.

To charge your phone, just attach it to the SideWinder and start cranking. The SideWinder comes with power adapter tips for the most popular cell phone models. Additional tips are available from the manufacturer.

Model: SideWinder
Manufacturer: Innovative Solutions & Technologies (www.sidewindercharger.com)
Price: $24.95

Cellboost

Cellboost is a compact, low-cost, disposable battery/charger. It works with most cell phone models and provides instant power for a run-down phone.

Each Cellboost provides 60 minutes of talk time, while simultaneously charging your phone. Just plug it into the bottom of your phone, and you're good to go.

Model: Cellboost
Manufacturer: Compact Power Systems, Inc. (www.cellboost.com)
Price: $9.95

ZIP-CELL-M01 USB Phone Charger

The ZIP-CELL is a phone charge cable that lets you connect your cell phone to the USB port of your notebook computer and recharge directly from your PC. The cord is retractable, so it's easy to pack; with the ZIP-CELL, you no longer need to carry your phone's bulky charger with you when you travel.

Versions of the ZIP-CELL are available for most popular cell phone models. You can also attach an optional wall adapter or cigarette lighter adapter for more traditional AC or DC charging options.

Model: ZIP-CELL-M01
Manufacturer: ZIP-LINQ (www.ziplinq.com)
Price: $19.99

Other Cool Phone Gadgets

Walk into any cellular phone or consumer electronics store and you see a ton of different gadgets you can use with your mobile phone. Most of these accessories are somewhat generic, and not worth specific mention here. But there are a handful of truly unique gadgets you can use with your phone, and they bear attention.

The first gadget is the Dock-N-Talk, which lets you use your normal home phones with your cellular service. It's a great device if you're thinking of shutting off your land-line service to go all cellular.

Next up are a couple of phone-specific gadgets. The Nokia Music Stand works with specific FM-enabled Nokia phones to play music from your cell phone in a desktop music system. The Sony Ericsson Bluetooth Car Kit lets you use your

Sony Ericsson phone to control a small radio-operated toy car. Both are worth looking at if you have compatible Nokia or Sony Ericsson phones.

The PowerSwipe is a gadget of use in very specific applications—notably, if you're trying to run a business on the road. It lets you use just about any mobile phone to obtain credit card authorizations. It's great if you're a salesperson on the road or offer any kind of in-home service.

Finally, the Pretender isn't a cell phone gadget per se, but it can be used with any telephone. It generates a variety of background noises you can use to annoy telemarketers or lets you disguise your voice digitally. It's a lot more fun than you might think.

Read on to learn more.

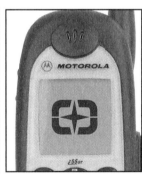

PhoneLabs Dock-N-Talk

PhoneLabs's Dock-N-Talk is a docking station that turns your wireless service into wired phone service. Dock your cell phone in the Dock-N-Talk, and then use your normal home phones (corded or cordless) to make and receive calls via your cellular phone service.

This is the perfect gadget if you want to completely get rid of traditional land-line phone service. Just dock your cell phone, and then use any phone in your house to connect to your mobile service. You can even take advantage of the new local number portability to move your land-line number to a cell phone but retain use of your land-line phones.

The Dock-N-Talk works with more than 150 cell phone models. It utilizes and transfers features like voice recognition, caller ID, and SMS message alerts from your cell phone to other phones in your house. You can even switch an active call seamlessly from cell phone to home phone, and vice versa.

PhoneLabs also sells an optional Bluetooth Module ($69.99) that you can use to connect your cell phone wirelessly to the main Dock-N-Talk unit.

Model: Dock-N-Talk
Manufacturer: PhoneLabs (www.phonelabs.com)
Price: $139.99

CAR-100 Bluetooth Car Kit

The CAR-100 isn't a phone kit for your car, but rather a car for your phone. That is, it's a match-box-sized toy electric car that can be radio-controlled by any Sony Ericsson phone, using Bluetooth wireless technology.

Use the keys on the phone's keypad to control the car. The car runs for an hour on a charge and recharges by connecting to the bottom of your phone. Totally useless, I know—but lots of fun!

Model: CAR-100
Manufacturer: Sony Ericsson (www.sonyericsson.com)
Price: $93

Nokia Music Stand

Nokia's Music Stand works with compatible Nokia cell phones that have built-in FM radios. Just insert your phone into the Music Stand and get ready to listen to room-filling music. It also charges your phone while it's inserted.

The Music Stand contains a built-in stereo amplifier and pair of speakers. It also has a built-in microphone, which lets you use the unit for hands-free speaker phone calls.

Model: Music Stand
Manufacturer: Nokia (www.nokia.com)
Price: $99

Creditel PowerSwipe

The Creditel PowerSwipe lets you swipe and transmit credit card information via selected Internet-enabled cell phones. It's ideal for accepting business payments in the field; you don't have to call the main office to obtain credit card authorization.

Your cell phone sits in the PowerSwipe dock. Swipe the credit card through the slot in the dock, and then securely transmit the encrypted credit card information via your cell phone. Approval numbers are displayed on your cell phone's display.

Model: PowerSwipe
Manufacturer: Creditel
(www.creditelcorp.com)
Price: $249, plus monthly subscription and per-transaction charges

The Pretender

This is a fun little gizmo that performs two functions. First, it generates four sounds you can play into your telephone handset to get you off the hook when you receive an unwanted call. Press a button and generate a baby cry, a dog bark, a doorbell ring, or a call waiting sound. "Sorry, I have another call coming in." Clever!

In addition, the Pretender also functions as a digital voice changer. You get six settings to distort your voice and make yourself unrecognizable to whomever you're talking to. A single woman can give herself a man's voice, or a mischievous male can make himself sound like a robot, whatever works for you. Sounds like fun to me.

Model: The Pretender P8970
Manufacturer: Safety Technology
(www.safetytechnolgoy.com)
Price: $79

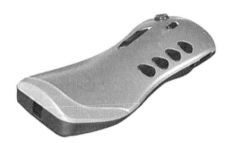

Game Gadgets

7

Game Controllers

Playing games is serious business, as you can tell from the plethora of game controllers on the market today. You can find game controllers to fit just about any type of game you want to play.

When you're shopping for a controller, here are the major styles to choose from:

- **Gamepad**—The default controller for most videogame consoles, complete with a variety of buttons and the directional D-pad. It's versatile enough for just about any type of game.

- **Flight/combat stick**—A type of joystick with 360° movement and firing buttons; it's ideal for flight games.

- **Racing wheel**—Combines a full-function steering wheel, gear shift, and gas and brake pedals for playing racing games. (Some wheels implement the gas and brake functions as buttons on the wheel.)

- **Light gun**—Lets you shoot at onscreen objects; it's ideal for all types of shooting games.

What should you look for in a game controller? No matter which type of controller you use, here are some of the most important features:

- **Force feedback**—Using one or more built-in motors and controlling software, it vibrates the controller to correspond with onscreen action.

- **Programmable buttons**—On PC game controllers, these let you dedicate one or more push buttons to specific game actions.

- **Wireless operation**—Cuts the cord between you and the game console.

- **Cooling technology**—Puts a fan at your hands to keep you cool during hot gaming sessions.

Most important, make sure you like how the controller feels and how it plays. Make sure it's sturdy enough to hold up through intense game play, is comfortable enough for long gaming sessions, and has a quality feel. Then plug it in, settle back, and start playing!

Logitech Cordless RumblePad

This award-winning game controller is one of the best general gamepads on the market—and it's wireless, to boot!

The Cordless RumblePad connects to your PC via 2.4GHz RF signals, no cables necessary. It has a 20-foot range, so you can put some space between you and the screen. And the wireless operation gives you the freedom to twist, turn, and move around without tangling or unplugging any cables.

As to the gamepad itself, the RumblePad incorporates realistic vibration feedback effects that let you feel every explosion as you play. Two independent vibration feedback motors provide maximum tactile feedback, and you can customize the amount of feedback generated.

The gamepad features dual analog mini-sticks, an eight-way D-pad, 11 programmable buttons, and a slide throttle. The mini-sticks are particularly responsive, with precise 360° movement. Even better, you can customize all the buttons and "double" the number of buttons by using the shift button.

Logitech's software lets you quickly switch between different controller configurations for different games. The RumblePad includes profiles for hundreds of popular games, and you can easily download new game profiles from the Internet.

All in all, a great force feedback game controller—with the added bonus of wireless operation.

> **Model:** Cordless RumblePad
> **Manufacturer:** Logitech (www.logitech.com)
> **Price:** $49.95

Nyko Air Flo EX

Just call me Cool Hand Leo. Nyko's Air Flo EX gamepad features patented hand-cooling technology with air vents to eliminate sweaty hands during long gaming sessions. It incorporates a multispeed fan for custom cooling—and it really works.

The gamepad features force feedback technology with a variable vibration function, comfortable rubberized grips, and pressure-sensitive analog buttons. Versions are available for the PlayStation 2, Xbox, and PC platforms.

Model: Air Flo EX
Manufacturer: Nyko (www.nyko.com)
Price: $29.99

Gravis Xterminator Force

If you want a no-compromise high-quality game controller, check out the Gravis Xterminator Force, one of the most popular controllers among hardcore gamers. The Xterminator Force offers one of the best force feedback systems today, with proportional-control D-pad and flippers. Just push the D-pad—and it pushes back!

This rugged gamepad offers six programmable buttons and an ultra-comfortable design. There's even a click-on Precision Mode for improved accuracy.

Model: Xterminator Force
Manufacturer: Gravis (www.gravis.com)
Price: $69.99

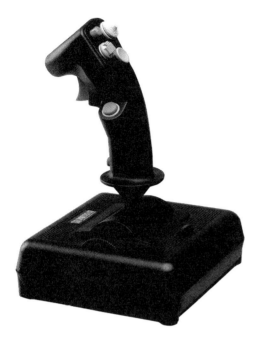

Belkin Nostromo SpeedPad n52

The Nostromo SpeedPad is a truly unique game controller, combining keyboard and gamepad functionality into one compact device. It's an unusual but extremely functional game controller, especially effective for first-person shooters.

This cool little gadget includes a 14-button keypad, a mouse wheel, and a directional pad, all in one cleverly designed unit. The keypad uses a variety of shift operations to provide up to 104 different functions.

Model: n52
Manufacturer: Belkin (www.belkin.com)
Price: $49.99

Combatstick 568 USB

The Combatstick 568 USB is simply the best flight stick controller available today. It has a realistic three-axis F-16 handle, side slide throttle wheel, and 18 buttons, complete with 34 programmable functions. You even get dual rotary trim controls for precision adjustment of ailerons and elevators.

The best thing about this flight stick is its sturdy base and solid feel. This is one controller that just feels right—and has excellent game play.

Model: Combatstick 568 USB
Manufacturer: CH Products
(www.chproducts.com)
Price: $109.95

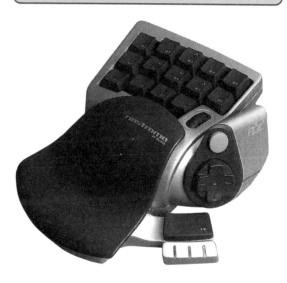

NASCAR Pro Digital 2 Racing Wheel

When it comes to racing games, why not drive with the big boys? This officially licensed racing wheel is notable for its 10 1/4" full-sized rubber-coated wheel, which makes it feel like you're driving an actual NASCAR car.

The wheel features four programmable buttons and two wheel-mounted shift paddles, or you can use the short-throw manual shifter. Below, you get two realistic racing-style pedals on a non-slide base. It's a great-feeling wheel!

Model: NASCAR Pro Digital 2
Manufacturer: Thrustmaster (us.thrustmaster.com)
Price: $59.99

Logitech MOMO Racing Force Feedback Wheel

From Logitech comes a force-feedback racing wheel designed by the racing professionals at MOMO—one of the world's leading designers of automotive accessories. The advanced force feedback lets you feel every turn, slide, and bump, and the comfortable grip offers precise steering.

The steering wheel includes two paddle shifters, just like the F1 drivers use, so you can shift without taking your hands off the wheel—or you can use the manual shifter for precise sequential shifting. The foot pedals are mounted on a large stable base with a unique carpet grip system.

Model: MOMO Racing Force Feedback Wheel
Manufacturer: Logitech (www.logitech.com)
Price: $99.95

Silent Scope Light Rifle

Microsoft's Xbox has a number of cool light gun games, but to play them you need a quality gun—which is where the Silent Scope comes in. This light rifle is constructed of neon green plastic with a rubberized butt and features a motion-activated scope. It offers realistic linear kickback, so it feels just like shooting a real rifle.

The Silent Scope operates in normal, burst auto reload, and auto reload auto fire modes. The stock, barrel, and scope are removable for storage, and it's fully HDTV-compatible—so you can practice your shooting with a big screen TV!

Model: Silent Scope
Manufacturer: Pelican
(www.pelicanperformance.com)
Price: $49.99

TrackIR 3-Pro

Now this is a different way to fly. The TrackIR 3-Pro is a high-performance optical head-tracking system that enables hands-free view control with many popular flight simulators, including Microsoft Flight Simulator 2004, Lock On: Modern Air Combat, and Falcon 4.0. It works by bouncing infrared light off your forehead; the reflected light is imaged by a CMOS sensor and the resulting video signal is passed to the pre-processing electronics.

Sit the TrackIR stand on top of your monitor and aim it at your forehead. A slight turn of your head causes your in-game view to pan in any direction, independent of mouse, joystick, or keyboard commands. It lets you look out windows and around the cockpit as if you were in a real plane!

Model: TrackIR 3-Pro
Manufacturer: NaturalPoint
(www.naturalpoint.com)
Price: $139

Adapters and Switchers

Connecting your videogame console used to be a straightforward affair—just plug it into the coaxial input on the back of your TV. But newer game consoles feature high-quality video and audio that require a more sophisticated connection. Microsoft's Xbox even has a high-definition video mode for the best-looking game screens imaginable. (To connect to an HDTV set, you need Microsoft's Xbox High Definition AV pack, which I'll discuss in a few pages.)

You should be sure to use the highest-quality connection available between your game box and TV, which is typically a composite or S-Video connection. Likewise, run the audio through your home audio system, so you can get big sound from big speakers.

If you don't have enough free connections on the back of your TV, invest in some type of A/V switcher. I already discussed JVC's all-digital switcher (p. 195), but that might be overkill for the average gamer. Instead, consider the push-button Pro System Selector, which offers just enough switching options to get the job done.

Finally, if you want to use your PlayStation 2 or Xbox to play games online, take a look at Nyko's Wireless Net Extender. This little gizmo lets you connect your game console to a broadband Internet connection wirelessly, so you can enjoy real-time online gaming. It's a great way to test your skills against other gamers worldwide.

    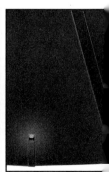

Nyko Wireless Net Extender

Enter the world of online gaming, over the Internet, with Nyko's Wireless Net Extender. This useful device connects your PlayStation 2 or Xbox console to the Internet—without wires—for real-time online game play.

You get two small cubes that connect your game console to your DSL or cable modem. The cubes use RF technology, so there's no need to run any wires; the system has a 100-foot range.

The Net Extender is compatible with any broadband modem and any router that has a built-in Ethernet port. Setup is plug-and-play, so anybody can do it.

With the Net Extender connected and configured, you can enjoy lag-free online gaming with any player connected to the Internet. You can even use multiple Net Extender pairs in the same house—they're matched and coded so there won't be any interference.

So, go online without worrying about running wires from here to there. Just connect the Net Extender and start playing!

Model: Wireless Net Extender
Manufacturer: Nyko (www.nyko.com)
Price: $129.99

Pro System Selector

If you find yourself disconnecting one device to connect another, it's time to invest in a decent audio/video switcher, such as Pelican's Pro System Selector. Connect everything once and then switch from one component to another with the touch of a front-panel button.

The Pro System Selector is the ultimate control device for your home gaming system. You get rear inputs for composite video, S-Video, component video, digital optical audio, analog audio (R/L), and Ethernet, as well as two full-function outputs. It's all packed in a sleek metal case with lighted interchangeable name plates for all your equipment.

Model: PL-957
Manufacturer: Pelican (www.pelicanperformance.com)
Price: $99.99

Xbox High Definition AV Pack

Ever see an Xbox game on a big high-definition television? You're in for a treat—the graphics are way impressive.

To connect your Xbox console to an HDTV set, you need the Xbox High Definition AV Pack. This device connects to your Xbox and provides a set of component video outputs to run to any TV that supports 480p, 720p, or 1080p component video signals. It also lets you hear your games in glorious Dolby Digital surround sound; just connect a digital optical cable to any 5.1 channel A/V receiver.

Model: Xbox High Definition AV Pack
Manufacturer: Microsoft (www.xbox.com)
Price: $19.99

Other Cool Game Gadgets

The world of gaming offers ample opportunity to purchase all manner of cool gadgets. I only have room to discuss a few here, but I think you'll agree that these have a high "wow" factor.

First up is a new type of hardware component, the PC game console. This is, quite simply, a stripped-down personal computer tweaked especially for playing games. You connect the game console to any television set, plug in a game controller, and start playing, just as you would with a videogame console. In essence, this type of gadget lets you play PC games the same way you play videogames in the comfort of your living room. Prices are surprisingly affordable—only a little higher than a PlayStation 2 or Xbox console.

Speaking of game consoles, how about a game machine without a console? The TV Games controllers pack a variety of classic video and arcade games into a vintage game controller, which hooks up directly to your TV set. It's kind of cool to once again play Centipede with a real Atari joystick—and not have to bother with hooking up a game console!

Of course, when you're serious about your game play, you want a comfortable gaming environment. That's provided by the PyraMat game chair, which is like a futon with built-in speakers. Just lay back and listen to the game sounds coming from the headrest. It's an extremely comfortable—and surprisingly immersing—way to play the latest videogames.

Finally, how would you like to get to the highest levels of today's most complex videogames—without having to work your way there? Then you need GameShark, a collection of secret codes and cheats that let you skip right to the good stuff. It's a way to play like the pros—even if you're not nearly that good.

    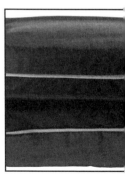

ApeXtreme Media and Game Console

Here's a cool idea: A game console that lets you play PC games on your home TV. The ApeXtreme (pronounced "Apex Extreme," but certainly not spelled that way) brings console functionality to PC games and connects to any TV or home theater system.

The ApeXtreme (I still want to call it the "Ape Extreme," even though I know better) combines a specialized PC, DVD player, and PVR hard-disk recorder in one component-sized unit. Hardware-wise, it has a 40GB hard drive and 256MB memory; it uses an AMD Athlon XP 2000+ microprocessor, with NVIDIA nForce 2 IGP video. The unit has five USB connections, as well as a broadband video connection, and it sells for just $399—cheap for all you get.

Up to four players can connect to the ApeXtreme at the same time. You can also use the unit to view digital photos on your TV (in a slideshow presentation), record television programming to hard disk, and listen to CDs or digital audio files—which makes the ApeXtreme a fairly versatile media center for your living room.

Of course, the ApeXtreme is designed as a PC game machine. To that end, it incorporates Digital Interactive Systems's DISCover Drop and Play engine that lets you load a PC game and play it almost immediately. The engine also automatically installs patches and mods for more than 2,000 games.

Admit it—it's kind of cool to be able to play all your PC games from the comfort of your living room couch!

Model: ApeXtreme
Manufacturer: Apex (www.apexdigitalinc.com)
Price: $399

Phantom Game Receiver/Service

Here's another PC-based gaming device disguised as a game subscription service. The Phantom Network, scheduled to launch in November 2004, offers a library of PC game titles. You can try, rent, or buy games on demand and then have the games streamed to you on demand over the Internet.

The Phantom Game Receiver is free when you purchase a two-year subscription to the Phantom Network or $199 if you buy it outright. It connects to your TV and any broadband Internet connection and lets you play the games you buy right in your living room.

> **Model:** Phantom Gaming Service
> **Manufacturer:** Infinium Labs
> (www.phantom.net)
> **Price:** $29.95/month (Phantom Game Receiver available separately for $199)

TV Games Game Consoles

TV Games let you experience old-school gaming on any TV—no PC or game console required. These are portable, self-contained game systems; everything is contained in the joystick controller device. Just connect the joystick to your TV and start playing.

Each joystick device contains six or so popular games. Different models include Activision (Pitfall, River Raid, and so on), Atari (Pong, Asteroids, Centipede, and so on), Atari Paddle (Breakout, Street Racer, and so on), Classic Arcade Pinball, Ms. Pac-Man (Ms. Pac-Man, Pole Position, Galaga, and so on), NAMCO (Pac-Man, Dig Dug, Galaxian, and so on), and special Spiderman and SpongeBob SquarePants collections.

> **Model:** TV Games
> **Manufacturer:** JAKKS Pacific, Inc.
> (www.jakkstvgames.com)
> **Price:** $20

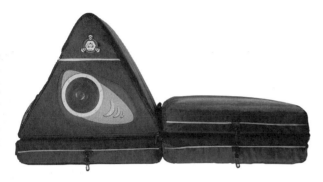

Pyramat PM300 Game Chair

This is one cool gadget. It's a gaming chair that unfolds like a futon or folds up into a 20" cube. The headset contains a powerful 25-watt sub-woofer and two surround-sound side speakers; connect it your videogame console for the ultimate gaming experience.

It's an extremely comfortable chair/mat/whatever, with form-fitting cushions that support your back and neck during long gaming sessions. There's even a wired remote control that lets you adjust the volume and rumble intensity. Connect multiple units together for multiplayer gaming—if you have enough floor space!

Model: PM300
Manufacturer: Pyramat
(www.pyramat.com)
Price: $149.99

GameShark

The GameShark is a software-based game enhancer that lets you access final levels; hidden areas; and secret characters, weapons, and vehicles in your favorite videogames. Load it up and get access to an incredible number of secret codes and game saves; you can download additional codes from the GameShark.com website.

Different versions of GameShark are available for PlayStation 2, Xbox, GameCube, and Game Boy Advance. It's the perfect accessory for the hardcore gamer—or for anyone who wants to get to the highest levels, as fast as possible!

Model: GameShark
Manufacturer: GameShark (www. gameshark.com)
Price: $24.99 (Xbox), $29.99 (GameCube), $39.99 (Game Boy Advance), $44.99 (PS2)

Automotive Gadgets

8

GPS Navigation Systems

Back on p. 101 I talked about portable GPS navigation devices. These gadgets are great for all sorts of navigation purposes, but they can be a little awkward to use when you're driving. A better solution is one that's purpose-built—the automotive GPS device.

A car GPS system comes with either a windshield or dashboard mount and is typically battery powered, although some can also tap into your car's DC power. Like the portable devices, they track your location using a dozen or so geostationary global positioning system satellites and display maps and directions on a large LCD screen.

Car GPS devices typically come configured for auto travel, with a variety of points of interest—gas stations, restaurants, hotels, ATMs, and so on—preprogrammed into memory. You also get built-in road maps, of course, as well as turn-by-turn driving instructions.

The best of the car GPS systems let you read the driving instructions onscreen or hear them from a computer-generated voice. The latter option is particularly useful when you're driving, so you don't have to take your eyes off the road.

If you do take your eyes off the road, look for the different kinds of displays offered by various devices. You typically have your choice of traditional overhead-view road maps or text instructions; some devices even provide a 3D view of the road as you drive it.

The other big difference between devices is whether the maps and points of interest are preloaded onto the device's hard drive or have to be downloaded from your computer (typically onto media cards) as you need them. The advantage of preloading is convenience, of course; the advantage of load-as-you-go systems is that you can download updated maps as they become available. In any case, make sure you get adequate map coverage for whatever regions you frequently travel.

Other features to look for are portability, which lets you take the unit with you when you change cars or use it in a rental car when you travel; audible alerts when you near turns; and the ability to quickly recalculate your route if you make a detour or take a wrong turn. Also make sure you're comfortable with the size and viewability of the display. Purchase the right unit, and you'll never get lost again!

Magellan RoadMate 500

Leo's Pick

My favorite car GPS system is Magellan's RoadMate 500. This little puppy does just about everything you need it to, and does it accurately. It's built around the same technology Magellan uses in the NeverLost system you find in Hertz rental cars.

This is one of those units that doesn't come with any maps built in. Instead, you download maps of the regions you're traveling in to a memory card and insert the memory card into the device. Magellan supplies some very accurate U.S. and Canadian maps on four CD-ROMs.

The RoadMate provides turn-by-turn instructions, with voice prompting. You can choose from three onscreen views: True View (a cool 3D view with actual road layout), Map View (standard overhead map), and Maneuver List (text instructions). I really like the True View, which provides a somewhat realistic first-person visual view of your route as you drive it.

When it comes to choosing a route, you have four options: shortest time, shortest distance, least use of freeways, and most use of freeways. You can use the Road Exclusion feature to avoid a certain road or route, and the Auto Reroute function automatically calculates a new route when you decide to take a detour or make a wrong turn.

Magellan's Points of Interest (POI) database provides comprehensive listings of more than two million businesses, banks, hotels, airports, gas stations, ATMs, and restaurants, so it's easy to find just about anything you want near wherever you are. The unit itself is lightweight and easily portable, and it tracks 12 GPS satellites for accuracy within 3 meters.

Model: RoadMate 500
Manufacturer: Magellan (www.magellangps.com)
Price: $1,199.99

Garmin StreetPilot 2620

Unlike the other car GPS units, Garmin's StreetPilot 2620 has all the maps preloaded onto the unit's hard drive. This lets the StreetPilot store detailed maps of the entire United States, plus metropolitan areas of Canada—no downloading necessary. The unit also has a huge database of five million points of interest—including lodging, restaurants, gas stations, and local attractions.

Feature-wise, Garmin provides everything you'd expect—a high-resolution color touch-screen display, voice-prompted turn-by-turn instructions, and road segment and area avoidance. It comes with an integrated dash mount and portable bean-bag mount.

Model: StreetPilot 2620
Manufacturer: Garmin (www.garmin.com)
Price: $1,500

Navman iCN 630

The Navman iCN 630 provides many of the same features as the Magellan RoadMate, but at a much lower price. Like the RoadMate, the Navman unit is easily portable, so you can move it from car to car; it even comes with its own carrying case.

You get turn-by-turn directions, of course, as well as voice directions. You can choose from either a male or female voice in one of six languages (English, French, German, Dutch, Spanish, and Italian). Navman even provides its own 3D map views and includes map data for the United States and Canada. If you take the wrong turn, the Back-on-Track function automatically recalculates your route.

Model: iCN 630
Manufacturer: Navman
(www.navmanusa.com)
Price: $799.95

Hands-free Car Phone Kits

If you have a cell phone and a car (and you probably have both), the next must-have gadget is a hands-free car phone kit. Talking while driving is tricky enough, but when you have to juggle holding a cell phone while you shift and turn, things can get more than a little dangerous. This is why many states and countries are making car phone kits mandatory; it's a matter of safety.

The typical car phone kit connects to your phone and then plugs into your car's cigarette lighter for power. Calls are routed from your phone to the car kit, which usually has a built-in speaker and microphone. Some kits route your phone's audio through your car's stereo system. Other kits have a clip-on microphone instead of the normal speakerphone-type mic. There are even some wireless kits out there that eliminate the need for any connecting cables.

Of course, you don't have to use a dedicated car phone kit. Another viable option is to use a standard cell phone headset, like the ones I discussed on p. 210. The goal is to get the phone out of your hand, however you go about it.

By the way, if you have a Bluetooth-enabled phone, pay particular attention to my Leo's Pick kit: Anycom's Car Kit Blue. This is a kit that combines a Bluetooth wireless headset with a wireless hands-free car kit. The Bluetooth technology makes for a seamless transition from headset to car kit; just place the earphone in the car kit holder to hand off the call to your car kit's speaker and microphone. It's a pretty neat little system, probably the way all hands-free car kits will go sometime in the future.

   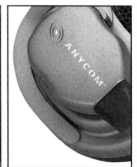 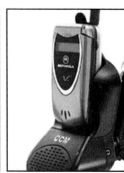

Anycom Car Kit Blue HCC-110

This kit does it all. It combines a wireless headset with a wireless hands-free car kit, thanks to remarkable Bluetooth technology.

The headset is of the Bluetooth wireless variety and works with any Bluetooth-equipped cellular phone. Just attach the earpiece/microphone unit around your ear, synch it up with your phone, and you can start talking. The headset delivers 3 hours of talk time on a charge and has a 10 meter range.

Use the headset normally; then when you get into the car, place the headset into the cradle of the car kit adapter. Now the car kit piece of the system is activated and all your calls are routed through the car kit's speaker and microphone. The car kit adapter plugs into your car's cigarette lighter and also serves to recharge the wireless headset.

The unique combination of headset/car kit lets you switch between hands-free and headset in the middle of a call, which is great if you need more privacy—or have to leave your car. The car kit also includes a wireless clip-on microphone that can be placed anywhere in your car for the best fidelity.

If you have a Bluetooth phone, this is definitely the way to go. It doesn't really matter whether you're talking and walking or talking and driving—you're covered no matter what.

Model: HCC-110
Manufacturer: Anycom (www.anycom.com)
Price: $130

CCM Roadster
Hands-free Kit

CCM is the largest manufacturer of third-party car kits for cellular phones, and the Roadster is its most popular model. Just slide your phone into the Roadster's cradle and plug the Roadster into your car's cigarette lighter; it turns your cell phone into a hands-free speakerphone without any attachments or other external accessories.

The Roadster incorporates a powerful built-in microphone and speaker, located in the front of the unit. It features full duplex sound quality, noise reduction technology, and an auto answer function. Roadsters are available for most popular cellular phone models; the company also sells a universal model that fits all phones.

Model: Roadster
Manufacturer: CCM
(www.alternativewireless.com)
Price: $49.95

FoneFree Hands-free
Speakerphone

The FoneFree is a wireless car kit that works with any cell phone. It has a built-in microphone and uses your car's speakers to broadcast audio from your calls—effectively turning your car stereo system into a giant speakerphone.

The FoneFree's universal mount clips to any cellular phone; the matching unit mounts on your car's dashboard. It routes all calls through your car's stereo system using FM frequency 88.7 or 106.5.

Model: FoneFree
Manufacturer: FoneFree
(www.meritline.com)
Price: $19.99

Satellite Radio Receivers

If you're on the road a lot, you know how frustrating it is to have radio stations fade out as you drive out of their broadcast areas. Satellite radio offers the much better alternative of nationwide coverage—you're never out of range. Plus, you get 100 or so channels of entertainment, with a good mix of music and talk, all with high-quality digital sound.

As I first discussed on p. 190, there are two competing satellite radio systems—XM (www.xmradio.com) and Sirius (www.sirius.com). They both offer a great selection of rock, country, jazz, and classical music channels, as well a dozens of news, talk, and sports channels. XM costs $9.99 per month to subscribe; Sirius costs $12.95.

Audio-wise, both sound pretty good in the car—much better than regular FM radio. That said, XM sounds slightly better to my ears; Sirius has some noticeable audio compression that bothers some listeners.

To listen to either XM or Sirius in your car, you need to invest in a satellite radio tuner. You can choose to replace your old car radio with an XM- or Sirius-capable model, add a separate XM or Sirius tuner to your existing in-dash receiver, or use a portable radio "shuttle" unit that sends the satellite radio signals through your car's FM radio or cassette deck. The advantage of a portable unit is that you can move it between your car and home, with an optional home adapter. Of course, you'll also need to install a satellite antenna, which is one more thing to hang on the outside of your car.

One of the things I really like about both the XM and Sirius systems is that the digital stream transmits more than music; there's room for the service to transmit data about the music that's playing, including artist and song information. Most satellite radio receivers have big multiline LCD displays for just this purpose.

Once you get everything installed and subscribed to, you can settle back for a long, enjoyable drive. Satellite radio signals never fade out, which means you can listen to the same station from New York to San Francisco. And, unlike AM or FM radio, most XM and Sirius channels are commercial free!

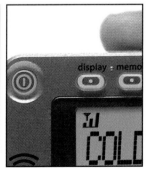

Kenwood Sirius Satellite Radio System

Kenwood's Sirius satellite radio system lets you add satellite radio to virtually any current car stereo system. It consists of the KTC-SR903 satellite tuner and the KCA-R70FM FM adapter/controller (and a matching satellite antenna, of course). Mount the satellite tuner under your dash and the FM adapter/controller in your dash, alongside your current receiver. The Sirius signal is received by the satellite tuner and then fed through your car's existing FM radio—or an auxiliary input, if your receiver has one.

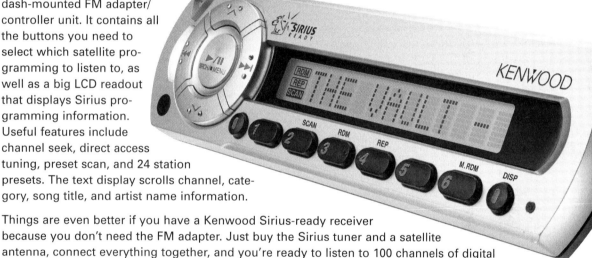

You control everything via the dash-mounted FM adapter/controller unit. It contains all the buttons you need to select which satellite programming to listen to, as well as a big LCD readout that displays Sirius programming information. Useful features include channel seek, direct access tuning, preset scan, and 24 station presets. The text display scrolls channel, category, song title, and artist name information.

Things are even better if you have a Kenwood Sirius-ready receiver because you don't need the FM adapter. Just buy the Sirius tuner and a satellite antenna, connect everything together, and you're ready to listen to 100 channels of digital programming.

Model: KTC-SR903 (tuner), KCA-R70FM (FM adapter/controller)
Manufacturer: Kenwood (www.kenwoodusa.com)
System: Sirius
Price: $200 (tuner), $100 (FM adapter/controller)

JVC Plug 'n' Play Sirius Radio

JVC's KT-SR1000 is an in-dash Sirius radio with a unique PDA-like look. It's a vertical design, with the 132 × 65 pixel LCD display sitting on top of the operating buttons.

The unit is relatively small, so it won't infringe too much on passenger space, and it easily connects to your existing car stereo system. It even comes with a wireless remote control, in case you have your seat pushed too far back to reach the dash.

> **Model:** KT-SR1000
> **Manufacturer:** JVC (www.jvc.com) **System:** Sirius
> **Price:** $99.95

Audiovox Sirius Shuttle Receiver

Audiovox's SIRPNP2 is a portable satellite receiver. You can use it in your car (with the optional SIRCK2 car kit) or in your home (with the optional SIRHK1 home docking kit or SIRBB1 boombox). At just 5.2" × 3.4" × 1.9", it's small enough to fit in a shirt pocket.

The SIRPNP2 and the car kit together will set you back around $150, which is quite affordable. The unit itself has a large, easy-to-read orange LCD display; the big channel selector knob provides quick access to all 100 Sirius programming streams. Even neater is the Memory Capture function that stores 20 of your favorite songs, searches incoming streams, and then alerts you when your songs are playing.

> **Model:** SIRPNP2
> **Manufacturer:** Audiovox
> (www.audiovox.com)
> **System:** Sirius
> **Price:** $99.95 (SIRPNP2), $49.99 (SIRCK2 car kit)

Delphi XM Roady

Delphi's XM Roady is similar to Audiovox's Sirius SIRPNP2, in that it's a portable receiver you can use either in your car or at home. The big difference (aside from the XM versus Sirius thing) is that the Roady comes with everything you need to use it in any car—micro-antenna, universal mounting bracket, and cassette adapter. (An optional wireless FM adapter is also available.)

The Roady is a stylish little unit that you can personalize with seven back-lit color displays and three interchangeable faceplates. You can even take it with you and use at home, with the optional Roady Home Kit.

Model: Roady
Manufacturer: Delphi (www.xmradio.com)
System: XM
Price: $119.99

Alpine In-Dash AM/FM/XM/CD Receiver

This Alpine unit is the world's first integrated in-dash XM radio/CD tuner. Just add an XM antenna and pay your subscription fee, and you're ready to listen to satellite radio anywhere in the United States.

Spec-wise, this puppy has a 50W × 4 power amplifier, full CD/CD-R/CD-RW playback, sub-woofer level control, and MediaXpander tone controls. It can also be used to control an optional CD changer. If you're in the mood for a new car audio system and you want the benefits of satellite radio, this is the one to get!

Model: CDA-9820XM
Manufacturer: Alpine (www.alpine-usa.com)
System: XM
Price: $350

DVD Video Systems

Back when I was a kid, the only entertainment I had on long car trips was a good book. Today, you have lots of ways to keep your kids entertained—the best of which might be an in-car DVD video system.

A mobile video system consists of a DVD player (which doubles as a CD player, of course), an LCD screen, and some sort of audio connection. Most video systems connect to and use your car's existing stereo system; some even have dual-zone operation, which lets you listen to the radio in the front seat while your kids listen to movie sound in the back. For more privacy, consider having your kids use headphones—maybe even a set of wireless phones, for best mobility.

When it comes to screen placement, you have some choices. Most in-car systems are dash-mounted, with the screen sliding out and flipping up for viewing. The only problem with this type of system is that rear-seat passengers have to view the screen from between the front seats, which can be problematic. The benefit of an in-dash system is that you can use it for more than video; the touch-screen can display map and navigation data, be connected to a rear-firing video camera (great for when you're backing up), or be used to control the entire audio system.

The other option is to mount one or more displays in the rear passenger compartment. You can find screens that mount on the roof and fold down for viewing, screens that attach to the rear of your car's front seats, and screens built in to the back of front-seat headrests. See your installer for additional options.

Of course, mobile video systems aren't just for watching movies. Most systems have input jacks that let your kids connect their favorite videogame systems—which is another great way to keep them happy during long trips.

Whichever type of system you get, you have a major installation challenge ahead of you. It's probably best to have a professional installer tackle the job, especially if you get any type of rear-seat displays. There's a lot of cable-running to do, and unless you're well-versed in what goes where, it's a job for a pro!

Pioneer Front/Rear Seat DVD System

Leo's Pick

Combine Pioneer's P6600DVD front-seat video system and AVD-W6200 rear-seat display and you get the best of two worlds. You get yourself a monitor up front to watch, and your kids get a seatback-mounted monitor of their own. (You can even add a second rear-seat display if you like.)

Up front, the dash-mounted DVD player plays both DVDs and CDs, so you're all set for a full multi-media experience. The 6.5" color LCD touch-screen display pops out and flips up when in use and even comes with a wireless remote control, so your rear-seat passengers can rewind and fast forward while you're driving.

The rear-seat display mounts to the headrest pole of a front passenger seat and then pivots into the best position for viewing or stowing. It's a 6.5" widescreen active-matrix color LCD, plenty big for watching movies or playing videogames.

Audio-wise, this is a dual-zone system, so you can listen to audio in the front while your kids watch videos in the back. It incorporates a 50W × 4 power amplifier for big, high-fidelity sound.

The P6600DVD also incorporates an XM radio tuner, so you're all set for satellite reception anywhere in the United States. And, because you already have the display in your dash, you can also add an optional Pioneer Mobile Navigation system for maps and directions.

For all you get, it's an excellent buy—lower priced than some competing dash-only systems. You can add a second rear-seat display and still have a very affordable system.

Model: P6600DVD ($1,600); AVD-W6200 ($600)
Manufacturer: Pioneer (www.pioneerelectronics.com)

Kenwood Excelon In-Dash DVD Receiver

Kenwood's Excelon KVT-915DVD is a self-contained in-dash multimedia system. You get an AM/FM tuner, a DVD/CD player, and (unique among these units) a built-in TV tuner. You can listen to the radio, listen to CDs, watch movies on DVD, or watch local television broadcasts, all from this one unit.

The flip-up display is a 7" 16:9 widescreen unit, with an onscreen GUI interface and touch-screen control. The audio part of the system has built-in Dolby Digital/DTS 5.1 surround sound; you get a 50W × 4 power amplifier, plus a 47W center channel. It's Sirius-ready if you want to go the satellite radio route.

Model: KVT-915DVD
Manufacturer: Kenwood
(www.kenwoodusa.com)
Price: $2,800

Blaupunkt Chicago In-Dash Monitor/DVD/Receiver

The Blaupunkt Chicago is a quality in-dash entertainment system designed to be used with a separate power amplifier. You get a 7" motorized retractable in-dash monitor, a DVD/CD player, and an AM/FM tuner; the unit features a fully integrated Dolby Digital/DTS 5.1 surround sound decoder.

As with most Blaupunkt receivers, the front panel of this one is detachable for increased security. And it lets you download up to seven pictures you can use for video wallpaper when you're not playing movies—very cool.

Model: IVDM-7002
Manufacturer: Blaupunkt
(www.blaupunktusa.com)
Price: $1,599.95

JVC KD-AV7000 In-Dash System

JVC's KD-AV7000 is a full-featured in-dash video entertainment system, based around a 7" touch-screen display with graphical user interface. The display is fully detachable and has motorized tilt (fore and aft) adjustment.

The KD-AV7000 has a 50W × 4 power amplifier, with 35W center channel, and a built-in Dolby Digital/DTS 5.1 surround sound decoder. It's a dual-zone system, which lets you listen to audio in front while playing video sound in the rear. Options include a DVD/CD changer, Sirius satellite radio tuner, TV tuner, and rear-seat mounting cradle.

Model: KD-AV7000
Manufacturer: JVC (www.jvc.com)
Price: $1,599

Alpine Mobile Multimedia Station

Alpine's Mobile Multimedia Station features a unique 7" PulseTouch touch-panel display that uses different vibrations and pressures to simulate pushing a real mechanical button. Audio-wise, it incorporates a 50W × 4 power amplifier; you can add an optional Dolby Digital/DTS surround sound decoder if you want.

Of course, the Mobile Multimedia Station includes a DVD/CD player for your viewing and listening pleasure. It's XM satellite-ready and includes an input for an optional rear camera.

Model: IVA-D300
Manufacturer: Alpine (www.alpine-usa.com)
Price: $1,500

Other Cool Automotive Gadgets

Our final category (of the entire book!) is another "other" category, in this instance featuring cool automotive gadgets that don't fit in any other category. There are lots of automotive accessories out there, but I tried to focus on those that (in general) are technologically interesting.

What types of car-related gadgets are worth your attention? I particularly like Magna Donnelly's VideoMirror, which is a rear-view mirror with a small flip-down monitor attached. Use the VideoMirror with either a rear-seat or bumper-mounted camera to keep tabs on either rear-seat passengers or potential obstacles when you're backing up; it's a good use of existing technology.

Another interesting type of gadget is the data logger. The DriveRight CarChip taps into your car's electronics to monitor performance and troubleshoot problems; it's just like the analysis devices pro mechanics used. Also used by the pros are external performance timers, like the Vector FX2. This little gizmo times your performance in the quarter mile, which can help you hone your racing skills.

I also have a soft spot for electronic entry systems. The typical system, like the one from Essex Electronics, uses a touchpad instead of a key. More unusual is the Knock-In-Key, which lets you unlock your doors by knocking a pattern on the window glass—great if you ever lock your keys in the car.

The other gadgets I discuss are more varied. In order, they include a unique new car washing system (Mr. Clean AutoDry Carwash), a talking tire gauge, an electronic parking aid, and a gizmo you can use to turn red lights into green lights. This last one is designed for emergency personnel only, but it's still pretty neat!

  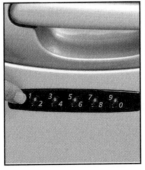  

Magna Donnelly VideoMirror

Leo's Pick

Here's a cool use of two fairly common technologies—small video displays and even smaller video cameras.

Magna Donnelly's VideoMirror is a rear-view mirror with a small flip-down video monitor attached. Combined with a separate mini-camera, the VideoMirror can be used in a number of ways.

For example, the ReversAid system provides an enhanced view behind your car or truck. Mount the mini-camera to the rear of your vehicle, and the rearview image automatically appears on the video screen whenever you shift into reverse.

Similarly, the TowCheck system uses a rear-mounted camera to provide a clear view behind your vehicle whenever you're towing a trailer.

Inside your vehicle, the BabyVue system mounts the small camera in your car's headliner. Aim the camera at the rear-facing baby in your back seat, and you get a constant view of your child while you're driving.

Even better, BabyVue turns into CabinVue when your child is old enough to face forward. Just move the mini-camera to provide a view of all rear-seat passengers.

The nice thing about any of these VideoMirror systems is that, because the video display is forward of your driving position, your eyes stay pointed forward. You never have to turn your head or take your eyes off the road to see what's happening behind you.

> **Model:** VideoMirror
> **Manufacturer:** Magna Donnelly
> (www.donnelly.com)
> **Price:** $449 (TowCheck), $599 (ReversAid or BabyVue), $769 (ReversAid/BabyVue combo)

DriveRight CarChip Data Logger

The DriveRight CarChip is an automotive performance scan tool, just like your mechanic uses. It lets you troubleshoot your engine, log your car's performance, and monitor driver performance. You can identify specific engine problems and trace intermittent ones, as well as view time, date, distance, and speed data.

You can even use the CarChip to clear your car's check engine light and to tell you what triggered it. Just attach the CarChip to your car's OBDII connector, which should be somewhere under the dash; the CarChip starts logging data as soon as you start driving. Connect the serial cable to download data to your PC for further analysis.

Model: CarChip
Manufacturer: Davis Instruments (www.driveright.com)
Price: $139.99

Vector FX2 Performance Timer Accelerometer

Want to get fast and furious? If you're a serious boy racer, you need to check out the Vector FX2, a handheld computer that measures your car's acceleration time, 1/4-mile time, braking distance, G-force, cornering, and horsepower.

The Vector FX2 mounts on your car's windshield and displays the pertinent measurements on an alpine blue display. Just turn it on, press the start button, and put the pedal to the metal. When you pass the 1/4-mile mark, the unit stops recording and instantly displays the run information. It stores up to 10 runs in memory, and you can download the data directly to your PC or PDA.

Model: Vector FX2
Manufacturer: Beltronics (www.beltronics.com)
Price: $249.95

Essex Electronics KE-1600 Keyless Entry System

The KE-1600 is a keyless entry system that installs on any car or truck. Entry is via a horizontal keypad that mounts on your car door; the keypad is weatherproof and illuminated for easy visibility in darkened parking lots and garages.

To unlock the door, enter your personalized three- to eight-digit access code to unlock the door; you can also open the door remotely with a keyfob remote. Once you've entered the valid code, you can enter trailing digits to open the trunk, glove box, or whatever.

The KE-1600 is sold by professional auto installers, so the price varies depending on the dealer and type of installation.

Model: KE-1600
Manufacturer: Essex Electronics (www.keyless.com)
Price: Varies

Knock-In-Key Backup Entry System

From Germany comes this unique answer to the problem of locking your keys in the car. The Knock-In-Key system lets you operate your car's central door lock by knocking a predefined code on the car's side window. You pick a code of between 5 and 12 digits long; knock the right pattern, and your doors unlock.

As an added precaution, the Knock-In-Key system requires you to input a new code after it has unlocked your doors—just in case anyone was watching when you knocked. It installs on any car.

Model: Knock-In-Key
Manufacturer: Knock-In-Key (www.knockinkey.com.au)
Price: $129

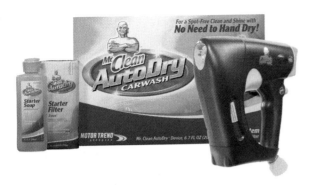

Talking Tire Gauge

Yes, a tire gauge can be cool. The Accutire gauge not only has a neat digital display, but it also tells you the current inflation in a computer-synthesized voice, which is pretty neat.

So, unless you have a high-priced BMW with run-flat tires (another category of gadget altogether!), get yourself a talking tire gauge. You'll find yourself checking your tires every day, just to hear the thing say, "eighteen point two pounds" or some such!

Model: MS-4440
Manufacturer: Measurement Specialties (www.msiusa.com)
Price: $24.99

Mr. Clean AutoDry Carwash

Admittedly, this is an unusual choice—but then again, I never thought such drudgery as washing my car could be so cool. The high-tech Mr. Clean AutoDry system gives your car a professional carwash-like cleaning, right in your own driveway—and you don't even have to dry it yourself!

A good wash is obtained by the special AutoDry soap and the AutoDray filter that clarifies the water stream and removes impurities that can cause spotting. A thin layer of deionized water is left on the car's surface, which quickly evaporates for a spot-free result. It's amazing to watch; water just sheets off your car for totally touchless drying.

Model: Mr. Clean AutoDry Carwash
Manufacturer: Procter & Gamble (www.autodry.com)
Price: $19.99

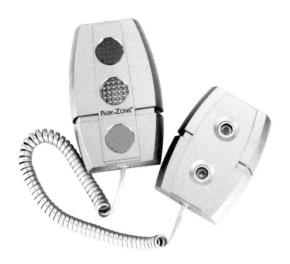

MIRT Mobile Infrared Transmitter

Like the idea of changing stoplights from red to green? Designed for emergency vehicles, the MIRT (mobile infrared transmitter) mounts on your dash and emits an infrared light that triggers traffic light changes from more than 1,500 feet away. The infrared light is invisible to anyone looking, and it can change traffic lights from red to green in less than 3 seconds.

The MIRT is authorized for use by police departments, fire fighters, state and city highway workers, emergency volunteers, doctors, EMS technicians, and the like. However, some (definitely not all) dealers will sell you one on the honor system, so it's your job not to get caught. It can definitely help clear your way through normally busy intersections!

Park-Zone Platinum Parking Aid

Here's a gadget for anyone who has a big car and a small garage. The Park-Zone uses an ultrasonic sensing mechanism to measure the distance from your car to the garage wall as you park; naturally, you have to set up the device beforehand, based on the size of your car and where you want it parked.

Here's how it works. Pull into the garage and see the green light illuminate. As you get closer to the wall, the light changes to yellow and then to red when you reach the correct parking spot. Go any further and you run into the wall—your bad.

Model: PL-957
Manufacturer: Pelican
(www.pelicanperformance.com)
Price: $475

Model: PZ-1500
Manufacturer: Measurement Specialties
(www.msiusa.com)
Price: $32.99

Index

Numbers

3*2*1 DVD Home Entertainment System (Bose), 185

3M Privacy Computer Filters, 45

35mm Slide to Video Adapter (Canon), 170

3650 camera phone (Nokia), 205

6800 mobile phone (Nokia), 199

7230 Wireless Handheld (BlackBerry), 208

A

Abacus Wrist Net Internet Watch, 107

accelerometer (Vector FX2), 256

accessories

iPod accessories

Altec Lansing inMotion Portable Audio System, 73

Belkin Digital Camera Link, 76

Belkin iPod Media Reader, 77

Belkin iPod Voice Recorder, 77

Belkin TuneDok car holder, 76

Griffin iTrip FM transmitter, 75

Groove Purse Tote, 79

iPod Armor, 79

iSkin eVo iPod protector, 78

Monster iCarPlay FM transmitter, 75

naviPod wireless remote control, 74

SportSuit Runabout case, 78

PDA accessories

iBIZ XELA Case/Keyboard, 65

overview, 63

Targus Universal Wireless Keyboard, 65

TomTom Navigator Bluetooth GPS, 64

Veo Photo Travele, 66

ZIP-LINQ Sync-N-Charge cable, 66

AccuCase cell phone cases, 216

Accutire gauge, 258

active noise-canceling headphones, 88

adapters (game)

Nyko Wireless Net Extender, 233

overview, 232

Pro System Selector, 234

Xbox High Definition AV Pack, 234

Addlogix

USB Beverage Warmer, 32

USB Glowing Aquarium, 33

Addonics MFR 18-in-1 Multi Function Recorder, 40

ADS Instant DVD 2.0, 165

ADVC300 (Canopus), 163

AIBO entertainment robot (Sony), 123

Air Flo EX (Nyko), 228

Air Flo Mouse (Nyko), 4

air purifier, 31

Aireo (SoniqCast), 70

AirZooka air gun (Unrealtoys), 123

All-In-Wonder 9800 PRO Video Card (ATI), 14

allways Headset (Cardo), 212

Alpine In-Dash AM/FM/XM/CD Receiver, 249

Altec Lansing inMotion Portable Audio System, 73

Ansmann Energy 16 battery charger, 113

anti-theft devices. *See* security products

Anycom Car Kit Blue HCC-110, 244

AOS Technologies iSeePet, 26

ApeXtreme Media and Game Console, 236

Apple iPod, 68-69, 72-79

Archos

    AV300 Series, 92

    Gmini 220, 70

ashtray, USB-powered, 31

ATI All-In-Wonder 9800 PRO Video Card, 14

audio players. *See* music players

audio/video gadgets. *See also* music players

    automotive DVD video systems

        Blaupunkt Chicago in-dash monitor/DVD/receiver, 252

        JVC KD-AV7000 in-dash system, 253

        Kenwood Excelon in-dash DVD receiver, 252

        overview, 250

        Pioneer front/rear seat DVD system, 251

    digital media hubs

        Escient FireBall DVDM-100, 174

        NETGEAR MP101, 176

        overview, 172

        Roku HD1000, 177

        Roku SoundBridge, 177

        Slim Devices Squeezebox, 176

        Sound Blaster Wireless Music, 175

        Turtle Beach AudioTron AT-100, 175

        Wurlitzer Digital Jukebox, 173

        Yamaha MusicCAST, 174

digital voice recorders

    Olympus DM-1, 99

    Olympus VN-240PC, 100

    overview, 98

    Sony ICD-ST25VTP, 100

DVD recorders

    JVC DR-MV1SUS, 181

    overview, 178

    Panasonic DMR-E55, 181

    Pioneer DVR-810H, 179

    Sony RDR-GX7, 180

Grundig Emergency Radio, 121

handheld GPS devices

    Cobra GPS 500, 103

    Garmin iQue 3600, 104

    Garmin Rino 130, 104

    Lowrance iFinder Pro, 103

    Magellan SporTrak Color, 102

    overview, 101

HTIB (home theater in a box) systems

    *Bose 3*2*1 DVD Home Entertainment System, 185*

    Niro 1.1PRO, 185

    overview, 182

    Panasonic SC-HT920, 183

    Samsung HT-DB390 Wireless Home Theater System, 184

    Sony DAV-FC7 DVD Dream System, 184

JVC Digital A/V Switcher, 195

Philips key019 wearable camcorder, 120

portable DVD players

    Audiovox D1500A, 96

    overview, 94

    Panasonic DVD-LX8, 97

    Sony DVP-FX700, 96

    Toshiba SD-P5000, 95

portable video players

    Archos AV300 Series, 92

    Creative Zen Portable Media Center, 93

    overview, 91

    RCA Lyra A/V Jukebox, 93

satellite radio

    Delphi SKYFi XM Audio System, 191

    Kenwood DT-7000S Sirius Tuner, 192

    overview, 190

    Tivoli Model Sirius, 192

Terk Leapfrog Wireless Audio/Video Transmitter/Receiver System, 195

Terk VR-1 TV Volume Regulator, 194

universal remote controls

    Harmony SST-659, 189

    One for All Kameleon 8-in-1 Remote, 189

    overview, 186

    Philips iPronto, 187

    Philips ProntoPro NG, 188

    Sony RM-AV3100, 188

AudioTron AT-100 (Turtle Beach), 175

Audiovox

  D1500A, 96

  Sirius Shuttle Receiver, 248

Auravision EluminX Illuminated Keyboard, 6

Auto Meter VF (Minolta), 144

automotive gadgets

  DVD video systems

    Blaupunkt Chicago in-dash monitor/DVD/receiver, 252

    JVC KD-AV7000 in-dash system, 253

    Kenwood Excelon in-dash DVD receiver, 252

    overview, 250

    Pioneer front/rear seat DVD system, 251

GPS navigation systems

    Garmin StreetPilot 2620, 242

    Magellan RoadMate 500, 241

    Navman iCN 630, 242

    overview, 240

hands-free car phone kits

    Anycom Car Kit Blue HCC-110, 244

    CCM Roadster Hands-free Kit, 245

    FoneFree hands-free speakerphone, 245

    overview, 243

miscellaneous automotive gadgets

    DriveRight CarChip data logger, 256

    Essex Electronics KE-1600 keyless entry system, 257

    Knock-In-Key backup entry system, 257

    Magna Donnelly VideoMirror, 255

    MIRT (Mobile Infrared Transmitter), 259

    Mr. Clean AutoDry Carwash, 258

    overview, 254

    Park-Zone Platinum Parking Aid, 259

    talking tire gauge, 258

    Vector FX2 performance timer accelerometer, 256

satellite radio receivers

    Alpine In-Dash AM/FM/XM/CD Receiver, 249

    Audiovox Sirius Shuttle Receiver, 248

    Delphi XM Roady, 249

    JVC Plug 'n' Play Sirius Radio, 248

    Kenwood Sirius Satellite Radio System, 247

    overview, 246

AV300 Series (Archos), 92

AVerMedia

    DVD EZMaker Pro, 164

    TVBox 9 TV Tuner, 14

B

backup devices

    CMS Velocity, 9

    Iomega REV drive, 10

    Maxtor OneTouch, 9

    Mirra Personal Server, 10

    overview, 7

    Western Digital Media Center, 8

bags and cases

    Bellagio leather PDA cases, 117

    e-Holster PDA/phone cases, 117

    overview, 114

    Star Case hard-sided PC and PDA cases, 116

    Targus Notebook PC and PDA cases, 115

    Tune Belt MP3 armband carrier, 116

Bar Master Deluxe pocket bartender (Excalibur), 122

batteries for cell phones

    Cellboost, 219

    overview, 217

    SideWinder Emergency Charger, 218

    ZIP-CELL-M01, 219

battery-related gadgets

    Ansmann Energy 16 battery charger, 113

    iSun Solar Charger, 111

    overview, 110

    Powerex intelligent battery charger and conditioner kit, 112

    Rayovac I-C3 15-minute battery charger, 112

    XPower Micro Inverter 175, 113

Belkin

    Digital Camera Link, 76

    iPod Media Reader, 77

    iPod Voice Recorder, 77

    Nostromo SpeedPad n52, 229

    TuneDok car holder, 76

Bellagio leather PDA cases, 117

Beltronics Vector FX2 performance timer accelerometer, 256

beverage warmer, USB-powered, 32

Bianchi AccuCase cell phone cases, 216

binoculars, 140

BlackBerry 7230 Wireless Handheld, 208

Blaupunkt Chicago in-dash monitor/DVD/receiver, 252

Boeckeler StudioSketch 2, 170

Bose

    3*2*1 DVD Home Entertainment System, 185

    QuietComfort 2, 89

C

C-8080 Wide Zoom (Olympus), 132

C.H.I.M.P. Monitor Mirror (ThinkGeek), 54

cables, Illuminated USB Cables, 33

camcorders

    accessories

        Eagletron PowerPod Robotic Mount, 160

        overview, 158

        Sony ECM-S930C Stereo Camcorder Microphone, 161

        Sony WCS-999 Wireless Microphone System, 161

        Sunpak Readylite 20 Video Light, 160

    Canon XL1S MiniDV Camcorder, 156

Canon ZR60 MiniDV Camcorder, 151

Canon ZR85 MiniDV Camcorder, 152

overview, 150, 154

Panasonic PV-DV953 MiniDV Digital
Palmcorder, 156

Panasonic PV-GS55 MiniDV Digital
Palmcorder, 152

Panasonic VDR-M70 DVD Palmcorder, 157

Sony DCR-IP1 MicroMV Handycam
Camcorder, 157

Sony DCR-PC109 MiniDV Handycam
Camcorder, 153

Sony DCR-TRV260 Digital8 Handycam
Camcorder, 153

Sony DCR-VX2100 MiniDV Handycam
Camcorder, 155

camera phones. *See also* hands-free car
phone kits; mobile phones; smart phones

LG VX6000, 205

Motorola V600, 204

Nokia 3650, 205

overview, 202

Sanyo SCP-5500/VM4500, 203

Sony Ericsson T610, 204

cameras. *See also* camcorders; camera
phones

digital camera accessories

CEIVA 2 Digital Photo Receiver, 147

EGG Photo 360° Pack First, 148

Hoodman LCD hoods, 145

Metz Mecablitz digital flash kits, 143

Minolta Auto Meter VF, 144

Norazza Digital Cleaning Kits, 145

overview, 141

SanDisk Digital Photo Viewer, 148

Smith-Victor KT500 Lighting Kit, 143

Tiffen digital camera lens filters, 142

VidPro TT-800 Tripod, 144

digital SLRs

Canon EOS Digital Rebel, 136

Nikon D70, 135

overview, 134

high-end digital cameras

Canon PowerShot Pro1, 133

Minolta DiMAGE A2, 132

Nikon CoolPix 8700, 133

Olympus C-8080 Wide Zoom, 132

overview, 130

Sony Cyber-shot DSC-828, 131

point-and-shoot digital cameras

Canon PowerShot S500, 127

Casio Exilim EX-Z4U, 129

Kyocera Finecam SL300R, 128

Minolta DiMAGE Xt, 128

overview, 126

Sony Cyber-shot DSC-T1, 129

specialty digital cameras

Ezonics EZBinoCam LX, 140

JB1 007 Digital Spy Camera, 138

overview, 137

Photo3-D 303 Kit, 140

*Sealife ReefMaster DC300
Underwater Digital Camera, 139*

*Sony Cyber-shot DSC-U60
Waterproof Digital Camera, 139*

*Veo Photo Traveler for Pocket
PC/Palm OS, 66*

webcams

*D-Link SecuriCam DCS-5300W
Wireless Internet Camera, 25*

Eagletron TrackerPod, 26

iSeePet, 26

Logitech QuickCam Orbit, 24

Logitech QuickCam Pro 4000, 25

overview, 23

Canon
    EOS Digital Rebel, 136
    FP100 35mm Slide to Video Adapter, 170
    PowerShot Pro1, 133
    PowerShot S500, 127
    XL1S MiniDV Camcorder, 156
    ZR60 MiniDV Camcorder, 151
    ZR85 MiniDV Camcorder, 152
Canopus ADVC300, 163
car gadgets. *See* automotive gadgets
Car Kit Blue HCC-110 (Anycom), 244
CAR-100 Bluetooth Car Kit (Sony Ericsson), 222
CarChip data logger (DriveRight), 256
Cardo allways Headset, 212
CardScan Executive (Corex), 21
cases and bags
    cell phones cases
        AccuCase cell phone cases, 216
        DIGITS, 215
        FastDraw cases, 216
        overview, 214
    PDA cases
        Bellagio leather PDA cases, 117
        e-Holster PDA/phone cases, 117
        overview, 114
        Star Case hard-sided PC and PDA cases, 116
        Targus Notebook PC and PDA cases, 115
    Tune Belt MP3 armband carrier, 116
Casio
    Color Wrist Camera Watch, 109
    Exilim EX-Z4U, 129
    TV Remote Control Watch, 109
CCM Roadster Hands-free Kit, 245

CD/Media Destroyer and Paper Shredder (Royal), 54
CDA-9820XM In-Dash AM/FM/XM/CD Receiver (Alpine), 249
CEIVA
    2 Digital Photo Receiver, 147
cell phones
    camera phones
        LG VX6000, 205
        Motorola V600, 204
        Nokia 3650, 205
        overview, 202
        Sanyo SCP-5500/VM4500, 203
        Sony Ericsson T610, 204
    cases/holders
        AccuCase cell phone cases, 216
        DIGITS, 215
        FastDraw cases, 216
        overview, 214
    chargers/batteries
        Cellboost, 219
        overview, 217
        SideWinder Emergency Charger, 218
        ZIP-CELL-M01, 219
    hands-free car phone kits
        Anycom Car Kit Blue HCC-110, 244
        CCM Roadster Hands-free Kit, 245
        FoneFree hands-free speakerphone, 245
        overview, 243
    headsets
        Cardo allways Headset, 212
        Logitech Mobile Bluetooth Headset, 213
        Logitech Mobile Earbud Miniboom, 212
        overview, 210

Plantronics M3500 Bluetooth Headset, 213

Shure QuietSpot Headset, 211

miscellaneous gadgets

CAR-100 Bluetooth Car Kit, 222

Creditel PowerSwipe, 223

Nokia Music Stand, 222

PhoneLabs Dock-N-Talk, 221

The Pretender, 223

mobile phones

Kyocera SE44/SE47, 200

Motorola V70, 201

Nokia 6800, 199

overview, 198

Samsung SPH-a460, 201

Siemens SL56, 200

smart phones

BlackBerry 7230 Wireless Handheld, 208

Handspring Treo 600, 207

Motorola MPx200, 209

overview, 206

Samsung SPH-i700, 209

Sony Ericsson P900, 208

Cellboost (Compact Power Systems), 219

CH Products Combatstick 568 USB, 229

chargers for cell phones

Cellboost, 219

overview, 217

SideWinder Emergency Charger, 218

ZIP-CELL-M01, 219

Chicago in-dash monitor/DVD/receiver (Blaupunkt), 252

CMS Velocity, 9

Cobra GPS 500, 103

Color Wrist Camera Watch (Casio), 109

Combatstick 568 USB (CH Products), 229

Compact Power Systems Cellboost, 219

computer gadgets

C.H.I.M.P. Monitor Mirror, 54

FrontX Front Panel Computer Port, 53

Griffin ControlKey, 50

GuitarPort, 51

IOGEAR MiniView III KVMP Switch, 53

Olympia Soundbug, 51

overview, 48

PhoneBridge Cordless Internet Phone, 52

Royal CD/Media Destroyer and Paper Shredder, 54

Sony Puppy Fingerprint Identity Token, 50

Streamzap PC Remote, 49

Super Cantenna Wireless Network Antenna, 52

ControlKey (Griffin), 50

ConvertX PX-402U (Plextor), 165

CoolPix 8700 (Nikon), 133

Cordless Presenter (Logitech), 5

Cordless RumblePad (Logitech), 227

Corex CardScan Executive, 21

Creative

GigaWorks S750, 17

Nomad MuVo TX, 71

Nomad MuVo2, 69

Sound Blaster Wireless Music, 175

Zen Portable Media Center, 93

Creature II (JBL), 18

Creditel PowerSwipe, 223

Crumpler DIGITS, 215

Cruzer Mini USB Flash Drive (Sandisk), 36

Cyber-shot DSC-828 (Sony), 131

Cyber-shot DSC-T1 (Sony), 129

Cyber-shot DSC-U60 Waterproof Digital Camera (Sony), 139

D

D-Link SecuriCam DCS-5300W Wireless Internet Camera, 25

D-SLRs, 134

D70 digital SLR (Nikon), 135

D1500A (Audiovox), 96

DAV-FC7 DVD Dream System (Sony), 184

Dazzle Digital Video Creator 150, 164

Dazzle Hi-Speed 10-in-1 Universal Reader/Writer (Zio), 41

DCR-IP1 MicroMV Handycam Camcorder (Sony), 157

DCR-PC109 MiniDV Handycam Camcorder (Sony), 153

DCR-TRV260 Digital8 Handycam Camcorder (Sony), 153

DCR-VX2100 MiniDV Handycam Camcorder (Sony), 155

DEFCON Security Devices (Targus), 44

Delphi SKYFi XM Audio System, 191

Delphi XM Roady, 249

Dexia Laptop Rack, 47

Digital A/V Switcher (JVC), 195

Digital Camera Link (Belkin), 76

digital cameras. See cameras

Digital Cleaning Kits (Norazza), 145

Digital Dream JB1 007 Digital Spy Camera, 138

digital media hubs

    Escient FireBall DVDM-100, 174

    NETGEAR MP101, 176

    overview, 172

    Roku HD1000, 177

    Roku SoundBridge, 177

    Slim Devices Squeezebox, 176

    Sound Blaster Wireless Music, 175

    Turtle Beach AudioTron AT-100, 175

    Wurlitzer Digital Jukebox, 173

    Yamaha MusicCAST, 174

digital media readers

    Addonics MFR 18-in-1 Multi Function Recorder, 40

    Dazzle Hi-Speed 10-in-1 Universal Reader/Writer, 41

    overview, 39

    Sandisk ImageMate 8-in-1 Reader/Writer, 41

digital music players

    Apple iPod, 68

    Apple iPod Mini, 69

    Archos Gmini 220, 70

    Creative Nomad MuVo TX, 71

    Creative Nomad MuVo2, 69

    earbuds

        Etymotic Research ER-6 Isolator, 86

        Future Sonics Ears EM3, 86

        overview, 84

        Sennheiser MX 500, 87

        Shure E3c sound isolating earphones, 85

        Sony Sports Series Fontopia Ear-Bud Headphones, 87

    headphones

        Grado SR60, 81

        Koss PORTAPRO Portable, 82

        overview, 80

        Panasonic Shockwave Brain Shaker Extreme Headphones, 83

        Sennheiser PX 100, 82

        Sony infrared cordless digital surround headphone system, 83

    iPod accessories, 72

        Altec Lansing inMotion Portable Audio System, 73

        Belkin Digital Camera Link, 76

Belkin iPod Media Reader, 77

Belkin iPod Voice Recorder, 77

Belkin TuneDok car holder, 76

Griffin iTrip FM transmitter, 75

Groove Purse Tote, 79

iPod Armor, 79

iSkin eVo iPod protector, 78

Monster iCarPlay FM transmitter, 75

naviPod wireless remote control, 74

SportSuit Runabout case, 78

iRiver iFP-390T, 71

noise-canceling headphones

Bose QuietComfort 2, 89

overview, 88

Panasonic RP-HC70, 90

Sony MDR-NC11, 90

overview, 67

SoniqCast Aireo, 70

Digital Photo Receiver (CEIVA), 147

Digital Photo Viewer (SanDisk), 148

digital photography. See cameras

digital SLRs

Canon EOS Digital Rebel, 136

Nikon D70, 135

overview, 134

digital voice recorders

Olympus DM-1, 99

Olympus VN-240PC, 100

overview, 98

Sony ICD-ST25VTP, 100

DIGITS, 215

DiMAGE A2 (Minolta), 132

diNovo Media Desktop (Logitech), 3

DM-1 (Olympus), 99

DMR-E55 (Panasonic), 181

Dock-N-Talk (PhoneLabs), 221

DocuPen (Planon), 22

DR-MV1SUS (JVC), 181

DriveRight CarChip data logger, 256

DT-7000S Sirius Tuner (Kenwood), 192

DVD EZMaker Pro (AVerMedia), 164

DVD gadgets. See also home movie gadgets

automotive DVD video systems

Blaupunkt Chicago in-dash monitor/DVD/receiver, 252

JVC KD-AV7000 in-dash system, 253

Kenwood Excelon in-dash DVD receiver, 252

overview, 250

Pioneer front/rear seat DVD system, 251

portable DVD players

Audiovox D1500A, 96

overview, 94

Panasonic DVD-LX8, 97

Sony DVP-FX700, 96

Toshiba SD-P5000, 95

DVD recorders

All-In-Wonder 9800 PRO Video Card, 14

JVC DR-MV1SUS, 181

overview, 178

Panasonic DMR-E55, 181

Pinnacle PCTV Deluxe , 12

Pioneer DVR-810H, 179

Sony RDR-GX7, 180

WinTV-PVR-350, 13

WinTV-PVR-USB2, 13

DVD-LX8 (Panasonic), 97

DVD Movie Writer dc4000 (HP), 167

DVP-FX700 (Sony), 96

DVR-810H (Pioneer), 179

DVRs

All-In-Wonder 9800 PRO Video Card, 14

JVC DR-MV1SUS, 181

overview, 178

Panasonic DMR-E55, 181

Pinnacle PCTV Deluxe , 12

Pioneer DVR-810H, 179

Sony RDR-GX7, 180

WinTV-PVR-350, 13

WinTV-PVR-USB2, 13

E

e-Holster PDA/phone cases (Personal Electronics Concealment), 117

E3c sound isolating earphones (Shure), 85

Eagletron

PowerPod Robotic Mount, 160

TrackerPod, 26

earbuds. *See also* headphones

Etymotic Research ER-6 Isolator, 86

Future Sonics Ears EM3, 86

overview, 84

Sennheiser MX 500, 87

Shure E3c sound isolating earphones, 85

Sony Sports Series Fontopia Ear-Bud Headphones, 87

Ears EM3 (Future Sonics), 86

ECM-S930C Stereo Camcorder Microphone (Sony), 161

EGG Photo 360° Pack First, 148

electricknee (MIB), 32

EluminX Illuminated Keyboard (Auravision), 6

Emergency Radio (Grundig), 121

Energy 16 battery charger (Ansmann), 113

EOS Digital Rebel (Canon), 136

Epson Perfection 4870 Photo, 21

ER-6 Isolator (Etymotic Research), 86

Ericsson P900 smart phone (Sony), 208

Ericsson T610 camera phone (Sony), 204

Escient FireBall DVDM-100, 174

Essex Electronics KE-1600 keyless entry system, 257

Etymotic Research ER-6 Isolator, 86

eVo iPod protector (iSkin), 78

Excalibur Bar Master Deluxe pocket bartender, 122

Excelon in-dash DVD receiver (Kenwood), 252

Exilim EX-Z4U (Casio), 129

Eyetop Centra, 120

EZBinoCam LX (Ezonics), 140

F

fans, USB-powered, 30

FastDraw cell phone cases, 216

Felicidade Groove Purse Tote, 79

filters (Tiffen), 142

Finecam SL300R (Kyocera), 128

FireBall DVDM-100 (Escient), 174

FIU-180 Puppy Fingerprint Identity Token (Sony), 50

flash kits (Metx Mecablitz), 143

FlyFan USB Fan (Kensington), 30

FlyLight USB Notebook Light (Kensington), 30

Focus Enhancements MXProDV Digital Video Mixer, 169

FoneFree hands-free speakerphone, 245

Fontopia Ear-Bud Headphones (Sondy), 87

FP100 35mm Slide to Video Adapter (Canon), 170

Freecom USB Card, 37

Front Panel Computer Port (FrontX), 53

front/rear seat DVD system (Pioneer), 251

FrontX Front Panel Computer Port, 53

Fujifilm USB Drive, 35

Future Sonics Ears EM3, 86

G

Game Chair (Pyramat), 238

game gadgets

  adapters and switchers

    Nyko Wireless Net Extender, 233

    overview, 232

    Pro System Selector, 234

    Xbox High Definition AV Pack, 234

  game controllers

    Belkin Nostromo SpeedPad n52, 229

    Combatstick 568 USB, 229

    Gravis Xterminator Force, 228

    Logitech Cordless RumblePad, 227

    Logitech MOMO Racing Force Feedback Wheel, 230

    NASCAR Pro Digital 2 Racing Wheel, 230

    Nyko Air Flo EX, 228

    overview, 226

    Silent Scope Light Rifle, 231

    TrackIR 3-Pro, 231

  miscellaneous gadgets

    ApeXtreme Media and Game Console, 236

    GameShark, 238

    overview, 235

    Phantom Game Receiver/Service, 237

    Pyramat PM300 Game Chair, 238

    TV Games game consoles, 237

GameShark, 238

Garmin

  iQue 3600, 104

  Rino 130, 104

  StreetPilot 2620, 242

Gibson Audio Wurlitzer Digital Jukebox, 173

GigaWorks S7505.1 (Creative), 17

Glowing Aquarium, 33

Gmini 220 (Archos), 70

GPS 500 (Cobra), 103

GPS navigation systems

  automotive GPS systems

    Garmin StreetPilot 2620, 242

    Magellan RoadMate 500, 241

    Navman iCN 630, 242

    overview, 240

  handheld GPS devices

    Cobra GPS 500, 103

    Garmin iQue 3600, 104

    Garmin Rino 130, 104

    Lowrance iFinder Pro, 103

    Magellan SporTrak Color, 102

    overview, 101

  Timex GPS Watch, 106

  TomTom Navigator Bluetooth GPS, 64

GPS Watch (Timex), 106

Grado SR60, 81

Gravis Xterminator Force, 228

Griffin

  ControlKey, 50

  iTrip FM transmitter, 75

  PowerMate, 28

Groove Purse Tote (Felicidade), 79

Grundig Emergency Radio, 121

GuitarPort (Line 6), 51

Gyration Ultra GT Cordless Optical Mouse, 4

H

handheld GPS devices

  Cobra GPS 500, 103

  Garmin iQue 3600, 104

  Garmin Rino 130, 104

  Lowrance iFinder Pro, 103

Magellan SporTrak Color, 102
overview, 101

hands-free car phone kits
Anycom Car Kit Blue HCC-110, 244
CCM Roadster Hands-free Kit, 245
FoneFree hands-free speakerphone, 245
overview, 243

hands-free speakerphone (FoneFree), 245

Handspring Treo 600 smart phone (palmOne), 207

hard-sided PC and PDA cases (Star Case), 116

Harman/Kardon SoundsticksII, 18

Harmony SST-659 (Intrigue Technologies), 189

Hauppauge WinTV-PVR-350, 13

Hauppauge WinTV-PVR-USB2, 13

HCC-110 car kit (Anycom), 244

HD1000 (Roku), 177

headphones. See also earbuds
Grado SR60, 81
Koss PORTAPRO Portable, 82
noise-canceling headphones
Bose QuietComfort 2, 89
overview, 88
Panasonic RP-HC70, 90
Sony MDR-NC11, 90
overview, 80
Panasonic Shockwave Brain Shaker Extreme Headphones, 83
Sennheiser PX 100, 82
Sony infrared cordless digital surround headphone system, 83

headsets
Cardo allways Headset, 212
Logitech Mobile Bluetooth Headset, 213
Logitech Mobile Earbud Miniboom, 212
overview, 210

Plantronics M3500 Bluetooth Headset, 213
Shure QuietSpot Headset, 211

heating blanket, USB-powered, 32

Hewlett-Packard. See HP

high-end camcorders
Canon XL1S MiniDV Camcorder, 156
overview, 154
Panasonic PV-DV953 MiniDV Digital Palmcorder, 156
Panasonic VDR-M70 DVD Palmcorder, 157
Sony DCR-IP1 MicroMV Handycam Camcorder, 157
Sony DCR-VX2100 MiniDV Handycam Camcorder, 155

high-end digital cameras
Canon PowerShot Pro1, 133
Minolta DiMAGE A2, 132
Nikon CoolPix 8700, 133
Olympus C-8080 Wide Zoom, 132
overview, 130
Sony Cyber-shot DSC-828, 131

holders for cell phones
AccuCase cell phone cases, 216
DIGITS, 215
FastDraw cases, 216
overview, 214

home audio/video gadgets
digital media hubs
Escient FireBall DVDM-100, 174
NETGEAR MP101, 176
overview, 172
Roku HD1000, 177
Roku SoundBridge, 177
Slim Devices Squeezebox, 176
Sound Blaster Wireless Music, 175
Turtle Beach AudioTron AT-100, 175

Wurlitzer Digital Jukebox, 173

Yamaha MusicCAST, 174

DVD recorders

All-In-Wonder 9800 PRO Video Card, 14

JVC DR-MV1SUS, 181

overview, 178

Panasonic DMR-E55, 181

Pinnacle PCTV Deluxe , 12

Pioneer DVR-810H, 179

Sony RDR-GX7, 180

WinTV-PVR-350, 13

WinTV-PVR-USB2, 13

HTIB (home theater in a box) systems

Bose 3*2*1 DVD Home Entertainment System, 185

Niro 1.1PRO, 185

overview, 182

Panasonic SC-HT920, 183

Samsung HT-DB390 Wireless Home Theater System, 184

Sony DAV-FC7 DVD Dream System, 184

JVC Digital A/V Switcher, 195

satellite radio

Delphi SKYFi XM Audio System, 191

Kenwood DT-7000S Sirius Tuner, 192

overview, 190

Tivoli Model Sirius, 192

Terk Leapfrog Wireless Audio/Video Transmitter/Receiver System, 195

Terk VR-1 TV Volume Regulator, 194

universal remote controls

Harmony SST-659, 189

One for All Kameleon 8-in-1 Remote, 189

overview, 186

Philips iPronto, 187

Philips ProntoPro NG, 188

Sony RM-AV3100, 188

home movie gadgets. See also home audio/video gadgets

camcorder accessories

Eagletron PowerPod Robotic Mount, 160

overview, 158

Sony ECM-S930C Stereo Camcorder Microphone, 161

Sony WCS-999 Wireless Microphone System, 161

Sunpak Readylite 20 Video Light, 160

camcorders

Canon XL1S MiniDV Camcorder, 156

Canon ZR60 MiniDV Camcorder, 151

Canon ZR85 MiniDV Camcorder, 152

overview, 150, 154

Panasonic PV-DV953 MiniDV Digital Palmcorder, 156

Panasonic PV-GS55 MiniDV Digital Palmcorder, 152

Panasonic VDR-M70 DVD Palmcorder, 157

Sony DCR-IP1 MicroMV Handycam Camcorder, 157

Sony DCR-PC109 MiniDV Handycam Camcorder, 153

Sony DCR-TRV260 Digital8 Handycam Camcorder, 153

Sony DCR-VX2100 MiniDV Handycam Camcorder, 155

Canon FP100 35mm Slide to Video Adapter, 170

MXProDV Digital Video Mixer, 169

StudioSketch 2, 170

tape-to-DVD burners

    HP DVD Movie Writer dc4000, 167

    Iomega Super DVD QuikTouch Video Burner, 167

    overview, 166

video capture devices

    ADS Instant DVD 2.0, 165

    AVerMedia DVD EZMaker Pro, 164

    Canopus ADVC300, 163

    Dazzle Digital Video Creator 150, 164

    overview, 162

    Plextor ConvertX PX-402U, 165

home theater in a box (HTIB) systems

    Bose 3*2*1 DVD Home Entertainment System, 185

    Niro 1.1PRO, 185

    overview, 182

    Panasonic SC-HT920, 183

    Samsung HT-DB390 Wireless Home Theater System, 184

    Sony DAV-FC7 DVD Dream System, 184

Hoodman LCD hoods, 145

HP (Hewlett-Packard), 20

    DVD Movie Writer dc4000, 167

    iPAQ h1940/h1945, 62

    iPAQ h4350/h4355, 62

    iPAQ h5550/h5555, 61

    Scanjet 4670, 20

HT-DB390 Wireless Home Theater System (Samsung), 184

HTIB. *See* home theater in a box systems

I

I-C3 15-minute battery charger (Rayovac), 112

i-Duck (Solid Alliance), 38

iBIZ XELA Case/Keyboard, 65

iCarPlay FM transmitter (Monster), 75

ICD-ST25VTP (Sony), 100

iCN 630 (Navman), 242

ICP Solar Technologies iSun Solar Charger, 111

iFinder Pro (Lowrance), 103

iFP-390T (iRiver), 71

Illuminated USB Cables (ThinkGeek), 33

ImageMate 8-in-1 Reader/Writer (Sandisk), 41

In-Dash AM/FM/XM/CD Receiver (Alpine), 249

Infinium Labs Phantom Game Receiver/Service, 237

infrared cordless digital surround headphone system (Sony), 83

inMotion Portable Audio System (Altec Lansing), 73

Innovative Solutions SideWinder Emergency Charger, 218

input devices

    Auravision EluminX Illuminated Keyboard, 6

    Gyration Ultra GT Cordless Optical Mouse, 4

    iBIZ XELA Case/Keyboard, 65

    IOGEAR Phaser Handheld Wireless Mouse, 5

    Logitech Cordless Presenter, 5

    Logitech diNovo Media Desktop, 3

    Logitech io Personal Digital Pen, 6

    Nyko Air Flo Mouse, 4

    overview, 2

    Targus Universal Wireless Keyboard, 65

Instant DVD 2.0 (ADS), 165

Internet cameras. *See* webcams

Intrigue Technologies Harmony SST-659, 189

io Personal Digital Pen (Logitech), 6

IOGEAR

MiniView III KVMP Switch, 53

Phaser Handheld Wireless Mouse, 5

Iomega

Micro Mini, 36

REV drive, 10

Super DVD QuikTouch Video Burner, 167

iPAQ h1940/h1945 (HP), 62

iPAQ h4350/h4355 (HP), 62

iPAQ h5550/h5555 (HP), 61

iPod accessories, 72

Altec Lansing inMotion Portable Audio System, 73

Belkin Digital Camera Link, 76

Belkin iPod Media Reader, 77

Belkin iPod Voice Recorder, 77

Belkin TuneDok car holder, 76

Griffin iTrip FM transmitter, 75

Groove Purse Tote, 79

iPod Armor, 79

iSkin eVo iPod protector, 78

Monster iCarPlay FM transmitter, 75

naviPod wireless remote control, 74

SportSuit Runabout case, 78

iPronto (Philips), 187

iQue 3600 (Garmin), 104

IRISPen Executive (I.R.I.S.), 22

iRiver iFP-390T, 71

iRobot Roomba Pro robotic vacuum cleaner, 119

iSeePet, 26

iSkin eVo iPod protector, 78

iSun Solar Charger (ICP Solar Technologies), 111

iTrip FM transmitter (Griffin), 75

IVDM-7002 Chicago in-dash monitor/DVD/receiver (Blaupunkt), 252

J-K

JAKKS Pacific TV Games game consoles, 237

JB1 007 Digital Spy Camera, 138

JBL Creature II, 18

JVC

Digital A/V Switcher, 195

DR-MV1SUS, 181

KD-AV7000 in-dash system, 253

Plug 'n' Play Sirius Radio, 248

Kameleon 8-in-1 Remote (One for All), 189

KD-AV7000 in-dash system (JVC), 253

KE-1600 keyless entry system (Essex Electronics), 257

Kensington

FlyFan USB Fan, 30

FlyLight USB Notebook Light, 30

Wi-Fi Finder, 47

Kenwood

DT-7000S Sirius Tuner, 192

Excelon in-dash DVD receiver, 252

Sirius Satellite Radio System, 247

key019 wearable camcorder (Philips), 120

keyboards

Auravision EluminX Illuminated Keyboard, 6

iBIZ XELA Case/Keyboard, 65

Logitech diNovo Media Desktop, 3

overview, 2

Targus Universal Wireless Keyboard, 65

keychain storage devices

Freecom USB Card, 37

Fujifilm USB Drive, 35

i-Duck, 38

Iomega Micro Mini, 36

Meritline Mobile Pen Drive, 38

overview, 34

    Sandisk Cruzer Mini USB Flash Drive, 36

    SWISSMEMORY USB Swiss Army Knife, 37

keyless entry systems, 257

Klipsch ProMedia Ultra 5.1, 17

Knock-In-Key backup entry system, 257

Koss PORTAPRO Portable, 82

KT-SR1000 Plug 'n' Play Sirius Radio (JVC), 248

KT500 Lighting Kit (Smith-Victor), 143

KVT-915DVD in-dash DVD receiver (Kenwood), 252

Kyocera

    Finecam SL300R, 128

    SE44/SE47, 200

L

LapCool Notebook Cooler (Vantec), 43

laptop accessories. *See* portable computer accessories

Laughing Rabbit Photon Freedom Micro keychain LED flashlight, 122

LCD hoods (Hoodman), 145

Leapfrog Wireless Audio/Video Transmitter/Receiver System (Terk), 195

leather PDA cases (Bellagio), 117

lens filters (Tiffen), 142

Leo's picks

    Addonics MFR 18-in-1 Multi Function Recorder, 40

    Altec Lansing inMotion Portable Audio System, 73

    Anycom Car Kit Blue HCC-110, 244

    ApeXtreme Media and Game Console, 236

    Apple iPod, 68

    Bose QuietComfort 2, 89

    Canon EOS Digital Rebel, 136

Canon PowerShot S500, 127

Canon ZR60 MiniDV Camcorder, 151

Canopus ADVC300, 163

Delphi SKYFi XM Audio System, 191

DIGITS, 215

Grado SR60, 81

Griffin PowerMate, 28

Handspring Treo 600, 207

HP iPAQ h5550/h5555, 61

HP Scanjet 4670, 20

iSun Solar Charger, 111

JB1 007 Digital Spy Camera, 138

Kenwood Sirius Satellite Radio System, 247

Logitech Cordless RumblePad, 227

Logitech diNovo Media Desktop, 3

Logitech QuickCam Orbit, 24

Logitech Z-680, 16

Magellan RoadMate 500, 241

Magna Donnelly VideoMirror, 255

naviPod wireless remote control, 74

Nikon D70, 135

Nokia 6800, 199

Nyko Wireless Net Extender, 233

Olympus DM-1, 99

palmOne Tungsten T3, 57

Panasonic SC-HT920, 183

Philips iPronto, 187

PhoneLabs Dock-N-Talk, 221

Pinnacle PCTV Deluxe , 12

Pioneer DVR-810H, 179

Pioneer front/rear seat DVD system, 251

Sanyo SCP-5500/VM4500, 203

Shure QuietSpot Headset, 211

SideWinder Emergency Charger, 218

Sony Cyber-shot DSC-828, 131

Sony DCR-VX2100 MiniDV Handycam Camcorder, 155

Streamzap PC Remote, 49

Targus DEFCON Security Devices, 44

Targus Notebook PC and PDA cases, 115

Terk VR-1 TV Volume Regulator, 194

Tiffen digital camera lens filters, 142

Timex GPS Watch, 106

TomTom Navigator Bluetooth GPS, 64

Toshiba SD-P5000, 95

Vantec LapCool Notebook Cooler, 43

Western Digital Media Center, 8

Wurlitzer Digital Jukebox, 173

LG VX6000, 205

Line 6 GuitarPort, 51

Linksys Wireless Compact USB Adapter, 29

LOAS USB Vacuum Cleaner, 29

Logitech

Cordless Presenter, 5

Cordless RumblePad, 227

diNovo Media Desktop, 3

io Personal Digital Pen, 6

Mobile Bluetooth Headset, 213

Mobile Earbud Miniboom, 212

MOMO Racing Force Feedback Wheel, 230

QuickCam Orbit, 24

QuickCam Pro 4000, 25

Z-680, 16

Lowrance iFinder Pro, 103

Lyra A/V Jukebox (RCA), 93

M

M3500 Bluetooth Headset (Planatronics), 213

Magellan

RoadMate 500, 241

SporTrak Color, 102

Magna Donnelly VideoMirror, 255

Marware SportSuit Runabout case, 78

Matias iPod Armor, 79

Maxtor OneTouch, 9

MDR-DS8000 infrared cordless digital surround headphone system (Sony), 83

MDR-NC11 (Sony), 90

Measurement Specialties

Park-Zone Platinum Parking Aid, 259

talking tire gauge, 258

Mecablitz digital flash kits (Metz), 143

Media Center (Western Digital), 8

media readers

Addonics MFR 18-in-1 Multi Function Recorder, 40

Dazzle Hi-Speed 10-in-1 Universal Reader/Writer, 41

overview, 39

Sandisk ImageMate 8-in-1 Reader/Writer, 41

memory devices

Freecom USB Card, 37

Fujifilm USB Drive, 35

i-Duck, 38

Iomega Micro Mini, 36

Meritline Mobile Pen Drive, 38

overview, 34

Sandisk Cruzer Mini USB Flash Drive, 36

SWISSMEMORY USB Swiss Army Knife, 37

Meritline

Mobile Pen Drive, 38

Powerex intelligent battery charger and conditioner kit, 112

Meritline RIST Memory Watch, 107

Metz Mecablitz digital flash kits, 143

MFR 18-in-1 Multi Function Recorder (Addonics), 40

MHL Communications PhoneBridge Cordless Internet Phone, 52

MIB USB heating blanket, 32

mice

Gyration Ultra GT Cordless Optical Mouse, 4

IOGEAR Phaser Handheld Wireless Mouse, 5

Logitech Cordless Presenter, 5

Logitech diNovo Media Desktop, 3

Logitech io Personal Digital Pen, 6

Nyko Air Flo Mouse, 4

overview, 2

Micro Mini (Iomega), 36

microphones, 161

Microsoft Xbox High Definition AV Pack, 234

MiniView III KVMP Switch (IOGEAR), 53

Minolta

Auto Meter VF, 144

DiMAGE A2, 132

DiMAGE Xt, 128

Mirra Personal Server, 10

MIRT (Mobile Infrared Transmitter), 259

Mobile Bluetooth Headset (Logitech), 213

Mobile Earbud Miniboom (Logitech), 212

mobile gadgets. See portable gadgets

Mobile Infrared Transmitter (MIRT), 259

Mobile Pen Drive (Meritline), 38

mobile phones. See also camera phones; hands-free car phone kits; smart phones

Kyocera SE44/SE47, 200

Motorola V70, 201

Nokia 6800, 199

overview, 198

Samsung SPH-a460, 201

Siemens SL56, 200

Model Sirius (Tivoli), 192

MOMO Racing Force Feedback Wheel (Logitech), 230

Monster iCarPlay FM transmitter, 75

Motorola

MPx200, 209

V600, 204

V70, 201

moviemaking gadgets. See home movie gadgets

MP101 (NETGEAR), 176

MPx200 (Motorola), 209

Mr. Clean AutoDry Carwash, 258

MS-4440 talking tire gauge, 258

music players

Apple iPod, 68

Apple iPod Mini, 69

Archos Gmini 220, 70

Creative Nomad MuVo TX, 71

Creative Nomad MuVo2, 69

earbuds

Etymotic Research ER-6 Isolator, 86

Future Sonics Ears EM3, 86

overview, 84

Sennheiser MX 500, 87

Shure E3c sound isolating earphones, 85

Sony Sports Series Fontopia Ear-Bud Headphones, 87

headphones

Grado SR60, 81

Koss PORTAPRO Portable, 82

overview, 80

Panasonic Shockwave Brain Shaker Extreme Headphones, 83

Sennheiser PX 100, 82

Sony infrared cordless digital surround headphone system, 83

iPod accessories, 72

    Altec Lansing inMotion Portable Audio System, 73

    Belkin Digital Camera Link, 76

    Belkin iPod Media Reader, 77

    Belkin iPod Voice Recorder, 77

    Belkin TuneDok car holder, 76

    Griffin iTrip FM transmitter, 75

    Groove Purse Tote, 79

    iPod Armor, 79

    iSkin eVo iPod protector, 78

    Monster iCarPlay FM transmitter, 75

    naviPod wireless remote control, 74

    SportSuit Runabout case, 78

iRiver iFP-390T, 71

noise-canceling headphones

    Bose QuietComfort 2, 89

    overview, 88

    Panasonic RP-HC70, 90

    Sony MDR-NC11, 90

overview, 67

SoniqCast Aireo, 70

Music Stand (Nokia), 222

MusicCAST (Yamaha), 174

MX 500 (Sennheiser), 87

MXProDV Digital Video Mixer, 169

NETGEAR MP101, 176

Nikon

    CoolPix 8700, 133

    D70, 135

Niro 1.1PRO (Nirotek), 185

Nirotek Niro 1.1PRO, 185

noise-canceling headphones

    Bose QuietComfort 2, 89

    overview, 88

    Panasonic RP-HC70, 90

    Sony MDR-NC11, 90

Nokia

    3650, 205

    6800, 199

    Music Stand, 222

Nomad MuVo (Creative), 69-71

Norazza Digital Cleaning Kits, 145

Nostromo SpeedPad n52 (Belkin), 229

notebook accessories. *See* portable computer accessories

notebook light, USB-powered, 30

Notebook PC and PDA cases (Targus), 115

Nyko

    Air Flo EX, 228

    Air Flo Mouse, 4

    Wireless Net Extender, 233

N

NASCAR Pro Digital 2 Racing Wheel (Thrustmaster), 230

NaturalPoint TrackIR 3-Pro, 231

navigation systes. *See* GPS navigation systems

Navigator Bluetooth GPS (TomTom), 64

naviPod wireless remote control, 74

Navman iCN 630, 242

O-P

Olympia Soundbug, 51

Olympus

    C-8080 Wide Zoom, 132

    DM-1, 99

    VN-240PC, 100

One for All Kameleon 8-in-1 Remote, 189

OneTouch (Maxtor), 9

P6600DVD front/rear seat DVD system
  (Pioneer), 251
Palm OS PDAs
  overview, 56
  palmOne Tungsten C, 58
  palmOne Tungsten T3, 57
  palmOne Zire 31, 59
  palmOne Zire 72, 58
  Tapwave Zodiac, 59
palmOne
  Handspring Treo 600, 207
  Tungsten C, 58
  Tungsten T3, 57
  Zire 31, 59
  Zire 72, 58
Panasonic
  DMR-E55, 181
  DVD-LX8, 97
  PV-DV953 MiniDV Digital Palmcorder, 156
  PV-GS55 MiniDV Digital Palmcorder, 152
  RP-HC70, 90
  SC-HT920, 183
  Shockwave Brain Shaker Extreme
    Headphones, 83
  VDR-M70 DVD Palmcorder, 157
Park-Zone Platinum Parking Aid, 259
parking aid, 259
passive noise-canceling headphones, 88
PC Remote (Streamzap), 49
PCTV Deluxe (Pinnacle), 12
PDAs
  accessories
    iBIZ XELA Case/Keyboard, 65
    overview, 63
    Targus Universal Wireless Keyboard,
      65
    TomTom Navigator Bluetooth GPS,
      64

Veo Photo Traveler, 66
ZIP-LINQ Sync-N-Charge cables, 66
cases
  Bellagio leather PDA cases, 117
  e-Holster PDA/phone cases, 117
  overview, 114
  Star Case hard-sided PC and PDA
    cases, 116
  Targus Notebook PC and PDA cases,
    115
Palm OS PDAs
  overview, 56
  palmOne Tungsten C, 58
  palmOne Tungsten T3, 57
  palmOne Zire 31, 59
  palmOne Zire 72, 58
  Tapwave Zodiac, 59
Pocket PC PDAs
  HP iPAQ h1940/h1945, 62
  HP iPAQ h4350/h4355, 62
  HP iPAQ h5550/h5555, 61
  overview, 60
Pelican
  MIRT (Mobile Infrared Transmitter), 259
  Pro System Selector, 234
  Silent Scope Light Rifle, 231
Perfection 4870 Photo (Epson), 21
Personal Electronics Concealment e-Holster
  PDA/phone cases, 117
Personal Server (Mirra), 10
Phantom Game Receiver/Service (Infinium
  Labs), 237
Phaser Handheld Wireless Mouse (IOGEAR), 5
Philips
  iPronto, 187
  key019 wearable camcorder, 120
  ProntoPro NG, 188

phone gadgets. *See* telephone gadgets

PhoneBridge Cordless Internet Phone (MHL), 52

PhoneLabs Dock-N-Talk, 221

Photo 360° Pack First (EGG Solution), 148

Photo Traveler (Veo), 66

Photo3-D 303 Kit, 140

Photon Freedom Micro keychain LED flashlight (Laughing Rabbit), 122

Pinnacle Systems

    Dazzle Digital Video Creator 150, 164

    PCTV Deluxe, 12

Pioneer

    DVR-810H, 179

    front/rear seat DVD system, 251

Planon DocuPen, 22

Plantronics M3500 Bluetooth Headset, 213

Plextor ConvertX PX-402U, 165

Plug 'n' Play Sirius Radio (JVC), 248

PM300 Game Chair (Pyramat), 238

Pocket PC PDAs

    HP iPAQ h1940/h1945, 62

    HP iPAQ h4350/h4355, 62

    HP iPAQ h5550/h5555, 61

    overview, 60

point-and-shoot digital cameras

    Canon PowerShot S500, 127

    Casio Exilim EX-Z4U, 129

    Kyocera Finecam SL300R, 128

    Minolta DiMAGE Xt, 128

    overview, 126

    Sony Cyber-shot DSC-T1, 129

Portable Anti-Theft System (TrackIT), 45

portable computer accessories

    3M Privacy Computer Filters, 45

    Dexia Laptop Rack, 47

    Kensington Wi-Fi Finder, 47

    overview, 42

    Targus DEFCON Security Devices, 44

    Targus Power Accessories, 46

    TrackIT Portable Anti-Theft System, 45

    Vantec LapCool Notebook Cooler, 43

    ZIP-LINQ Road Warrior Kit, 46

portable gadgets

    bases and bags

        Bellagio leather PDA cases, 117

        e-Holster PDA/phone cases, 117

        overview, 114

        Star Case hard-sided PC and PDA cases, 116

        Targus Notebook PC and PDA cases, 115

        Tune Belt MP3 armband carrier, 116

    battery-related gadgets

        Ansmann Energy 16 battery charger, 113

        iSun Solar Charger, 111

        overview, 110

        Powerex intelligent battery charger and conditioner kit, 112

        Rayovac I-C3 15-minute battery charger, 112

        XPower Micro Inverter 175, 113

    digital music players

        Apple iPod, 68

        Apple iPod Mini, 69

        Archos Gmini 220, 70

        Creative Nomad MuVo TX, 71

        Creative Nomad MuVo2, 69

        iRiver iFP-390T, 71

        overview, 67

        SoniqCast Aireo, 70

    digital voice recorders

        Olympus DM-1, 99

        Olympus VN-240PC, 100

overview, 98

Sony ICD-ST25VTP, 100

earbuds

Etymotic Research ER-6 Isolator, 86

Future Sonics Ears EM3, 86

overview, 84

Sennheiser MX 500, 87

Shure E3c sound isolating earphones, 85

Sony Sports Series Fontopia Ear-Bud
Headphones, 87

handheld GPS devices

Cobra GPS 500, 103

Garmin iQue 3600, 104

Garmin Rino 130, 104

Lowrance iFinder Pro, 103

Magellan SporTrak Color, 102

overview, 101

headphones

Grado SR60, 81

Koss PORTAPRO Portable, 82

overview, 80

Panasonic Shockwave Brain Shaker
Extreme Headphones, 83

Sennheiser PX 100, 82

Sony infrared cordless digital surround headphone system, 83

iPod accessories, 72-79

micellaneous gadgets

AirZooka air gun, 123

Bar Master Deluxe pocket bartender,
122

Eyetop Centra, 120

Grundig Emergency Radio, 121

overview, 118

Philips key019 wearable camcorder,
120

Photon Freedom Micro keychain LED
flashlight, 122

Roomba Pro robotic vacuum cleaner,
119

Skymaster Weathermaster portable
weather station, 121

Sony AIBO entertainment robot, 123

noise-canceling headphones

Bose QuietComfort 2, 89

overview, 88

Panasonic RP-HC70, 90

Sony MDR-NC11, 90

Palm OS PDAs

overview, 56

palmOne Tungsten C, 58

palmOne Tungsten T3, 57

palmOne Zire 31, 59

palmOne Zire 72, 58

Tapwave Zodiac, 59

PDA accessories

iBIZ XELA Case/Keyboard, 65

overview, 63

Targus Universal Wireless Keyboard,
65

TomTom Navigator Bluetooth GPS,
64

Veo Photo Traveler, 66

ZIP-LINQ Sync-N-Charge cables, 66

Pocket PC PDAs

HP iPAQ h1940/h1945, 62

HP iPAQ h4350/h4355, 62

HP iPAQ h5550/h5555, 61

overview, 60

portable DVD players

Audiovox D1500A, 96

overview, 94

Panasonic DVD-LX8, 97

Sony DVP-FX700, 96

Toshiba SD-P5000, 95

portable video players

Archos AV300 Series, 92

Creative Zen Portable Media Center, 93

overview, 91

RCA Lyra A/V Jukebox, 93

watches

Abacus Wrist Net Internet Watch, 107

Casio Color Wrist Camera Watch, 109

Casio TV Remote Control Watch, 109

Meritline RIST Memory Watch, 107

overview, 105

Speedtech Weather Watch Pro, 108

Timex GPS Watch, 106

Xact Wristlinx 2-Way Radio Watch, 108

PORTAPRO Portable (Koss), 82

Power Accessories (Targus), 46

Powerex intelligent battery charger and conditioner kit (Meritline), 112

PowerMate (Griffin), 28

PowerPod Robotic Mount (Eagletron), 160

PowerShot Pro1 (Canon), 133

PowerShot S500 (Canon), 127

PowerSwipe (Creditel), 223

Privacy Computer Filters (3M), 45

The Pretender (Safety Technology), 223

Pro System Selector (Pelican), 234

Proctor & Gamble Mr. Clean AutoDry Carwash, 258

ProMedia Ultra 5.1 (Klipsch), 17

ProntoPro NG (Philips), 188

prosumer digital cameras. See high-end digital cameras

Puppy Fingerprint Identity Token (Sony), 50

PV-DV953 MiniDV Digital Palmcorder (Panasonic), 156

PV-GS55 MiniDV Digital Palmcorder (Panasonic), 152

PX 100 (Sennheiser), 82

Pyramat PM300 Game Chair, 238

PZ-1500 Park-Zone Platinum Parking Aid, 259

Q-R

QuickCam Orbit (Logitech), 24

QuickCam Pro 4000 (Logitech), 25

QuietComfort 2 (Bose), 89

QuietSpot Headset (Shure), 211

radio

Griffin iTrip FM transmitter, 75

Monster iCarPlay FM transmitter, 75

satellite radio

Delphi SKYFi XM Audio System, 191

Kenwood DT-7000S Sirius Tuner, 192

overview, 190

Tivoli Model Sirius, 192

satellite radio receivers

Alpine In-Dash AM/FM/XM/CD Receiver, 249

Audiovox Sirius Shuttle Receiver, 248

Delphi XM Roady, 249

JVC Plug 'n' Play Sirius Radio, 248

Kenwood Sirius Satellite Radio System, 247

overview, 246

Rayovac I-C3 15-minute battery charger, 112

RCA Lyra A/V Jukebox, 93

RDR-GX7 (Sony), 180

Readylite 20 Video Light, 160

ReefMaster DC300 Underwater Digital Camera (Sealife), 139

REV drive (Iomega), 10

Rino 130 (Garmin), 104

RIST Memory Watch (Meritline), 107

RM-AV3100 (Sony), 188

Road Warrior Kit (ZIP-LINQ), 46

RoadMate 500 (Magellan), 241

Roadster Hands-free Kit (CCM), 245

Roady (Delphi XM), 249

Roku HD1000, 177

Roku SoundBridge, 177

Roomba Pro robotic vacuum cleaner (iRobot), 119

Royal CD/Media Destroyer and Paper Shredder, 54

RP-HC70 (Panasonic), 90

RP-HS900 Shockwave Brain Shaker Extreme Headphones (Panasonic), 83

S

Safety Technology's The Pretender, 223

Samsung

HT-DB390 Wireless Home Theater System, 184

SPH-a460, 201

SPH-i700, 209

Sandisk

Cruzer Mini USB Flash Drive, 36

Digital Photo Viewer, 148

ImageMate 8-in-1 Reader/Writer, 41

Sanyo SCP-5500/VM4500, 203

satellite radio

Alpine In-Dash AM/FM/XM/CD Receiver, 249

Audiovox Sirius Shuttle Receiver, 248

Delphi SKYFi XM Audio System, 191

Delphi XM Roady, 249

JVC Plug 'n' Play Sirius Radio, 248

Kenwood DT-7000S Sirius Tuner, 192

Kenwood Sirius Satellite Radio System, 247

overview, 190, 246

Tivoli Model Sirius, 192

SC-HT920 (Panasonic), 183

Scanjet 4670 (HP), 20

scanners

Corex CardScan Executive, 21

Epson Perfection 4870 Photo, 21

HP Scanjet 4670, 20

IRISPen Executive, 22

overview, 19

Planon DocuPen, 22

SCP-5500/VM4500 camera phone (Sanyo), 203

SD-P5000 (Toshiba), 95

SE44/SE47 mobile phone (Kyocera), 200

Sealife ReefMaster DC300 Underwater Digital Camera, 139

SecuriCam DCS-5300W Wireless Internet Camera (D-Link), 25

security gadgets

Griffin ControlKey, 50

Royal CD/Media Destroyer and Paper Shredder, 54

Sony Puppy Fingerprint Identity Token, 50

Targus DEFCON Security Devices, 44

TrackIT Portable Anti-Theft System, 45

Sennheiser

MX 500, 87

PX 100, 82

Shockwave Brain Shaker Extreme Headphones (Panasonic), 83

Shure

E3c sound isolating earphones, 85

QuietSpot Headset, 211

SideWinder Emergency Charger, 218

Siemens SL56, 200

Silent Scope Light Rifle (Pelican), 231

Sirius Satellite Radio System (Kenwood), 247

Sirius Shuttle Receiver (Audiovox), 248

SIRPNP2 Sirius Shuttle Receiver (Audiovox), 248

SKYFi XM Audio System (Delphi), 191

Skymaster Weathermaster portable weather station (Speedtech), 121

SL56 mobile phone (Siemens), 200

Slim Devices Squeezebox, 176

smart phones. *See also* hands-free car phone kits; mobile phones; camera phones

    BlackBerry 7230 Wireless Handheld, 208

    Handspring Treo 600, 207

    Motorola MPx200, 209

    overview, 206

    Samsung SPH-i700, 209

    Sony Ericsson P900, 208

Smith-Victor KT500 Lighting Kit, 143

Solid Alliance i-Duck, 38

SoniqCast Aireo, 70

Sony

    AIBO entertainment robot, 123

    CAR-100 Bluetooth Car Kit, 222

    Cyber-shot DSC-828, 131

    Cyber-shot DSC-T1, 129

    Cyber-shot DSC-U60 Waterproof Digital Camera, 139

    DAV-FC7 DVD Dream System, 184

    DCR-IP1 MicroMV Handycam Camcorder, 157

    DCR-PC109 MiniDV Handycam Camcorder, 153

    DCR-TRV260 Digital8 Handycam Camcorder, 153

    DCR-VX2100 MiniDV Handycam Camcorder, 155

    DVP-FX700, 96

    ECM-S930C Stereo Camcorder Microphone, 161

    Ericsson P900, 208

    Ericsson T610, 204

    ICD-ST25VTP, 100

    infrared cordless digital surround headphone system, 83

    MDR-NC11, 90

    Puppy Fingerprint Identity Token, 50

    RDR-GX7, 180

    RM-AV3100, 188

    Sports Series Fontopia Ear-Bud Headphones, 87

    WCS-999 Wireless Microphone System, 161

Sound Blaster Wireless Music (Creative), 175

sound players. *See* music players

SoundBridge (Roku), 177

SoundsticksII (Harman/Kardon), 18

Soundbug (Olympia), 51

speakers

    Creative GigaWorks S750, 17

    Harman/Kardon SoundsticksII, 18

    JBL Creature II, 18

    Klipsch ProMedia Ultra 5.1, 17

    Logitech Z-680, 16

    Olympia Soundbug, 51

    overview, 15

specialty digital cameras

    Ezonics EZBinoCam LX, 140

    JB1 007 Digital Spy Camera, 138

    overview, 137

Photo3-D 303 Kit, 140

Sealife ReefMaster DC300 Underwater Digital Camera, 139

Sony Cyber-shot DSC-U60 Waterproof Digital Camera, 139

Speedtech

Skymaster Weathermaster portable weather station, 121

Weather Watch Pro, 108

SPH-a460 mobile phone (Samsung), 201

SPH-i700 (Samsung), 209

SporTrak Color (Magellan), 102

Sports Series Fontopia Ear-Bud Headphones (Sondy), 87

SportSuit Runabout case (Marware), 78

Spy Camera, 138

Squeezebox (Slim Devices), 176

SR60 (Grado), 81

Star Case hard-sided PC and PDA cases, 116

stereo pairs, 140

Streamzap PC Remote, 49

StreetPilot 2620 (Garmin), 242

StudioSketch 2, 170

Sunpak Readylite 20 Video Light, 160

Super Cantenna Wireless Network Antenna (Wireless Garden), 52

Super DVD QuikTouch Video Burner (Iomega), 167

SWISSMEMORY USB Swiss Army Knife, 37

switchers (game)

Nyko Wireless Net Extender, 233

overview, 232

Pro System Selector, 234

Xbox High Definition AV Pack, 234

Sync-N-Charge cables (ZIP-LINQ), 66

T

talking tire gauge, 258

tape-to-DVD burners

HP DVD Movie Writer dc4000, 167

Iomega Super DVD QuikTouch Video Burner, 167

overview, 166

Tapwave Zodiac, 59

Targus

DEFCON Security Devices, 44

Notebook PC and PDA cases, 115

Power Accessories, 46

Universal Wireless Keyboard, 65

telephone gadgets

camera phones

LG VX6000, 205

Motorola V600, 204

Nokia 3650, 205

overview, 202

Sanyo SCP-5500/VM4500, 203

Sony Ericsson T610, 204

cases/holders

AccuCase cell phone cases, 216

DIGITS, 215

FastDraw cases, 216

overview, 214

chargers/batteries

Cellboost, 219

overview, 217

SideWinder Emergency Charger, 218

ZIP-CELL-M01, 219

hands-free car phone kits

Anycom Car Kit Blue HCC-110, 244

CCM Roadster Hands-free Kit, 245

FoneFree hands-free speakerphone, 245

overview, 243

headsets

Cardo allways Headset, 212

Logitech Mobile Bluetooth Headset, 213

Logitech Mobile Earbud Miniboom, 212

overview, 210

Plantronics M3500 Bluetooth Headset, 213

Shure QuietSpot Headset, 211

miscellaneous gadgets

CAR-100 Bluetooth Car Kit, 222

Creditel PowerSwipe, 223

Nokia Music Stand, 222

PhoneLabs Dock-N-Talk, 221

The Pretender, 223

mobile phones

Kyocera SE44/SE47, 200

Motorola V70, 201

Nokia 6800, 199

overview, 198

Samsung SPH-a460, 201

Siemens SL56, 200

smart phones

BlackBerry 7230 Wireless Handheld, 208

Handspring Treo 600, 207

Motorola MPx200, 209

overview, 206

Samsung SPH-i700, 209

Sony Ericsson P900, 208

TEN Technology naviPod wireless remote control, 74

Terk

Leapfrog Wireless Audio/Video Transmitter/Receiver System, 195

VR-1 TV Volume Regulator, 194

ThinkGeek

C.H.I.M.P. Monitor Mirror, 54

Illuminated USB Cables, 33

USB Air Purifier, 31

USB Ashtray, 31

Thrustmaster NASCAR Pro Digital 2 Racing Wheel, 230

Tiffen digital camera lens filters, 142

Timex GPS Watch, 106

tire gauge, 258

Tivoli Model Sirius, 192

ToCAD Sunpak Readylite 20 Video Light, 160

TomTom Navigator Bluetooth GPS, 64

Toshiba SD-P5000, 95

TrackerPod (Eagletron), 26

TrackIR 3-Pro (NaturalPoint), 231

TrackIT Portable Anti-Theft System, 45

Treo 600 smart phone (palmOne), 207

tripods, VidPro TT-800 Tripod, 144

truck gadgets. See automotive gadgets

TT-800 Tripod (VidPro), 144

Tune Belt MP3 armband carrier, 116

TuneDok car holder (Belkin), 76

Tungsten C (palmOne), 58

Tungsten T3 (palmOne), 57

Turtle Beach AudioTron AT-100, 175

TV Games game consoles (JAKKS Pacific), 237

TV Remote Control Watch (Casio), 109

TV tuners, 11

All-In-Wonder 9800 PRO Video Card, 14

AVerMedia TVBox 9 TV Tuner, 14

Pinnacle PCTV Deluxe , 12
WinTV-PVR-350, 13
WinTV-PVR-USB2, 13

U

UHK-01A/B heating blanket (MIB), 32
Ultra GT Cordless Optical Mouse (Gyration), 4
underwater cameras, 139
universal remote controls
    Harmony SST-659, 189
    One for All Kameleon 8-in-1 Remote, 189
    overview, 186
    Philips iPronto, 187
    Philips ProntoPro NG, 188
    Sony RM-AV3100, 188
Universal Wireless Keyboard (Targus), 65
Unrealtoys AirZooka air gun, 123
USB gadgets
    FlyFan USB Fan, 30
    FlyLight USB Notebook Light, 30
    Griffin PowerMate, 28
    Illuminated USB Cables, 33
    Linksys Wireless Compact USB Adapter, 29
    memory devices
        Freecom USB Card, 37
        Fujifilm USB Drive, 35
        i-Duck, 38
        Iomega Micro Mini, 36
        Meritline Mobile Pen Drive, 38
        overview, 34
        Sandisk Cruzer Mini USB Flash Drive, 36
        SWISSMEMORY USB Swiss Army Knife, 37
    overview, 27
    USB Air Purifier, 31

USB Ashtray, 31
USB Beverage Warmer, 32
USB Glowing Aquarium, 33
USB heating blanket, 32
USB Vacuum Cleaner, 29

V

V70 mobile phone (Motorola), 201
V600 camera phone (Motorola), 204
vacuum cleaner, USB-powered, 29
Vantec LapCool Notebook Cooler, 43
VDR-M70 DVD Palmcorder (Panasonic), 157
Vector FX2 performance timer accelerometer, 256
Velocity (CMS), 9
Veo Photo Traveler, 66
video capture devices
    ADS Instant DVD 2.0, 165
    AVerMedia DVD EZMaker Pro, 164
    Canopus ADVC300, 163
    Dazzle Digital Video Creator 150, 164
    overview, 162
    Plextor ConvertX PX-402U, 165
video gadgets. *See* audio/video gadgets; home movie gadgets
VideoMirror (Magna Donnelly), 255
VidPro TT-800 Tripod, 144
Virtual Motion Sound System (VMSS), 83
VMSS (Virtual Motion Sound System), 83
VN-240PC (Olympus), 100
voice recorders
    Olympus DM-1, 99
    Olympus VN-240PC, 100
    overview, 98
    Sony ICD-ST25VTP, 100

VR-1 TV Volume Regulator (Terk), 194

VX6000 camera phone (LG), 205

W

watches

   Abacus Wrist Net Internet Watch, 107

   Casio Color Wrist Camera Watch, 109

   Casio TV Remote Control Watch, 109

   Meritline RIST Memory Watch, 107

   overview, 105

   Speedtech Weather Watch Pro, 108

   Timex GPS Watch, 106

   Xact Wristlinx 2-Way Radio Watch, 108

waterproof cameras, 139

WCS-999 Wireless Microphone System (Sony), 161

weather gadgets

   Abacus Wrist Net Internet Watch, 107

   Skymaster Weathermaster portable weather station, 121

   Speedtech Weather Watch Pro, 108

Weather Watch Pro (Speedtech), 108

Webcams

   D-Link SecuriCam DCS-5300W Wireless Internet Camera, 25

   Eagletron TrackerPod, 26

   iSeePet, 26

   Logitech QuickCam Orbit, 24

   Logitech QuickCam Pro 4000, 25

   overview, 23

Western Digital Media Center, 8

Wi-Fi Finder (Kensington), 47

WinTV-PVR-350 (Hauppauge), 13

WinTV-PVR-USB2 (Hauppauge), 13

Wireless Compact USB Adapter (Linksys), 29

Wireless Garden Super Cantenna Wireless Network Antenna, 52

Wireless Net Extender (Nyko), 233

Wrist Net Internet Watch (Abacus), 107

Wristlinx 2-Way Radio Watch (Xact), 108

Wurlitzer Digital Jukebox (Gibson), 173

X

Xact Wristlinx 2-Way Radio Watch, 108

Xantrex Energy 16 battery charger (Ansmann), 113

Xbox High Definition AV Pack (Microsoft), 234

XELA Case/Keyboard (iBIZ), 65

XL1S MiniDV Camcorder (Canon), 156

XPower Micro Inverter 175 (Xantrex), 113

Xterminator Force (Gravis), 228

Y-Z

Yamaha MusicCAST, 174

Z-680 (Logitech), 16

Zen Portable Media Center (Creative), 93

Zio Corp. Dazzle Hi-Speed 10-in-1 Universal Reader/Writer, 41

ZIP-CELL-M01 (Zip-LINQ), 219

ZIP-LINQ

   Road Warrior Kit, 46

   Sync-N-Charge cables, 66

   ZIP-CELL-M01, 219

Zire 31 (palmOne), 59

Zire 72 (palmOne), 58

Zodiac (Tapwave), 59

ZR60 MiniDV Camcorder (Canon), 151

ZR85 MiniDV Camcorder (Canon), 152